Investigating Old Buildings

Investigating Old Buildings

LANCE SMITH

Batsford Academic and Educational London

ISBN 0 7134 3633 6

Typeset by Keyspools Ltd, Golborne, Lancs
and printed in Great Britain by
Anchor Brendon Ltd
Tiptree, Essex
for the publishers.
Batsford Academic and Educational
a division of B. T. Batsford Ltd
4 Fitzhardinge Street
London W1H 0AH

00998176

PQ

Smith, Lance
    Investigating old buildings.
    1. Architecture—Great Britain—History
    2. Excavations (Archaeology)—Great Britain
    I. Title
    720'.941   NA961

Contents

Acknowledgments

My thanks are due to Dr Graham Webster for encouraging me to start on this book. I also owe particular thanks to my wife, Chris, for her patience and encouragement, and to friends and colleagues at Ironbridge Museum, in the Solihull Archaeological Group and in the Telford Historical and Archaeological Society. David de Haan, Curator of Art at Ironbridge, made many helpful suggestions for illustrations, and Keith Gale freely gave me the benefit of his technical knowledge.

ONE

Investigating old buildings

In the investigation of old buildings the common feature of all good work is the recognition of its archaeological status. It is not surprising, then, that we can turn to the work of the 'father' of archaeology, General Pitt-Rivers, the first Inspector of Ancient Monuments, for a precedent of good recording, just as we can turn to his work for a precedent for modern scientific methods of excavation.

When, in 1880, Pitt-Rivers inherited the medieval hunting lodge known as King John's House at Tollard Royal, with his estates at Cranborne on the Wiltshire and Dorset border, he carried out an analysis of the house and the surviving evidence for its history before commencing the restoration work. His study of the building shows the art of recording at its best.[1] The General was far ahead of his time in his scientific approach to archaeology, and although this is now recognised in his contributions to the understanding of the Iron Age and the Romano-British periods, his advanced approach to the study of upstanding buildings is less well known. His insistence on the value of studying evidence in context is now orthodoxy, and 'recording', in its widest sense, is the tool of that methodical study.

The meticulous illustration of architectural features was, of course, nothing new in the late nineteenth century. For 50 years or more a large number of excellently illustrated architectural dictionaries and textbooks existed; and, against these, the illustrations in the monograph on King John's House are of good, but by no means outstanding quality. They are pioneering, however, as an integral part of a unified documentary and archaeological study. The example of King John's House points to the first requirement of architectural observation and recording: both may be done with the eye of the artist, but they are essentially matters of exact scholarship.

It could be wished that every nineteenth-century architect employed to restore a building of antiquity or importance had had the patience and foresight to produce at least annotated record drawings. Today, with a rather more widespread interest in the study of antiquities amongst both amateurs and professionals, the failure to record is more reprehensible. At the time of the King John's House monograph, the study of even a royal hunting lodge may have seemed low in the scale of architectural interest, but now the importance of even the lowest levels of domestic, agricultural and industrial buildings is recognised.

KING JOHN'S HOUSE, TOLLARD ROYAL, WILTSHIRE.

GROUND PLAN.

FIRST FLOOR PLAN.

ATTIC PLAN

FOUNDATIONS OF TOWER

13TH CENTURY WORK.

TUDOR OR JACOBEAN WORK.

SCALE OF FEET.

1 Tollard Royal: a thirteenth-century first-floor house with later additions, recorded by General Pitt Rivers in 1890 (A. H. Pitt-Rivers, *King John's House, Tollard Royal, Wiltshire*, 1890, Plate III)

The monograph on King John's House starts with a discussion of the history of the site and its documentary evidence. There follows a profusely illustrated description of the house as found, with an account of the clues which led to the appreciation of the possibility of making detailed discoveries regarding its original form. This leads to a room by room account of the architectural discoveries. Relics, or 'small finds' as they would now be termed, are described, and there is a description of the excavation of the surviving foundations and floor of detached service buildings which originally stood nearby.

In the first section of the report the author uses every scrap of documentary or circumstantial evidence which could be found. There is a discussion of the place name, the 'field archaeology' of the site, as it would now be termed, the ancient boundaries, the holding of a court-leet nearby, and the descent of the manor down to the present day. The uninteresting external appearance of the house and the uninformative and misleading nature of the only published drawing of it, in the *Gentleman's Magazine* in 1811, is mentioned.

Two lithographs illustrate the start and finish of the investigation, both

Gent. Mag. Sep. 1811. Pl. II. p. 217.

KING JOHN'S HUNTING SEAT near TOLLARD ROYAL, WILTS.

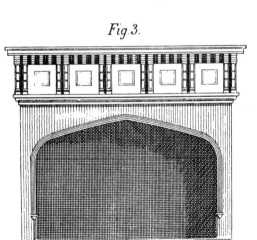

Fig. 3.

Fig. 2.

views taken in perspective from the same position. One shows the appearance of the house with its recent covering of stucco removed. The outlines of blocked windows are visible, but none of the modern masonry has yet been removed. The second view shows the house with its early openings restored, and lean-to structures of recent date removed. The windows are all numbered for reference.

2 Uninformative recording: King John's House depicted in the *Gentleman's Magazine* in 1811 (A. H. Pitt-Rivers, *King John's House, Tollard Royal, Wiltshire*, 1890, Plate IV)

WINDOW Nᵒ XVI, ON FIRST FLOOR OF KING JOHN'S HOUSE.

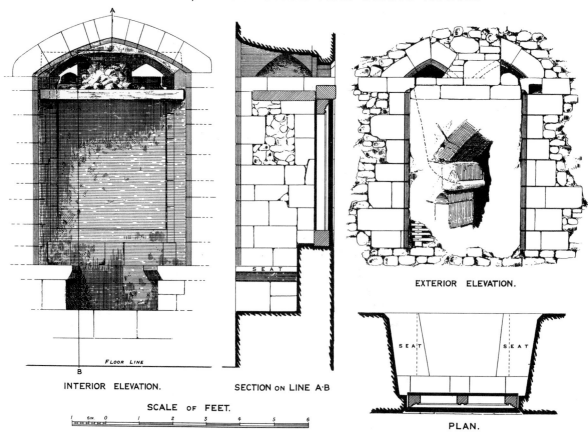

INTERIOR ELEVATION.

SECTION ON LINE A·B

EXTERIOR ELEVATION.

PLAN.

SCALE OF FEET.

3 A window detail from the Monograph on Tollard Royal (A. H. Pitt-Rivers, *King John's House, Tollard Royal, Wiltshire*, 1890, Plate XV)

With the stucco removed, the first close examination showed that there were two main periods, Early English and Tudor, and it was decided that 'the work of both periods should be preserved, only removing that of the later period where it completely hid the earlier work'. It is clear from the room by room account of the discoveries that the General was very much present on site, directing operations. Two windows in particular proved to be of special importance, and, as some reconstruction was necessary, the evidence for their condition as found was recorded: 'Careful models have been made of both windows, showing their exact condition at the time they were found, and the position of each stone and brick is given by means of which architects and antiquaries will be able to see clearly what has been done, and what authority exists for the slight restorations that have been made.' Detailed drawings serve the same purpose.

The study of King John's House is marked by its use of published sources in support of the purely archaeological examination of the fabric. The house was unusual at the time it was studied in that it was within the scope of the already published royal archives, particularly King John's Patent Rolls, which had been published in 1837. The emphasis placed by nineteenth-century historical researchers on the buildings of the Church and of royalty is partly explained by the lack of access at that time to 'popular' archives. The system of County Record Offices, regularly open to the public, only came into being in the inter-war years of the present century. The modern investigator of old buildings, likely to be concerned exclusively with buildings from a lower social level than that of the royal household, has the same duty to use available documentary sources, and has good facilities to do so.

RESEARCH AND RESCUE

Enjoyment apart, the purpose of forming records of old buildings might be summed up in two words: research and 'rescue'. Ideally, any fieldwork of an archaeological nature should satisfy both of these aims. Fieldwork serves a research purpose if it contributes to the common pool of information in an area where questions are being asked and where information is inadequate. Investigators have long been warned of the importance of coherent research: 'the temptation to desultory research must in every case be great, and desultory research, however it may amuse or benefit the investigator, seldom adds much to the real stock of human knowledge'.[2] The great risk to this coherence comes from too great an emphasis on the other main aim, rescue. Fieldwork serves a rescue purpose if it preserves information in the face of destruction where valuable facts would otherwise be lost for ever. Rescue is not to be confused with preservation: it is the information, and not the fabric, which is saved. The urgency of rescue in an age of decay and redevelopment hardly needs to be argued; the only dispute would be if the rescue effort were undirected by any sense of research. In architectural recording, rescue makes good sense, in that buildings being dismantled can be studied far more intensively than can those which are preserved.

It is a matter of tragedy to leave even the poorest fragment of medieval construction to disappear unrecorded. Buildings of lesser age might be treated more selectively, but if any lower limit of age is to be imposed, it must be a matter of personal judgement where the line is to be drawn. Some investigators may like to draw a line at a date when they consider that building at the popular level ceases to be 'vernacular', i.e. regionally characteristic. With the changing emphasis in the climate of historical research towards technical, social and economic subjects, there has in recent years been a marked tendency for younger and younger buildings to fall under the eye of active research. The recording activities of the Royal Commission on Historical Monuments were originally confined to buildings before 1700, then 1714, and now 1850 or, exceptionally, later.

The boom of interest in industrial archaeology has led to a great attention being paid to buildings which were part of the milieu of the factory system from the late eighteenth century onwards, both in the sense of those which incorporate the new materials of the period, such as cast iron, and those which served industrial purposes such as mills or workers' cottages. Architecture may gain a research importance, as much for reasons of economic or social history as for reasons of constructional detail.

The houses of the yeoman and tenant-farmer level of pre-industrial rural society have survived in very much greater numbers than those of the common labourers. Cottages of the poorest labourers built as recently as the early nineteenth century hardly survive at all – the campaign of the sanitary reform movement during the mid-nineteenth century (a fascinating subject to follow in the contemporary literature) having succeeded very well in their supression. The success of the sanitary reformers has left an important chapter in housing history well documented but with hardly any specimens on the ground as tangible evidence. Any surviving specimens of the dwellings of the very lowest orders of society of that period will merit the investigator's time and attention before many 'better' structures of a century or two of greater antiquity.

Another reason to turn one's attention to the buildings of the comparatively recent past is that it may well be that the most significant period of English history is the Industrial Revolution. English innovations in the structural and decorative uses of cast iron and other new industrial materials are of particular importance. Developments in the design of buildings for industrial purposes were also important; it is as necessary to assess buildings as solutions to practical needs as to see them just as problems of material and construction.

The architectural investigator who does not prefer to concentrate on the work of a particular patron, architect or builder, in other words one whose architectural investigations are not a side-line to biography, will wish to study those buildings which are typical of their time and place rather than those which are unusual. The definition, through extensive recording work, of what is truly typical is one of the longstanding problems of research. Information on what is a typical plan is valuable to the excavating archaeologist. The long concentration by students of standing buildings on those of superior status has led to an unnatural divide between these two branches of archaeology, the excavators seeming to study a different world to that of the students of standing buildings. This was a problem examined by Beresford and Hurst in their study of deserted medieval villages and the types of dwelling found in excavated sites, published in 1971;[3] the gap will perhaps never be completely bridged.

In trying to define what is typical, the investigator should try to have a realistic view of what are likely to have been the thoughts and preoccupations of the practical builder, whether a peasant building his cottage with stones cleared from his field, or a professional builder working to contract. Old buildings are sometimes treated as if they were natural history specimens in a taxonomic debate. The real builder's concerns are likely to have been first and foremost with the buying of the materials he is selling to his customer, the employment of labour, and the achievement of a stable structure simply erected.

Beginning

A number of avenues are open to the interested beginner wishing to find out what local recording work is going on in his vicinity. A number of universities have thriving extra-mural departments which organise courses for all aspects of archaeological and related studies. Studentship is open to all interested people, regardless of how little formal qualification they may possess. A letter to the administrative section will elicit information about courses, or help to put the beginner in touch with local amateur research groups and societies. Courses may be available similarly under the local education authority or the WEA. Conferences designed to enable local groups to meet and show their work are organised in the same way.

Local historical societies or county archaeological societies should also be able to advise the interested amateur on local research and recording. Membership of such societies, with the contact it gives with local enthusiasts and local academic researchers, is bound to be worthwhile, and most such societies try to carry out fieldwork in their area.

Museums are particularly useful as a means of finding out about local activity in recording. In the field of vernacular buildings, one might write to Avoncroft Museum of Buildings, Stoke Prior, Bromsgrove, Worcestershire, or to the Weald and Downland Open Air Museum, Singleton, Chichester, West Sussex. In the field of industrial archaeological buildings, one might write to Ironbridge Gorge Museum, The Wharfage, Ironbridge, Telford, Shropshire, or to the North of England Open Air Museum, Beamish, Nr Stanley, County Durham.

Local Authority Conservation Officers are another possible source of local information. Not necessarily personally involved in recording, they are concerned to foster the fullest possible local interest in the buildings of their areas. Civic Societies may also be helpful, or one or other of the national societies specialising in a particular aspect of the architectural scene – the Vernacular Architecture Group, the Georgian Group and the Victorian Society.

Where groups of people are active in the recording of buildings in one's own district, it should be possible to find out about them from one or other of these sources. The easiest introduction for the beginner is to offer to assist, if only by holding the end of a tape measure. Slightly harder, but a quicker way to learn new skills, is the decision to jump in at the deep end and start work on one's own initiative. It is still best to collaborate with one or two other people, though to do recording work on one's own is perfectly possible.

TRADITIONAL BUILDING AND BEYOND

In 1932 Sir Cyril Fox put forward a principle which has been of great influence on the study of popular culture, including the commonplace buildings of the past. This was the division of the country into two zones, the highlands and the lowlands, the lowlands being those parts lying to the south and east of the belt of Jurassic limestone which runs from Lincolnshire to Dorset.[4]

The distinction is not so much a matter of altitude as of proximity to or remoteness from the south-east and the Continent. Both in the succession of prehistoric cultures and in the history of recent centuries as manifested in folk-life and in the common traditions of building, Fox observed that, whereas in the lowlands one culture (one coherent body of custom) tended to *succeed* its predecessor, in the highlands each new culture tended to be *absorbed*, merely modifying that which existed before. Thus in the highland region of Yorkshire, at the end of the sixteenth century, the gentry were building stone houses, but the architectural tradition shows continuity with their former timber buildings. In Devon, likewise, new architectural forms grew out of the earlier prototypes, preserving features of the longhouse and the first-floor hall. In the highland district of the Welsh Marches, much of it physically low-lying but counted as part of the highland zone, a vigorous timber-frame tradition, with both box-frame and cruck methods of construction, persisted. In lowland England quite new forms were appearing in those areas where economic conditions called for new building rather than the improvement of what already existed. In Essex and Kent and in other areas near London the changes occurring in the late Tudor period took the form of improvements to earlier houses; in more provincial parts of the lowland zone, substantial rebuilding took place. A new type of house, first appearing extensively in the late sixteenth century in East Anglia, was based on the axial positioning of the chimney stack, a change sometimes brought about in an older structure by blocking the former cross-passage. At the humbler level of society, the single room cottage was giving way to the two-room plan, incorporating the axial chimney learned from the example of superior houses. On the limestone uplands on the fringe of the lowland zone, a new tradition of stone building was making its first appearance.

Professor Barley's work on farmhouses and cottages takes the highland and lowland distinction as its basis: 'Throughout the study of small houses in the centuries prior to the industrial revolution runs one persistent fact: the difference between lowland England . . . and the highland zone beyond it.'[5] More recently, the emphasis on this contrast has been played down because too great a reliance on a geographical principle directs attention away from the subtler details of the historical pattern of building.[6] It is through the efforts of people observing and recording that the amount of weight to give to general principles can be found. Also to be determined is how much weight to give to general distinctions of a cultural geographical nature, and how much to the rather more demonstrable contrasts in geology, agriculture and economic prosperity underlying the architecture of different districts and regions.

Early work by members of the Vernacular Architecture Group on the distribution of medieval and post-medieval carpentry methods culminated in a classification of historical roof types by Professor R. A. Cordingley in 1961.[7] It was recognised that there were two carpentry traditions, *cruck* construction being representative of one and *box-frame* construction of the the other. A modified version of the highland and lowland distinction was apparent in the distribution of examples of each of the two methods. For this purpose a 'cruck frame homeland' was recognised in a reduced highland zone, covering essentially Wales and the Pennines. The 'box-frame homeland' lay in the counties between and east of Lincolnshire and Sussex. Between these lies an extensive tract, the West Country, the Midlands and the low-lying parts of the north-west and the north-east, in which intermediate zone was found a mixture of traditions. In the south of the intermediate zone box-framing was found to be predominant; in the Midlands and north, cruck framing predominated.

In deciding which types to regard as belonging to a cruck tradition and which to a box-frame tradition, Fox drew attention to the relationship of tie-beam and wall-plate.[8] Cordingley, on the other hand, chose the method of securing the purlins to the principal rafters or other support as the crucial feature. In 1965 J. T. Smith threw doubt on the soundness of the distinction between cruck and box-frame,[9] and drew attention instead to a new hypothesis of three carpentry schools: eastern, western and northern. The characteristic feature of the eastern school was the use of close-studding; that of the western school, square panelling and angle-bracing; and that of the northern, the interrupted sill.

Although surviving early buildings include a number of medieval houses of manorial and better status[10] and a number of fine medieval barns, for much of the country the last quarter of the sixteenth century and the early part of the seventeenth is the earliest period for which non-ecclesiastical buildings survive in any quantity. In his article in *Past and Present*[11] in 1953, Professor W. G. Hoskins drew attention to the spate of secular building activity which happened in the period from 1570 onwards, and to its causes. This period has been called the 'great rebuilding' or the 'housing revolution'.

During the reign of Elizabeth, wealth and increasing population gave constant work to the mason and the carpenter. In some regions where timber building had formerly been the rule, new stone houses were built with material from quarries hardly used since the Church had needed them before the Reformation. In other regions, forests were depleted to an extent which caused concern that timber supplies for the Navy might be exhausted.

The upper ranks of rural society rebuilt or modernised their manor houses, inserting chimneys to increase their standard of domestic comfort. As open fireplaces gave way to chimneys, and hence a clean and smoke-free living space, the type of house based on the hall open to the roof gave way to one with ceilings and a complete upper floor. The farmsteads and dwellings of the lesser ranks of society were also transformed in the same period of rebuilding, though not now surviving in great numbers from that time. The evidence with which to refine the picture of the great rebuilding has come partly from a large amount of local work in the recording of old buildings, and partly from documentary research. Much new evidence has been brought into currency by the meticulous though very slowly advancing work of the Royal Commission on Historical Monuments.

Industrial Revolution

For some students of the architecture of ordinary buildings, the Industrial Revolution may mark an end to their interest, perhaps prematurely. In addition to the effects of the revolution in transport, the nineteenth century saw mass production of building materials. Both factors led to a universalising of constructional detail, so that nowadays it is hardly possible to distinguish the suburban architecture of one county from another. A third factor, not obvious on the surface, is that there was a profound change in the organisation of the building industry, with the growth of the 'contract in gross' and the emergence of the general contractor in place of the array of separate independent tradesmen of the earlier period.[12]

It might be tempting to make a divide in the historical continuum of architecture at the Industrial Revolution, for the illegitimate reason that at

4 Model Houses at Copley, near Halifax, c.1860: though still built in the back-to-back manner for economy (and condemned by *The Builder* for that reason), Edward Ackroyd's two-storey cottages had coal and provisions cellars, mains water and drainage, and well separated privies and pigsties. (J. Hole, *The Homes of the Working Classes*, 1866, Plate IX)

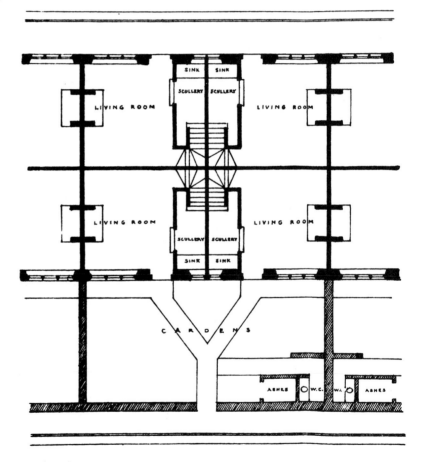

this point the subject matter seems to become less aesthetically appealing; but it is in the practical considerations of trade organisation and building economics that a justification for this divide exists.

It is only in the present century that building has become to any extent part of the factory system, so that modern building is now largely a matter of assembling proprietory materials. Throughout the nineteenth and through much of the present century, building remained a matter of using natural materials or non-patentable manufactured ones. Work on site was still largely untouched by ideas of factory organisation.

The effects of the Industrial Revolution appear in transport becoming easier, changes in the manner of organising investment in development and contracting, and changes in the types of building required for housing and industry. The exploitation of new materials and innovation in site methods are much more a matter of civil engineering construction than of architecture at a domestic scale.

In building at the domestic scale, innovations such as fireproof construction occur, but as a second-hand technique borrowed from the earlier experience of builders of mills and warehouses (*see Figs. 52 and 53*).[13] The technical interest of small details of construction usually diminishes as building methods become settled into those illustrated in early editions of still current constructional textbooks. There remains, however, much of importance for the architectural investigator, provided the issues of the time are taken into account. The dominant issue in housing is sanitary reform – both in a planning sense and in the sense of providing for proper building services.

The nineteenth century brings us into a time when common housing begins to be documented by contemporaries. Since the cholera and typhoid scares of the 1840s, sanitary authorities have been concerned with identifying unfit housing and thinking about slum clearance. Some informally gathered information about housing is found in local evidence collected by Poor Law Commissioners or committees of physicians, submitted to Edmund Chadwick's Sanitary Inquiry[14] or to the 398 local Board of Health reports.[15] Thus there are useful records of plans of houses in Birmingham, showing not only the houses themselves but the important ancillary details of water pump, brewhouse, privy and boghole or midden.[16]

Amongst better houses, and model cottages such as estate gate-houses and *cottages ornés*, there was, in the nineteenth century, an increasing adoption of arbitrary, mostly historically inspired or deliberately rustic, 'style' which had little or nothing to do with plan or construction. New ideas in building materials are particularly interesting from a practical manufacturing or art-historical viewpoint: terracotta, ceramics, encaustic tiles, wrought ironwork, castings, and the early stages leading towards modern construction in steel and concrete.

Ninteenth-century building, domestic or otherwise, is a much broader subject than that of earlier centuries, since it becomes more a matter of how it serves the needs of a technically and culturally ambitious age.

TWO

Materials and construction

Most structural material is timber, stone or brick. Iron is only a minor sideline in traditional building, but its importance in the development of the art in recent centuries cannot be over-estimated. Also to be considered is lime, which, as mortar and plaster, has always been the most conspicuous of materials.

The framed construction of the carpenter contrasts with the amassed construction of the mason: its origins lie in the north of Europe. The south of Europe, with its copious limestone and its mild climate, has always depended heavily on the techniques of stone, lime, cement and concrete work, but it is a poor region for timber construction, and there is no Latin word for 'carpenter'. As framing materials, timber and iron are quite different to the others in their application. Iron construction is, in a sense, a development of carpentry, just as brickwork is a development of the craft of the mason. All materials are used in ways heavily influenced by how they are produced, and the observer of old buildings should be alert to their peculiarities.

TIMBER

Timber is the one material common to practically all buildings, and whether or not the architectural investigator and recorder concentrates on timber-framed buildings, he needs a familiarity with the structure of wood as a substance and how its natural characteristics govern its use. Wood has natural planes of strength and of weakness which affect how it is converted from the log into usable timbers, and how these are put together in construction.

Most trees grow by the addition of outer layers, and in temperate climates the succession of growing and dormant seasons causes the wood to be arranged in a series of clearly marked annual growth rings. The old botanical term *exogen* classifies those plants which generate their new growth in this manner at the external surface. The cells in wood where new generation takes place are called collectively *meristem* (as a substance), or *cambium* (viewed as a layer). Meristem appears as a moist green layer surrounding the solid wood when the bark is scraped off. A small residue of meristem may also be visible in the central pith of young wood. In the

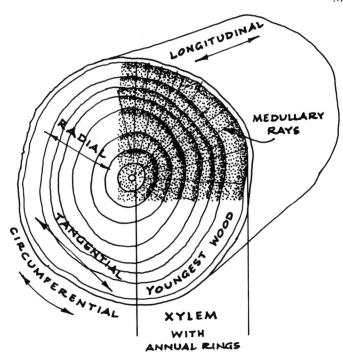

5 A log in cross section

study of timber used in buildings, we are hardly concerned with types of tree such as the palm in which the new wood is generated in a different manner. With any type of tree conventionally used to provide timber, it is an important fact that the new wood, once generated, occupies a static place in the tree, thus creating a building material of considerable strength.

Examining a log in cross section (*Fig. 5*), there is a core of pith at the centre. This disappears in time and there is unlikely to be any detectable pith in timber mature enough for constructional use, though a fissure may remain. The greater part of the log consists of tissue called *xylem*, usually visibly divided into annual rings. Outside this is the growing or mobile part, consisting of cambium, bast, bark-cambium, and finally the bark itself. On closer examination, each annual ring of the xylem is seen to consist mostly of longitudinal cells. Each annual growth-ring starts abruptly with the large, spongy and relatively light-coloured cells of the spring growth. These merge more or less gradually into the smaller, denser and relatively dark coloured summer and autumn cells. The sharply defined lines are where the dense autumn cells abut the open-textured spring growth of the following year. There are thus several features revealing the position and orientation of any fragment of timber in the log from which it was cut.

Furthermore, since the width of an annual ring between a pair of sharply defined lines is indicative of the quality of the growing conditions experienced that year, the pattern formed by the succession of rings of varying widths should show some similarity in all trees of the same species growing together in one locality and at one period. The pattern may be used as a means by which timber may be dated with absolute accuracy, provided enough specimens are studied to build up sets of reference series, and provided all matching of one specimen with another is sufficiently close

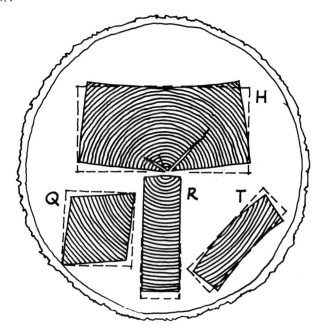

6 Warping of timber: halved timbers (H) typically show two plane surfaces slightly folded back from the central fissures; quartered timbers (Q) distort to a lozenge section; tangentially-sawn timbers (T) tend to 'cup'; rift-sawn timbers (R) shrink radially but maintain their shape.

to satisfy strict statistical theory. This technique, *dendrochronology*, is in its infancy, but promises to revolutionise the dating of buildings.

The predominance of longitudinal cells causes timber to be more stable longitudinally than in other directions. With the movements known as warping occurring with changes in the moisture content, distortions tend to be seen more in the cross-sectional shape of a timber than in its length. Second in order of strength is the radial direction, in which the timber is strengthened by the presence of *medullary rays*. These rays consist of a different type of wood cells, and are conspicuous in oak and beech.

The weakest direction in timber is around the circumference. 'The illustration of a closing fan affords the best example of the principle of shrinking during seasoning.'[17] This inequality in strength between the three directions governs how timber tends to split and distort (*Fig. 6*). The commonest plane of a split is one passing through the central axis of the log. Under different conditions a split may start either at the centre or at the outer edge. Timbers are stable in length, a fact which makes timber-framed construction possible, though they may twist.

Only the youngest wood in a tree, typically the outer 20 or 30 rings of annual growth in the case of an oak, is active in the living tree as a conductor of sap. The wood in this outer region is termed *sapwood*, and it is often of a lighter colour than the inactive *heartwood*. It is the task of the cells of the sapwood to conduct solutions of mineral salts from the soil to the leaves and to bring back the liquid food which the leaves produce. In the best carpentry this active wood is avoided because it is seldom durable. It is very common, however, to see some traces of sapwood on the corners of timbers of old buildings, where it is conspicuous by its lighter colour and because it is often riddled with beetle holes and softened with decay. The darker colour of the heartwood is due to the deposits of gum, resin and tannin in the cells when they cease to be used for conducting sap.

The choice of oak as a prestigious material in the nineteenth and early twentieth centuries has given rise to well-researched standards of practice for its use; but in previous centuries, when it was a common material, it was not so fastidiously used. Unseasoned 'green' timber is easier for the carpenter to work, regardless of the splits and distortions which might later occur. Timber might also be felled at too young or too old an age for optimum quality. Modern practice requires oak to be felled at its prime age of about 100 years. At a younger age, too high a proportion of the log will consist of sapwood; at an older age, the central heartwood becomes increasingly brittle and subject to decay.

Trees should be felled in autumn or winter, when there is the least amount of moisture in the wood, and the timber should then be seasoned, that is to say its moisture and sap content should be gradually reduced to an acceptable level for the particular situation for which the timber is to be used. Documentary evidence on the sale of timber and the evidence of old buildings examined in detail may show to what extent early carpenters took trouble to maintain standards. Trees might be felled in early spring, that being the best season for obtaining the valuable oak bark.

If timber is fixed in position before it has seasoned to the right extent, warping will occur. It is important, therefore, for the full seasoning process to be completed, because it is not the early loss of moisture from the cell cavities, but the later loss from the cell walls, which is the cause of movement.

Conversion

Once a tree is felled, it is 'converted' by being cross-cut into lengths which are then cut or split lengthwise to produce the required cross-sectional sizes of timbers required by the carpenter. The classic tools of conversion are the axe, the saw, the hammer and wedges and, for finishing the face of timber, the adze, all of which have been part of the carpenter's kit from prehistoric times. The conversion of a log into a timber fit for building by means of the axe and adze is likely to be little more than barking and squaring. Adzing, in the hands of a skilled worker, is easier than sawing; timbers halved or quartered by means of the saw are often observed to have been initially wrought on their outer faces by means of the adze. The adze and saw are complementary to each other. In examining carpentry it is interesting to note the tools used by their characteristic marks and to see how economy of labour was achieved.

The large two-man saw worked with a pair of trestles or a sawpit (*Fig. 7*) provided a method of dividing a log into two or more timbers which was in almost universal use down to the Industrial Revolution. The type of saw-mark it produces, straight but varying in angle, is distinctive.

According to the chosen method of cutting a timber, its face will reveal the annual ring pattern 'radially' or 'tangentially' (*see Fig. 5*). A radially-cut face passes through or near to the central axis of the log. The rings then appear as closely-spaced regular lines, and the medullary rays are sometimes conspicuous. A tangentially-cut face reveals the effect commonly seen in floorboards: the annual rings appear as widely-spaced swirling lines, and the face is often disfigured by splintering.

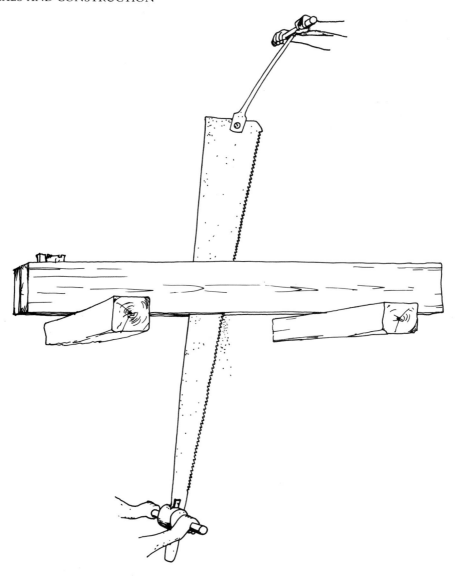

7 A common pit-saw, about 8ft (2.4m) long. The man above controls the direction of the sawcut. The lower handle is removable.

Logs converted into timber by the manual labour of sawyers may be *boxed*, *halved*, *quartered* or *slabbed* (*Fig. 8*).

Boxing is the simplest conversion, by which a timber of approximately square section is produced. Depending on the quality of the work, there may be sapwood or even bark present on the corners of the timber. Each face reveals, along its centreline, the characteristic swirling lines of tangentially-cut annual rings.

In halving, the saw passes through the central axis of the log to produce a pair of timbers which are then finished, commonly by adze, to a rectangular cross-section. The three outer faces reveal tangentially-cut wood, as in a boxed timber, but the sawn inner face is quite different. The ring pattern is more or less regular and there may be medullary rays, but, most conspicuously, there may be a central fissure where the pith grew, with fissures extending from it into the timber. Because of tangential shrinkage, the two halves of the saw-cut inner face may be slightly folded back to leave a small central ridge.

In quartering, the sawyer produces four timbers from the log, the timber faces showing the features described for halved timbers except that the central fissure of the log appears at the corner of the timber.

The other traditional type of conversion is slabbing, in which a large log is simply sawn through several times with parallel cuts to produce a set of planks. The appearance of the timber faces varies according to position, the innermost faces being radially-cut and the others more or less tangential.

The two-man saws used to convert timber were worked vertically in conjunction with a sawpit or a pair of trestles. The line of the intended cut was marked on the timber by means of a chalked string pulled taut and snapped with the fingers to deposit a line of chalk dust. The sawyer in charge stood above, lifting the saw and controlling the direction of the cut, the labourer beneath doing the harder part of the work.[18]

8 Boxed, halved, quartered and slabbed types of manual conversion

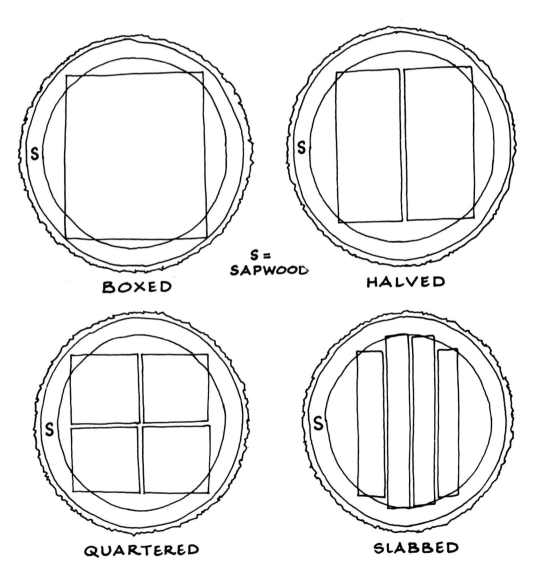

BOXED

S = SAPWOOD

HALVED

QUARTERED

SLABBED

The simpler of the two types of saw used for this purpose (*see Fig. 7*) had a deep blade, and a handle at each end. For insertion and extraction of the saw, the lower handle (the 'box') had to be removable, so it was designed to clamp on to the blade and was tightened by means of a wedge. The blade tapered from about 9in (*c.*225mm) at the upper end to about 3in (*c.*75mm) at the lower. Its depth made any curved cut impractical.

Alternatively, a shallow bladed saw was used, kept taut by being strained in a frame, the sides of which went either side of the log. In a fifteenth-century document this type of saw is called a *kytter*.[19] Whenever the sawcut reached a supporting beam or a trestle, the sawyers had to dismantle their saw, move the log on its supports, insert the saw again and continue. The width of cut of these early saws was about $\frac{1}{4}$in (*c.*5mm).

Sawpits were dug wherever the quantity of sawing to be done justified such labour. A specimen has been dug for demonstration at the Weald and Downland Open Air Museum. At a temporary workplace or wherever a pit would be impractical, trestles were used instead. The use of sawpits survived in remote parts of the country until the early years of this century.

When timber was converted by manual labour, the cost of sawing and the length of time taken were high in relation to the value of the timber. Consequently it made no sense economically to reduce the size of timbers used in building, provided they were small enough to be handled efficiently. In minor timber-framed buildings, the timber sizes were governed, therefore, by considerations of jointing rather than by any idea of structural sufficiency. It appears that trees were felled at stages of growth at which they could be converted with a minimum of work into generally useful sizes for posts, rafters and so forth, without close regard to minimising material.

The coming of mechanical sawmills revolutionised construction in timber. The cost of sawing became low and the speed of output high in relation to the cost of material. At the same time, softwoods became more general. The carpenter was provided with a large range of small sizes from which to choose, sizes better suited to nailed than to jointed construction. Economy came to depend on choosing the smallest sized piece of timber for each task, the mills and merchants tending to charge purely by the weight of timber purchased.

Carpenters' rules-of-thumb for the minimum safe sizing of timbers became commonly used, rules which were increasingly based on scientific material testing. For structural carpentry – joists, rafters, purlins etc., tables of minimum sizes were published. Once generally accepted, such minimum sizes became the carpenter's invariable choice: there was no justification in exceeding the safe structural minimum. The simple boxing, halving and quartering of hand-converted timber gave way to quite different categories of timber converted by the mechanical saw. With a demand for smaller sections, including thin planks and boards, a large log can be cut mechanically in three ways: slabbed, tangentially-sawn and rift-sawn.

Slabbing continued as a cheap method of conversion, for which a reciprocating frame saw with multiple blades was suited.

Tangentially-sawn timber was readily produced by means of a circular saw, the plank thickness being controlled by means of an adjustable fence

9 Mechanical plank sawing by steam power, illustrated in Tomlinson's *Cyclopaedia of Useful Arts and Manufactures*, 1854. 'A sawmill constructed by Mr Hague, of Radcliff... The saws are fixed and stretched in the frame by wedges, which are driven above through mortices in the upper part or bar of the saw. In this way a number of saws may be fixed on the frame, and to keep the saws at proper distances apart, and to prevent their tendency to twist in the plane of their direction, pieces of wood of the exact thickness of the planking are placed between the blades and secured by the pressure of the side screws' (C. Tomlinson ed., *Cyclopaedia of Useful Arts and Manufactures*, 1854, vol. II: unnumbered plate facing p. 582)

parallel to the line of the saw. This method produced timbers for floor joists with better resistance to bending than similarly sized rift-sawn timber. This type of conversion is also known as flat or plain sawing.

Rift-sawn timber is also easily produced with a circular saw, but the log is first quartered and then the quarters sawn into smaller pieces in a variety of ways to produce planks etc. in more or less radial positions relative to the original log (*Fig. 10*). The annual rings intersect the main sawn faces at more than 45°.

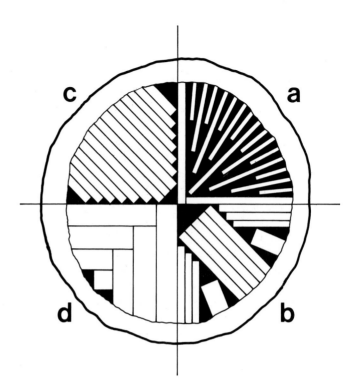

10 Types of rift-sawn conversion. These types were especially favoured for oak for joinery, as the pattern of medullary rays (the 'silver grain') was emphasised. The waste from type A was used for tiling laths. (Rivington's [ed. H. C. Seddon] *Notes on Building Construction*, Part III, 1879, p. 386)

Sawmills were first introduced in the eighteenth century, the early ones having vertically-mounted reciprocating blades. They were a straightforward adaptation to wind or water power of the traditional two-man frame-saw operated in a pit; but instead of the randomly-angled sawmarks of the hand-operated saw, the mechanical version produced parallel marks across the timber grain. The frame was driven by a crank arm and made to slide up and down in an outer frame rather like a sash window. The logical step then was to introduce multiple blades. In the naval dockyards of the Napoleonic era, multiple-blade vertical reciprocating frame-saws were powered by steam. A log could be sawn into a set of planks at one pass. 'There are wind-mills and water-mills which do the office of sawing wood, with infinitely more expedition and ease than is performed by hand.'[20]

Reciprocating saws working at high speed required thick blades to withstand the shocks of reversing movement, and were wasteful of timber and power. Reciprocating motion is appropriate for hand tools or for simple machinery in which the human muscles are involved, but for powered machinery, rotative and continuous motion is preferable. By the early nineteenth century, therefore, circular saws were coming into use, at least for the conversion of smaller logs. For larger logs, the bandsaw was introduced in about 1820. Both types allowed a thin blade to cut timber at high speed. All three types of saw, reciprocating, circular and band, were in common use in nineteenth-century sawmills; a rather primitive horizontally reciprocating single-blade saw of late nineteenth-century date is worked at Blists Hill Open Air Museum in Shropshire.

FRAMES AND JOINTS

Frames

Cottages, small dwelling houses and barns were frequently described in parish and manorial surveys as consisting of a certain number of 'bays': 'Joanna Minors, widow, claims to hold by custom of the manor ... a dwelling house of 4 bays, a barn of 3 bays, another barn of 2 bays ...' (Warwickshire, 1608). The division of most timber-framed buildings into bays was their most conspicuous feature. Bays are the units defined by cross frames. They may be of any size, depending on the purposes of the rooms or spaces enclosed, the smallest bay sizes being for entrance passages or for conducting smoke to a louvre in the roof. A cross frame may be a complete wall, often incorporating a truss, or simply a truss over a void between principal posts. Simple timber buildings are resolved into a series of two-dimensional frames plus roof and floor beams. The wall frames (parallel to the ridge) incorporate the principal posts of a series of two or more cross frames. The main additional structural elements are the purlins to carry rafters (or collars) and the binders to carry joists (*Fig. 11*).

The cross frames are the most significant, and here the sequence of erection is most clearly shown. The gable ends of a building should be studied early to see which type of cross framing is used, and it is important to enter the roof space, if possible, to see if the original bay arrangement is preserved in the roof trusses. Their spacing and detail may reveal the

11 Surviving timbers at 15a Holly Road, Little Dawley, a Shropshire longhouse: showing distinction between wall frame and cross frame, and between box framing (house part) and cruck framing (byre part)

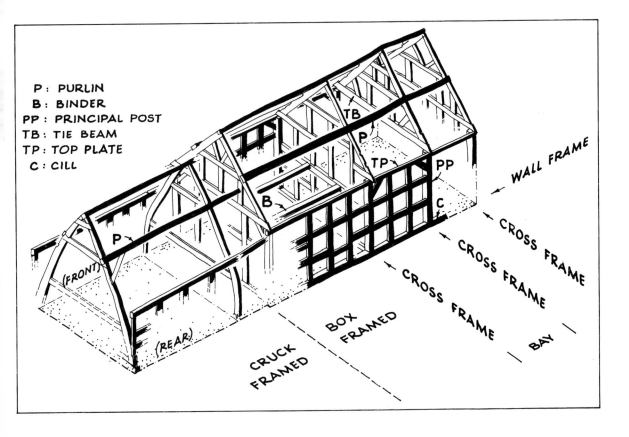

P : PURLIN
B : BINDER
PP : PRINCIPAL POST
TB : TIE BEAM
TP : TOP PLATE
C : CILL

INTERIOR OF THE HALL,
SUTTON COURTENAY, BERKSHIRE

12 Sutton Courtenay Hall, *c.*1330: the roof contains two large purlins derived from the arcade plates of the aisled arrangement, but freed from supporting posts. At the far (lower) end is the screens passage, beyond the spere truss. (J. H. Parker, *Some Account of Domestic Architecture in England from Edward I to Richard II*, 1857, facing p. 32)

original plan even when the partitioning below has been completely altered.

In *cruck* buildings a pair of inclined timbers lean inwards to give direct support to the purlins. They are often curved and tapered in a manner of great practical subtlety. Full crucks extend from the apex to near the ground, or at least are based in the wall stonework well below eaves level. There is no proof that they are a survival of a primitive form of construction with leaning poles; they may be a medieval innovation. Full crucks rising to the roof apex are distinguished from *base crucks*, the latter being a medieval variant introduced into the tradition of aisled construction, perhaps suggested by the example of full crucks.

Crucks may be a medieval innovation, but the tradition of *aisled construction* seems to be far more ancient. If a building is too wide to be spanned by one tie-beam, it may be planned as a nave with aisles. The line of posts supports an *arcade plate* serving the same purpose with regard to the nave roof as a *wall-plate* in an ordinary roof.

In some places the posts of an aisled building would coincide with walls and not be objectionable, but if a clear space was wanted, posts would be a nuisance and some ingenuity went into their elimination. In medieval halls base crucks were often used to free the floor area in the vicinity of the central hearth. The aisled form of cross frame may be preserved in a *spere truss* partitioning the hall from the cross passage (*Fig. 12*).

Box-frame (otherwise called *post and truss*) buildings may be divided into several types with regard to how the *purlins* are managed. These are the longitudinal timbers parallel to the ridge, carrying the main weight of the rafters. There is usually one, and sometimes there are two or three, *side purlins* to a roof slope, or the roof may contain a single *crown purlin* supporting a collar beam to each pair of common rafters. Side purlins may be carried on the backs or sides of the principal rafters, or they may be clasped ('trapped') between a collar beam and the under-face of the principal rafter.

In a classic study 'British Historical Roof types and their Members' in the *Transactions of the Ancient Monuments Society* for 1961, Professor Cordingley laid stress on the distinction between *butt purlin* and *through purlin* families of roof construction:

> A *butt purlin* is 'A purlin which is interrupted in its longitudinal course down the length of a building by the trusses spaced at bay intervals. The backs of the principal rafters of the trusses reach the underside of the roof covering, and the purlins thus butt against their sides, being secured there by various means. Butt purlins denote a type of carpentry construction normal to the Lowland Zone of England and Wales.'

> A *through purlin* is 'A side purlin which is free to run uninterruptedly from end to end of a building, limited only by the lengths of timber available. Such purlins are carried on the backs of trusses spaced at bay intervals down the length of a building, and their occurrence is indicative of a type of carpentry structure normal to the Highland Zone of England and Wales.'

In this classification there is a relationship between the through purlin types and cruck construction. Cruck construction and related types of roof construction of the through purlin class are a highland technique involving substantial principals, the crucks or the principal rafters, which occur considerably below the plane of the common rafters. The system of construction is *double*, in the sense that principals and common rafters are completely distinct. In box-frame buildings with roofs of the through purlin type the principal rafters are of a much heavier section than the common rafters. A ridge piece is generally present.

Lowland roof construction is less hierarchical: less distinction is made between principal and common rafters. Principal rafters are brought to the same plane as the common ones by the techniques of using butt, crown or clasped purlins, so that they share directly in the support of the battens and tiles. There is often no ridge piece. The principal rafters are of lighter section than would be the case with roofs in the highland tradition, and they are often reduced from collar level upwards to the same section as common rafters.

Every timber frame has an upper and a lower face. The rimbers are rarely all of one thickness, and, in setting out the frame flat on the ground for the preliminary purpose of fitting all the members together, the carpenter packs the thinner timbers up so that the top surface is all flush. He marks his identification numbers on this upper face and, in the final assembling on site, he drives his pegs in from the upper face also. The general rule is that the upper face is turned towards the more important side: wall frames face outwards, as do the first and last cross frames forming the gable or end walls. Inner cross frames face the more important of the two rooms or spaces they separate or, if intermediate, they face the more important end of the room. In barns, the frames on either side of the threshing floor face towards it.

When it was necessary to peg joints but retain some play in them during erection, loose temporary pins called *hookpins*[21] were used. When the frame was all in place they were withdrawn, and the final full-size pins were driven in tight.

Flooring almost always consists of a set of beams called *common joists*, more or less evenly spaced and acting in unison. They are sometimes called *bridging joists*. Where there is an opening, the extra joist at right angles to the rest is the *trimmer*; the shortened joists jointed into it are the *trimmed joists*.

Considered structurally, there are three types of floor: in *single floors* the common joists span from wall to wall directly; in *double floors* there are *binders* to break the joisted area up into shorter spans. For the largest spaces there may be a third structural element: the binders are themselves carried by still larger beams called *girders*. Only the latter type should be called a *framed floor*.

Joints

Timbers may be connected to each other by means of a variety of joints, with or without fastenings. A joint is formed by the interlocking cutting of two timbers, and by 'fastening' is meant the insertion of a third piece, not necessarily of the same material, to resist their being pulled apart. The choice of type of joint and fastening depends on the type of structural movement between the two timbers which the carpenter anticipates, as well as on the practical problems of assembly.

A well-formed joint fits snugly with some friction between the two timbers. Usually this is not enough, and a *fastening* is present which might be a peg, wedge, bolt, nail or strap. At the late medieval height of the carpentry tradition, craftsmen may have been reluctant to introduce an alien material into the best work, but in common carpentry the use of iron in the form of nails and straps can be found as far back as observations can be made. As metal fastenings grew in sophistication, however, they became more acceptable. There came to be less and less call on the skill of the carpenter to form sophisticated joints. In recent centuries the repertoire of metal fastenings has grown to such an extent that the modern carpenter now rarely has to form a true joint. The admired skills of the medieval carpenter have been priced out of existence.

The most common joints are too basic to be of any dating value. The commonest is the *mortise and tenon* (*Fig. 13a*), usually fastened by means of pegs or *trenails*. If a peg is cut off flush on both sides it is called a *dowel*. In the somewhat incongruous terminology of the carpenter, the peg serves to keep the *cheeks* of the mortise tight against the *shoulders* of the tenon. Many

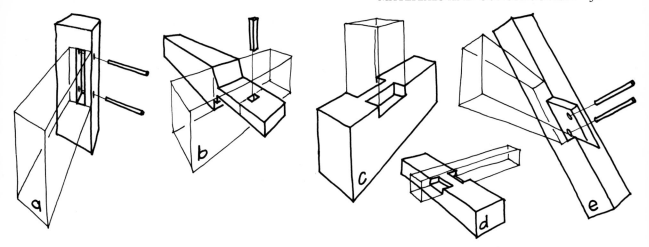

13 (a) Mortise and tenon; (b) tusk tenon; (c) bridle joint; (d) cogging; (e) lap joint; one member shown as if transparent

variations of this simple joint are found: the mortise may pass through the full thickness of the timber or it may be of limited depth. The latter is a *blind* or *stub* mortise. There may be more than one tenon to a joint, each in a separate mortise. A large mortise and tenon joint may be fastened by more than one peg. If the tenoned timber meets the mortised timber at an acute angle, the tenon may, none the less, be shaped so that it enters the mortise at right angles.

In joiner's work, wedges may be driven into the tenon end to spread it and make the joint more difficult to pull apart. When a new timber has to be inserted into an already assembled frame, the mortise at one end is extended into a slot, called a *chase*, to enable the tenon to be introduced. A variant seen in the framing of floors and in some furniture is the *tusk-tenon* joint, in which the tenon passes through the mortise, projects on the other side, and is held there by a cross-wedge (*Fig. 13b*).

A related and simpler joint called a *housing* occurs where the entering timber is not cut back to form a tenon but remains undiminished; risers and treads are usually 'housed' into the strings (sides) of a staircase. Alternatively the entering timber may be slightly sharpened to a point; this is the usual joint for ladder rungs and for the top ends of staves in wall panels in timber framing.

In a mortise and tenon joint, the mortise normally acts as a housing completely surrounding the tenon; but in some cases the main timber is twice corner-notched instead, and the branching timber is made to straddle the part between the notches; in effect, the positions of mortise and tenon are swapped. This is the *bridle* joint, the bridle being the uncut link of timber where the mortise would otherwise have been. The foot of a post standing on a beam is a typical situation (*Fig. 13c*). This was a popular nineteenth-century type recommended to ensure that the stress was thrown on to the centreline of the joint. The joint of two lengths of sill or wall-plate, where an open-topped or open-bottomed socket is cut in the end of one timber to receive a tenon cut on the end of the other, is now also called a bridle joint, and this type may be an element in a more complex joint (*see Figs. 15a and 16a*).

In a *cogged* joint the main timber is cut back on either side as for a bridle

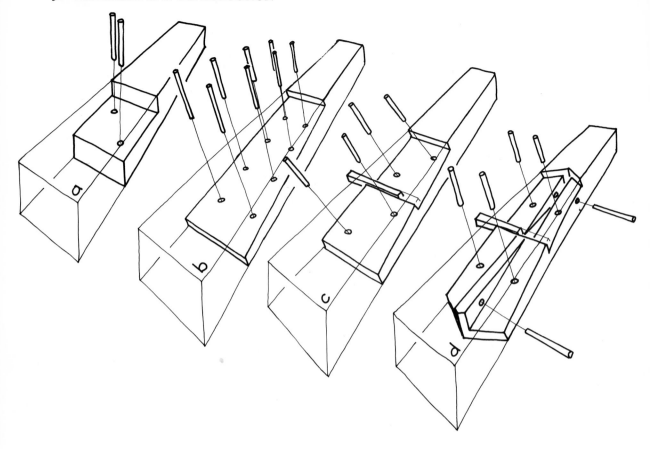

14 Some medieval types of scarf joint (after C. A. Hewett)

joint, but the other timber is notched and laid across it. This type came into popularity when the dovetail joint between tie-beam and wall-plate fell into disfavour (*Fig. 13d*).

A second basic principle is lapping: the entering timber is inserted sideways rather than endways. *Lap* joints were important in early medieval carpentry, and remained in use for the ends of collar beams. The lapping timber is usually shaped into a dovetail to resist withdrawal. These joints were invariably pegged (*Fig. 13e*).

Three types of more complex joint evolving over a long span of time are amongst those studied in the work of C. A. Hewett[22]: the *scarf*, the joint at the end of a tie beam and the joints of common floor joists.

Scarf joints are commonly found in the longitudinal members of wall frames and roofs: sill beams, wall-plates and purlins. A very early specimen of a scarf joint illustrated by Hewett is an edge-halving with two pegs, reported from Essex, *c*.1180–1200 (*Fig. 14a*). (The face and edge of a timber are, respectively, the broader and narrower sides; and in early carpentry these timbers were usually laid on face. So if a scarf is said to be edge-halved, the halving is visible on edge, or side, view. Likewise face-halving signifies a halving visible from above.)

In the thirteenth century, shallowly splayed edge-halved scarfs, with the splay stopped against sharply returning abutments, seem well established, the shallow angle of the splay creating a large area of contact (*Fig. 14b*). The

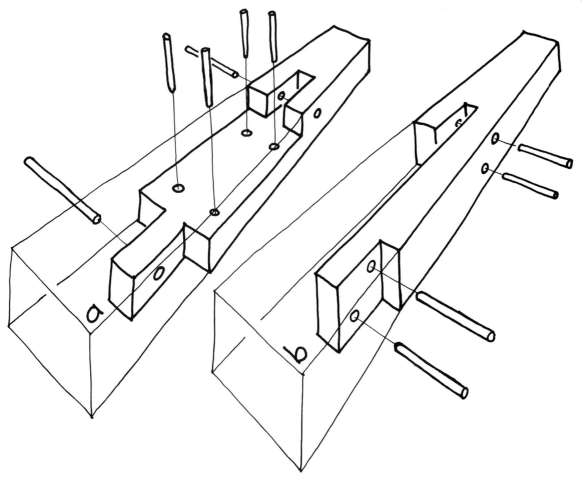

first major innovation was tabling, introduced before 1200. When a tabled scarf was formed with abutments it could be fastened by means of a wedge with a tightness impossible in a merely pegged joint (*Fig. 14c*). The wedge would be tightened before drilling for the pegs. This wedged type fell into disuse during the Middle Ages, but it re-appears in nineteenth-century engineering carpentry. The splayed and tabled scarf was then improved by the addition of tongues and grooves, leading to, in Hewett's words, 'the finest scarf joint known in England', at Place House, Ware, in Hertfordshire, *c.*1295 (*Fig. 14d*).

Much of the resistance of a scarf to bending depended on its length. As a second major innovation, a new principle was introduced into scarf design: *bridled abutments*, a projecting tenon at either end lying in a trench. It became evident that there was no further need to splay and table the main meeting surfaces, so these features were soon abandoned in favour of simple edge-halving. An edge-halved scarf with bridled abutments occurs in carpentry dated *c.*1375 in the Trig Lane excavation on the London waterfront (*Fig. 15a*).

Instead of using half-depth bridle tenons, an improvement could be achieved by face-halving, so that full height tenons could be formed (*Fig. 15b*). This joint would seem to be stronger against sagging or

15 An edge-halved and a face-halved scarf joint (after C. A. Hewett)

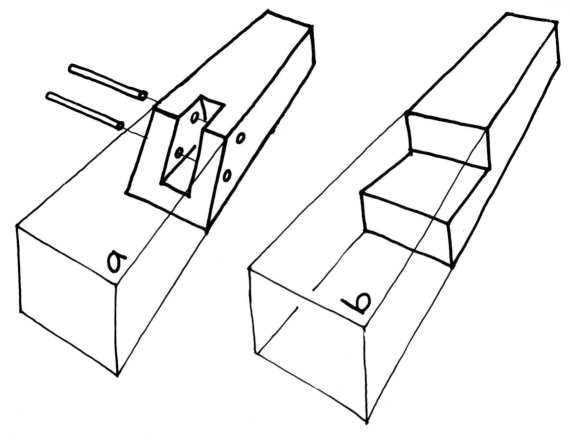

16 Simplified scarf joints

humping. It came into popularity in the fifteenth and sixteenth centuries, and was then commonplace down to modern times.

Also common in post-medieval carpentry is the *bridle scarf*, a simple adaptation of the mortise and tenon (*Fig. 16a*). For the scarfing of wall-plates resting on stone or brick walls in nineteenth-century work a simple halving was often used, with a slightly bevelled overlap (*Fig. 16b*).

Another evolving joint is the one of which the classic form is known as the *tie-beam lap-dovetail assembly*, though it reached its best form at an early date and became essentially invariable. It is found from the thirteenth to the eighteenth century, and occurs where the principal post, wall-plate and tie-beam are erected in that sequence. The assembly of the joint is complete before the majority of the roof members are added, and, as the weight of the roof is applied, pushing the top plate out, the effect is to tighten the joint (*Fig. 17*).

Hewett records a twelfth-century joint in which the post is tenoned into the wall-plate and the tie-beam laps over the wall-plate with a dovetail. The thirteenth-century innovation which greatly improved on this was to thicken the post so that a two-tier head could be formed in it, the lower tier carrying the wall-plate and the upper tier the tie-beam. Thus, of the three members, post, wall-plate and beam, each pair was independently jointed together. The thickening of the post that accommodated this detail is the *jowl*. With many minor variations, this joint remained in use until the discontinuation of the active tradition of timber-framing in the eighteenth century. In modified form it survived into stone or brick walled building.

In an interesting early eighteenth-century description of this joint in Richard Neve's Dictionary, to which Richard Harris draws attention,[23] contemporary names for the various parts of the joint are given. To Neve the tie-beam is simply the 'beam'; it rests on the wall-plate (or top plate), called the 'raison'; and this, in turn, where the wall is timber-framed, rests on the head of the principal post called simply a 'post'. The topmost of the three joints of the assembly, uniting the tie-beam and the wall-plate, is referred to by Neve as 'caulking down' ('which is the same as dovetailing across').[24] The middle joint, between tie-beam and principal post, is formed with a 'teazle tenon'. The surface from which the teazle tenon rises is the 'relish'. No special name is given to the mortise and tenon of the lowest joint, joining post to top plate.

Hewett also draws attention to the mortise and tenon joint between two members lying more or less horizontally, typically the joint between a floor joist and a binder, but also similar joints in roofs. In some early floors the joists were merely lodged on top of the beams carrying them, producing no carpentry joint. From the thirteenth century there are examples of floor joists tenoned into the sides of the beams carrying them, the tenon being at the mid-height of the joist.

In the first improvement of this detail, the tenon was moved down to the soffit level of the joist. As an intermediate stage, the tenon was at first moved down 1in (25mm) below mid-height. The first example of the

17 Tie-beam lap dovetail assembly. The head of the principal post PP is formed into two tenons, one parallel to the wall frame to engage with the top plate TP, the other parallel with the cross frame to engage with the tie-beam TB. In the first step of assembling (left), the top plate is mortised beneath and dovetail-trenched across above, and fitted on the lower tenon. The top plate is edge pegged. In the second step (right) the tie-beam is notched either side to form a dovetail and mortised to receive the second tenon on the principal post. The tie-beam is face pegged.

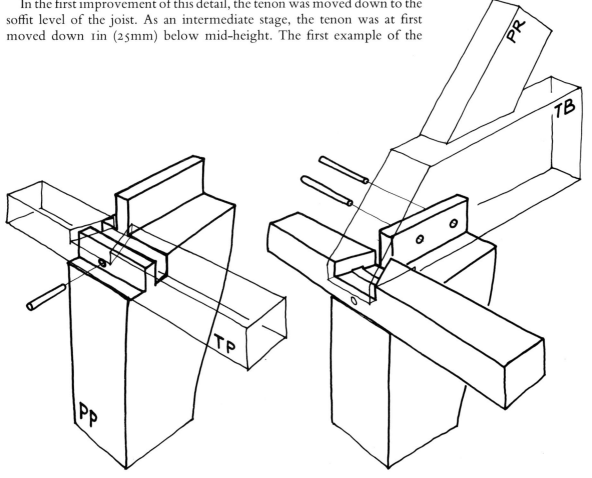

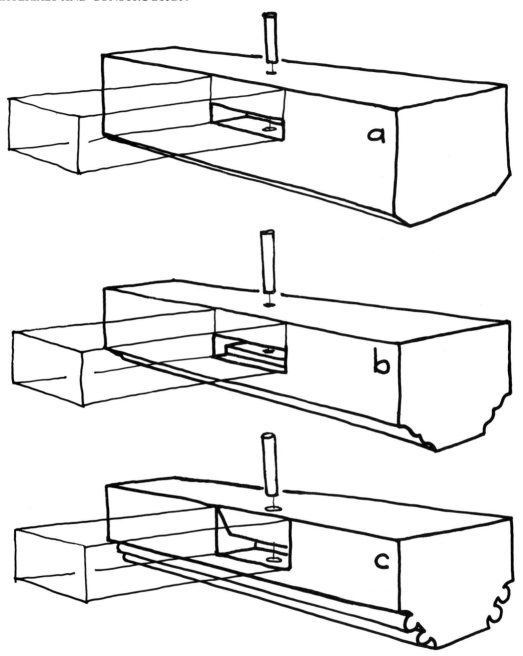

18 Medieval joist joints (after C. A. Hewett)

tenon at the soffit of the joist is at Winchester Cathedral in 1307 (*Fig. 18a*), in the floor beneath the choir stalls. This migration downward of the tenon had important advantages, lowering the bearing point of the joist and decreasing its tendency to split at the end. The main beam being rather deeper than the joist, the mortise in it was cut nearer to its central axis where continuity of fibre is least crucial. A late instance of this joint is in the Court House of Battle Abbey in 1398.

In the fifteenth century there was a preference for elaborate mouldings and chamfers on the undersides of beams. In high-quality work the profile of the joist mouldings might be scribed on the beam edge and a tight fitting housing cut for them. Two fifteenth-century technical innovations were the introduction of a soffit-spur and a housed soffit shoulder (*Fig. 18b*). These entailed a small return upwards of the level of the tenon.

A new form came into use in the sixteenth and seventeenth centuries. Once again the tenon migrated downwards; above the tenon a diminished haunch was provided (*Fig. 18c*), to be housed in a cavity above the mortise. This greatly strengthened the tenon against the weakness of its root, and helped to grip the joist against any tendency to rotate. It appears that the new type of joint was invented by Richard Russell, the King's Carpenter, and first used (as a roof purlin joint) in the completion of King's College Chapel, Cambridge, in 1510–12.

In terms of good carpentry, no advance was made thereafter. Variations are found, but it is not easy to see their technical justification.

The above is a very simplified summary of some of the evidence presented by Hewett, and any errors are those of the present writer. For the full account and the detailed use of joint development evidence for dating purposes, the original work should be consulted, especially *English Historic Carpentry*.

Modern building has caused the art of jointing to fall into disuse, but in high-quality nineteenth-century work, particularly in engineering applications, good jointing on scientific principles was favoured. This is noticeable especially in scarf joints. Designed in accordance with textbook principles rather than as handed down from craftsman to apprentice, they show at their best the 'economic' principle of engineering design. This holds that since 'the weakest part is the strength of the whole', the resistance to failure of every feature may be equalised. This was Tredgold's approach.[25] Rational design requires the carpenter to anticipate what force the joint must withstand. In a tabled scarf designed to withstand tension, the fibres across the neck should fail in tension at the same stress as that which would cause the fibres in the plane of the table to fail in shear. When hardwood wedges or iron fishplates were added their strengths were matched.

For pure compression a simple halving with bolted fishplates was preferred (*Fig. 19a*); for pure tension a splayed scarf with sharply returned abutments, fastened by means of opposed wedges (*Fig. 19b*). Hybrid forms arose from these two basic forms in other structural situations. A joint with wedges was used where either tension or compression was anticipated (*Fig. 19c*); to resist bending, which throws one face of the joint into tension and the other into compression, a solution was found which provided a splay, sharply returned abutment and a fishplate on the tensile face and a large square abutment on the other (*Fig. 19d*).

Both the tie-beam bearing detail and the joint between joists and binders were reduced in early modern carpentry to simple housing and cogging. As cast iron came into common use in the nineteenth century this also provided a substitute for traditional jointing. Cast iron is a brittle material best suited to resisting compression. It could be fashioned easily into any desired shape, subject only to the problem of freeing the finished casting from the mould. Cast iron shoes or sockets were introduced as standardised accessories. It was found that the work of the carpenter could be reduced to

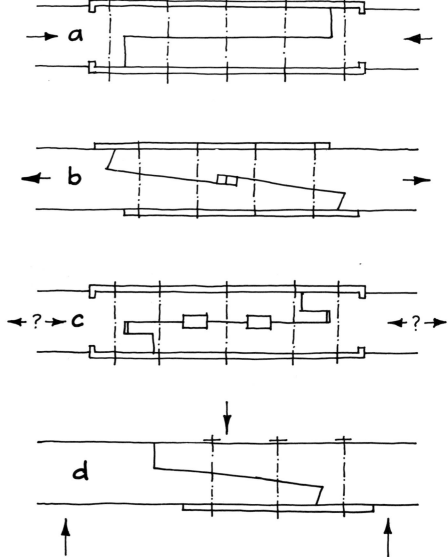

19 Engineers' bolted and fish-plated scarf joints: (a) to withstand compression; (b) to withstand tension; (c) to withstand either tension or compression; (d) to withstand bending

the simplest level: the cutting of notches to prevent sliding, the square-cutting of ends of timbers to fit into sockets, and the drilling of bolt holes. Cast iron joist-hangers could simply be nailed to the sides of beams, ready for the joists to be dropped in. In roof construction cast iron sockets were used in all the major joints of standardised trusses (*Fig. 20*).

Fastenings

The traditional joint fastening was the *trenail*, a slightly tapering oak peg driven into place and cut off about 1in (25mm) from each face. In inferior work the carpenter might not trouble to cut off the projecting parts. Temporary *hookpins* might be of ash, a more springy species of wood. Iron nails were used only in insignificant places, but their importance in such

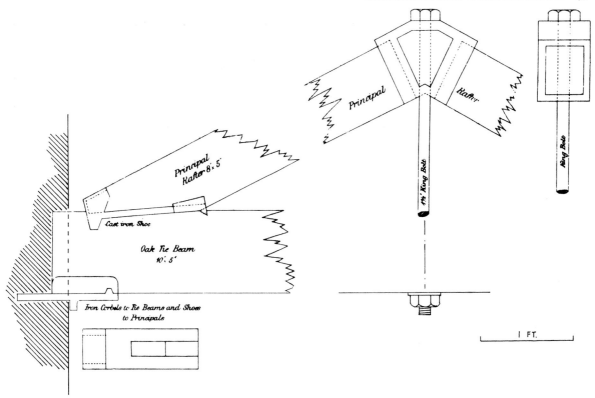

Principal

Rafter

1½" King Bolt

King Bolt

Principal Rafter 8 × 5"

Cast iron Shoe

Oak Tie Beam 10 × 5"

Iron Corbels to Tie Beams and Shoes to Principals

| 1 FT.

situations as the fixing of battens for a roof covering or the fixing of tiles was considerable.

The variety of iron nails is legion. Down to the end of the eighteenth century the production of nails was exclusively a hand craft, and one which was very sensitive to the needs of its market. Many types of nail were distinguished, and known either by their specific purpose or their price. Many common types were named in accordance with their purpose in boatbuilding and other trades. It is unlikely that the medieval range of nail types will ever be understood. Salzman's conclusion is very pessimistic: 'At first sight it would seem that such insignificant things as nails were scientifically graded and labelled; but examination shows that twenty different terms were applied to an identical article, while the same name may cover widely different objects.'[26] The nail trade was evidently very localised and local terminology very arbitrary; but nail users then, as now, would surely demand the correct nail for the job. They would refuse unsuitable nails or those which were too costly. A carpenter driving in hundreds or thousands of nails would soon have a very precise specification of what he preferred. The main reason for present-day confusion is perhaps that medieval scribes were only vaguely acquainted with the things they had to name.

The architectural recorder is in a similar position when remarking on nails used in old buildings. It may be helpful to use the sort of terms that were beginning to become standardised in the nineteenth century, when hand-made nail production was still a thriving trade. Nails might be classed according to the thickness of the shank as *fine*, *bastard* and *strong*.[27] The

20 Cast iron accessories for carpentry joints (adapted from Tarn's edition of Tredgold's *Carpentry*)

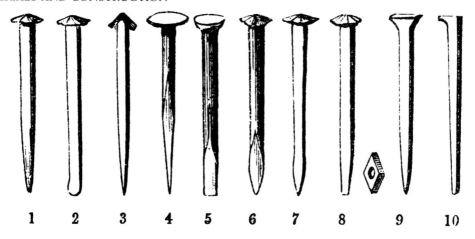

1   2   3   4   5   6   7   8   9   10

21 Nails: (1) rose sharp (for hardwood – a thinner variety for softwood); (2) rose with chisel point (the chisel point to be placed across the grain); (3) clasp (for deal, to be punched in and planed over); (4) clout (for nailing ironwork); (5) counterclout (wheelwrighting and smith's work); (6) dog (for nailing stout ironwork); (7) Kent hurdle or gate nails; (8) rose clench (with rove); (9) horse nail; (10) brad (for floorboarding) (C. Tomlinson ed., *Cyclopaedia of Useful Arts and Manufactures*, 1854, vol. II, p. 308, fig. 1489)

sectional shape of the shank might be *round, square, flat*, etc. Nail points were classed as *sharp, flat* (like a chisel or screwdriver) and *spear* (like a sharp point, but with a swelling behind the point). With some nails (brads, clinch nails) there is no point. The head of a nail might be *square* or *countersunk*.

Most important, for purposes of description, is the shape of the head seen from above. *Rose* nails have a large roundish head with four or more facets in a shallow pyramid. These may be decorative nails and are often found in door carpentry. Nails of about 2in (50mm) long with a rose head were very common.

Clasp nails have a head rising to a sharp apex with down-turned edges. Like modern oval nails, they were intended to be punched well below the surface of the timber to allow the surface to be smoothed.

Clout nails have large flat circular heads, and were used, for instance, to nail down iron straps.

The distinctive feature of a *clinch* ('clench') nail is that its tip is driven through the timber to reappear on the underside. A little lozenge-shaped plate called a *rove* is put over the nail tip and the nail is then hammered flat over the rove, to act as a rivet.

Nailmaking was at first a blacksmith's sideline, but could be carried out more economically by specialised workers. The tools of the specialised nailer were a hearth similar to that of the blacksmith, though somewhat smaller, and a spring-loaded foot-operated hammer known as an *oliver*, of which a specimen is to be seen in the Avoncroft Museum of Buildings at Bromsgrove, Worcestershire (and other museums). This equipment was in common use to the present century.

Early nails were made from wrought iron rods, and in 1617 Sir D. Bulmer devised a machine for rod cutting, leading to attempts to mechanise nail production. In 1786 Ezekiel Reed, an American, patented machinery for shearing nails from a strip of metal, and in 1790 Thomas Clifford of Bristol patented rolls for continuous forming of nails from a rod of iron. *Brads*, or nails cut from flat iron strips and possessing a projection on one side to serve as a head, were made in Birmingham and Sheffield from about 1805. (The word is a variant of *brod*, an older word for a round-headed nail.) Brads were cut out with a fly-press and became the standard nail for fixing deal floorboards.

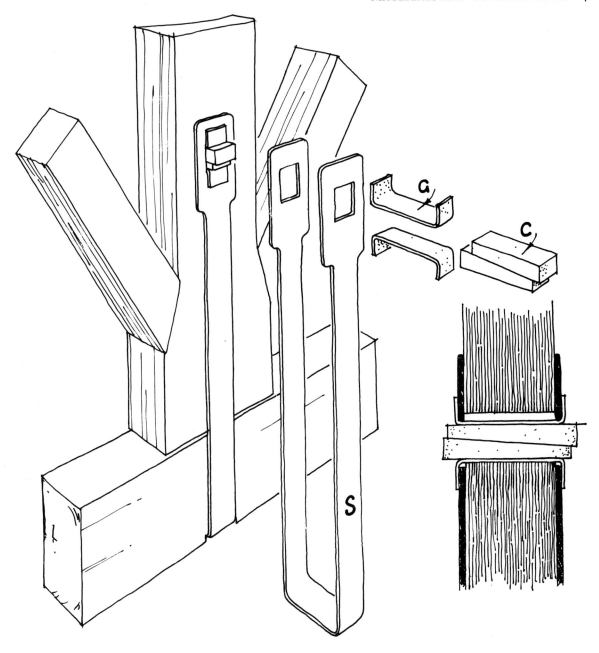

Dogs or *staples* consist of a rod of iron twice bent and pointed at each end. Staples are the smaller sort, used for instance driven into a doorframe to hold the bolt tongue.

Forelock bolts were a strong type of fastening learned from shipbuilding. A nail, even clinched, has limited resistance to withdrawal, and in massive carpentry there was sometimes a need for a stronger fixing. A long bolt slotted to take a wedge was invented, and remained in use from at least the sixteenth century to the time when mass-produced threaded bolts with nuts provided a cheaper and neater alternative in the nineteenth century.[28]

22 Gibs and cotters: a typical stirrup detail (at the foot of a king post). The upper cotter presses against the iron stirrup, the lower one against the timber as the cotters are driven in.

Gibs and *cotters* were alternatively used to tighten stirrup straps (*Fig. 22*). The gib is a little iron shield which is inserted first, and cotters are the wedges inserted behind. This is a common method of tightening a strap carrying a tie-beam from a king post in nineteenth-century carpentry.

BRICK AND TILE

Disregarding the re-use of Roman bricks, brickwork in the modern sense starts with imports of bricks from the Low Countries in the thirteenth century. A small-scale manufacture of bricks in the eastern counties, especially around Colchester and Hull, followed. As bricks and tiles are made of the same material, early scribes had some difficulty in distinguishing between them; but the earliest unequivocal reference to bricks specifically is found in 1335, when 18,000 *tegulae murales* were made for use at Ely. 'Tile' was the comprehensive word; 'brick' only comes into general currency in the fifteenth century.

When examining bricks of very early date which might be re-used Roman bricks or might be medieval, the crucial point is the ratio of dimensions. Medieval bricks are characterised by the 2:1 ratio of their two horizontal dimensions, giving a double-square appearance as seen from above. Roman bricks with a 2:1 or a 3:2 ratio are uncommon, though not unknown; the commonest proportions are a simple square.

Roman and medieval bricks were used for quite different constructional purposes. Roman bricks were essentially a facing and reinforcing material for concrete or masonry, following a technique developed in Italy which is appropriate for a region suffering from earth tremors. Roman bricks were of several sizes, the larger ones serving for bonding courses at intervals and the smaller ones for facing and for creating a firm surface for rendering. Roman bricks were laid with wide bed-joints, to enhance their adhesion to the concrete or masonry behind in the core of the wall. When stones were used as a facing, they were generally tapered to ensure that the joints at the rear would be wide for the same reason.

From the time of their introduction in northern Europe in the twelfth century, medieval bricks were predominantly of a double-square shape. These proportions enabled them to be laid in an alternating manner and achieve the maximum of cohesion through overlapping both along the length of a wall and through its thickness. This systematic alternation to achieve cohesion gave an improved quality of bond; the varieties of system are themselves known as *bonds*. Square bricks of one size could achieve bond in one direction only, double-square bricks could achieve it in two directions.

In the parts of England where brickmaking first flourished, Roman bricks were still to be seen in millions. A possible reason for changing to the new pattern was that in the north German lowlands there was neither any building stone nor remains of Roman buildings from which to rob bricks, so a new structural method had to be contrived to use brick on its own. Bricks of the new type spread to other areas in trading contact around the North Sea, being useful as ships' ballast. The manufacture of the new type was taken up in the Low Countries and in parts of northern France and

England where suitable alluvial clays were to be found. The new type of bricks could be laid with a much thinner joint.

English brickmaking started independently from two centres: Colchester and Hull. Once well established, its spread falls into phases. At first it was favoured by royal or noble patrons, and is mainly in evidence to the north of the Thames and east of the limestone belt. In 1434 the Duke of Suffolk built a brick church, school and hospital at Ewelme. At the same time Ralph Cromwell brought in a German brickmaker for the material for Tattershall Castle in Lincolnshire. Other early brick buildings of importance are Herstmonceaux Castle in Sussex, from 1440; Henry VI's work at Eton College, from 1442; Kirby Muxloe Castle in Leicestershire, from 1480, and the core, though not the facings, of the central tower of Canterbury Cathedral in the 1490s.

In the sixteenth century an ornate and ostentatious brick architecture was taken up in all regions of suitable clays for the mansions of the Tudor *nouveau riche* gentry. Chimneys were a novelty to be emphasised. Thus the earliest brick house in Shropshire, Plaish Hall, dated *c.*1540, has ornate chimneys with separate shafts decorated with a large corbelled-out coping, a string course and a pilaster of projecting bricks set cornerwise on each face, standing on a deep plinth with another string course, a shallow blind-arcade and a dentil course at the foot, all above roof level.

The main impetus to the introduction of brick as a popular material did not come until the seventeenth century. It was helped by the increasing scarcity of timber. During the reign of Elizabeth many proclamations show alarm at the loss of resources of timber; industry required great quantities of charcoal, and later in the century the troubles of the Commonwealth period were hardly favourable to the management of estates with long-term investment in timber in view. Brick finally supplanted timber as the dominant material for new buildings in London in consequence of the Great Fire of 1666. The Act for the Rebuilding made the use of stone or brick compulsory for the walls of new buildings. Types of urban brick house had been developed under strict fire regulations in Holland, and a similar architecture quickly gained fashionable status in London and elsewhere in England.

By the end of the seventeenth century brick was being used at all levels of society, and its later progress compared with alternative materials was no longer a matter of status but largely a matter of local price competition. In the eighteenth century old timber-framed buildings were often re-fronted in brick, not necessarily as an aesthetic sham but because it was the sensible material to use for the purpose. If frames had merely been panelled in brick, the wall thickness would have been inadequate. None the less, re-fronted buildings are often detectable from the odd proportions of their elevations, due to the survival of all or some of the framing behind the façade.

The last places for brick to penetrate into were those in which a plentiful supply of building stone was available. Parts of the Lake District, the Peak District, the limestone belt and the far south-west are all areas where bricks make their first substantial appearance with the coming of cheap transport.

Brick is far superior to stone as a practical material for the construction of hearths and chimneys, and its introduction for this limited purpose became general at an early date. A Worcester City regulation of 1467 stipulated that 'no chymneys of Tymber ne thacced houses be suffered wtyn the Cyte but that the owners do hem awey and make them chymneys of Stone or Bryke by midsomer day next commynge'.[29] In rural areas also, especially in the south-east in the sixteenth century, stone or brick fireplaces were being added to old houses in place of open hearths and to cottages previously unheated. In 1577 Harrison commented on the multitude of chimneys erected during the span of memory of the old men of his village.[30]

The main changes in the size of bricks have been in the height. Height is independent of the two other dimensions, but limited by the need to keep a brick within the weight which can readily be lifted by one hand repeatedly during a day's work. It is also limited by the skill of the brickmaker, thin bricks being easier to fire or burn; the thickness of a brick has, therefore, gradually increased over the centuries. The thirteenth-century bricks of Little Wenham Hall are about $2\frac{1}{4}$in (57mm) in height. Fourteenth- and fifteenth-century bricks are generally about 2in (50mm), but the Statute of 1477 sought to impose a minimum of $2\frac{1}{2}$in (63mm).[31] A Statute in 1729 required brickmakers within 15 miles (24km) of London to use a mould 3in (76mm) in depth, to produce a brick of about $2\frac{1}{2}$in (63mm). The introduction of a tax in 1784 levied per thousand bricks caused builders to demand a brick of the maximum volume permitted – 150 cu. in (2.46 litres) – above which a higher rate of tax applied. A brick height of about 3in (76mm) became common, and long outlived the repeal of the tax in 1850. During the late nineteenth century, many north of England brickmakers settled on $2\frac{7}{8}$in (73mm) as the standard height, with $2\frac{5}{8}$in (66mm) becoming similarly standardised in the south of England.

The colour of a brick (or tile) results mainly from the manner in which it was burned or fired and on the chemical composition of its clay. (The expression 'green brick' does not refer to colour: it signifies a brick not yet burned or fired.) In one class of brick the colours range from buff to salmon pink and red, the clays being mainly hydrated aluminium silicate. A second class contains bricks of a yellow colour, their clays containing a high percentage of calcium carbonate: these are from chalk or limestone districts. The latter class includes bricks derived from the alluvium of the London basin. A third class includes the blue bricks familiar in engineering works and used widely for decorative contrasts in Victorian buildings.

Reds   In the first of these classes the presence of a quantity of iron oxide ranging from about 2 to 10 per cent in the clay gives rise to a colour ranging from light buff to chocolate. Red bricks are found in the middle of this range. The presence of alkalis or an increase of firing temperature results in a darker or more purple colour; the presence of alumina tends to make the colour brighter and lighter.

In coal districts the brickmaking clays often contain a certain amount of organic matter, which has the effect of impairing the quality of bricks and giving them a speckled appearance.

Yellows   Brick clays with an admixture of chalk or limestone are known to the brickmaker as *marls*. Marls usually contain from 15 to 30 per cent of calcium carbonate and burn to a distinctive yellow colour; if the proportion is 40 per cent or more the result is a grey or a very pale buff colour.

Blues   The blue bricks commonly used in nineteenth- and twentieth-century engineering work contain from 7 to 10 per cent of iron oxide. At the end of the normal firing process these bricks are subjected to the reducing effect of a smoky kiln atmosphere. The red ferric oxide in the clay is reduced to a blue-green ferrous oxide or to metallic iron, which in turn combines with silica to produce a slag which melts and runs slightly, creating the slightly glazed appearance. The slag fills up the pores in the brick, adds greatly to the strength, and makes it impermeable to water. The surface of the brick is further darkened by particles of carbon from the fuel in the kiln.

Until the introduction of brickmaking machinery in the mid-nineteenth century, bricks were universally hand-made; that is to say, each brick was individually formed. Medieval bricks appear to have been made by treading the clay out on a floor by foot and then cutting it with knives. This method, coupled with uncertainty of firing or burning temperature, produced wide variations in the dimensions of individual bricks. Later bricks were made from a clay ground up and tempered to exactly the required texture, accurately formed by pressing a 'clot' of clay into a mould on a workbench. The use of a bench and a mould may have started very early, because it is hardly practical to form tiles in the primitive way, as they are too thin, need to be pinched up into 'nibs', or otherwise specially shaped. As bricks and tiles would usually be made together, the superior method of shaping them would soon be adopted generally. The mould was a wooden box, sometimes metal-faced internally, with no top or bottom but with projecting handles. The clot was thrown down vigorously into the mould and pressed to fill the corners. Any surplus clay was then struck off.

As the clay had to be in a very cohesive state, it tended to stick to the sides of the mould; to prevent this the mould was usually sprinkled with sand before the clot was put in, and this sand would be found adhering to the faces of the brick or tile on its removal from the mould. This is the origin of the custom of sand-facing bricks and tiles. It has an interesting consequence on the appearance of tiles: ordinary tiles, on the rear of which a nib is formed, have to be moulded face-down; ridge tiles, which have to be formed over a curved block and may have a finial, have to be moulded face-up. Ordinary tiles, therefore, show their sanded face to the outside of a roof, whilst ridge tiles show their smooth face. The contrast was often heightened by a slight glaze being given to ridge tiles.

Hack and *kiss* marks are indicative of the way bricks were stacked in the brickyard before firing or burning and in the kiln or clamp during the process. Water is present in the clay from which they are moulded, and they must be dried before any heat is applied, otherwise they would be ruined by the development of steam. As it would be wasteful of space in the brickyard to stack each brick separately, they are stacked in piles known as hacks. Often the wet bricks press into each other slightly, leaving indentations known as hack marks, which may be seen as lines along the length of a brick. As hack marks have nothing to do with firing or burning, they are not characterised by any difference in colour.

When bricks are stacked in the kiln for firing or in the clamp for burning, they are already in a dry state and will not be further marked with indentations. The stacking arrangement, however, causes a different type

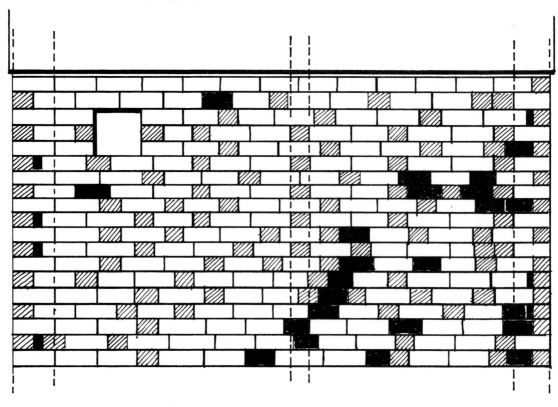

23 An inexpert attempt at Flemish bond (9in [225mm] wall of a midden-privy removed to Ironbridge Museum)

of mark to appear on the finished brick. As heat acts on the exposed surfaces far more than on the parts of the brick in contact with another brick, colour differences result. These marks are termed kiss marks and are not characterised by any indentation. Kiss marks reveal whether the bricks were lying parallel, at right angles or obliquely, and they may reveal whether tiles were being fired in the kiln or burned in the clamp at the same time.

Another recognisable surface texture is that of wire-cut bricks, made from the mid-nineteenth century. In this mechanical method of forming bricks they are extruded through an orifice, rather like toothpaste, and the resulting block of clay is then cut into individual bricks with wires, rather like cutting cheese. The appearance of wire-cut bricks is governed by the behaviour of the clay rubbing past the edge of the orifice, particles of grit tending to catch at the edge and to be held back as the mass of the clay passes, causing little furrows to appear with the speck of grit at the end.

When describing brickwork in detail it is often convenient to use a brick length as a unit of measurement. It may be a brick length with or without a joint, depending on the situation. A nominal brick length is usually taken to be 9in (225mm), although bricks may vary in precise size.

Bond

A *bond* has two purposes: it seeks to achieve the maximum firmness in a wall by overlapping the bricks and avoiding cavities, and it seeks to achieve the best appearance by means of regularity, symmetry and pattern on the visible faces of the brickwork, insofar as these two purposes are compatible. Using bricks of the standard double-square shape and of reasonably uniform size, it is practically impossible for a bricklayer not to conform to a regular system of disposing *headers* and *stretchers*, as the end-on and side-on bricks are called respectively. If there is a regular system to the work there must be an identifiable bond. Truly random work would be extremely difficult to achieve, except perhaps in the most irregularly-shaped medieval bricks. When one is tempted to describe the brickwork of an old building as 'randomly' bonded, it is far better merely to say that the bond is 'unclear'. Whatever the reasons for the obscurity, it is virtually certain that the original bricklayer consciously followed a systematic bond, which could be detected if the brickwork were to be dismantled for study.

To clarify the features of a bond, it may be helpful to trace the pattern of joints from a photograph and to shade headers, stretchers and cut bricks differently. Two cut bricks rarely occur together, so cut bricks might be shaded black, with headers shaded grey, and stretchers left white (*Fig. 23*). In this way the pattern of headers (often actually darker in colour than the stretchers in some nineteenth-century brickwork) will be emphasised, the bond may become clear, and the special features of bonding at corners and at the sides of openings will become apparent.

Stretcher bond (*Fig. 24a*)

Walls built in stretcher bond are necessarily only half a brick in thickness, unless the facing is fixed by concealed means to a backing, as in modern cavity wall construction.

Quoins and reveals: at each edge one course terminates with a stretcher, the other with a header (in the case of a quoin) or a half-bat (in the case of a reveal).

Setting out: the overall length of a wall and the widths of piers and openings within it should be to multiples of one brick (better rule) or to multiples of half a brick (inferior rule). The better rule preserves full symmetry.

Header bond (*Fig. 24b*)

This is more common in foundations than in facing work. It gives an even, net-like appearance. It can be built to any wall thickness of one brick or more, though if the wall is of $1\frac{1}{2}$ bricks thick or more, half-bats must be used alternately on face to create bonding through the depth of the wall.

Quoins and reveals: at every edge one course terminates with a stretcher and the other with a queen-closer and a header.

English bond (*Fig. 24c*)

In the main area of brickwork (disregarding edges at corners and openings) courses consisting entirely of stretchers alternate with courses consisting entirely of headers. Each header is centred over a joint or over a stretcher, and each stretcher is centred over a header.

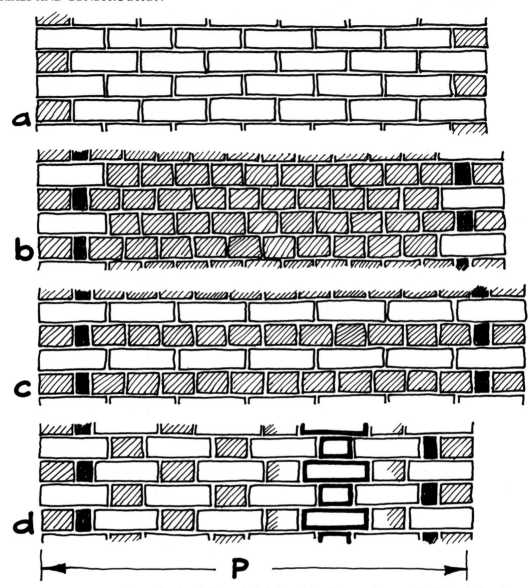

24 (a) stretcher bond: $P = n \times h$ (inferior rule) or $P = n \times s$ (better rule); (b) header bond: $P = (n \times h) + q$ (inferior rule) or $P = n \times h$ (better rule); (c) English bond: $P = n \times s$; (d) Flemish bond $P = (n \times (s+h)) + q$ (inferior rule) or $P = (n \times (s+h)) + s$ (better rule). P is a possible overall length where $s = $ a stretcher length, $h = $ a header length, $q = $ a quarter brick length and $n = $ any number. In each case the better rule achieves overall symmetry, the inferior rule (as illustrated) does not.

English is considered to be the strongest of the bonds. Its alternating header and stretcher courses give it a horizontally striped appearance. It can be built in walls of one brick or more in thickness. The strength of English bond lies in the fact that no cut bricks are used in the main area. In walls of over one brick in thickness, stretchers on face are backed by headers, and vice versa. In very thick walls the core is formed entirely in headers, making them very strong against overturning.

Quoins and reveals: quoins and plain reveals in English bond terminate with a header and an adjacent queen-closer in every header course. With recessed reveals the detail is different: as the timber frame is placed beside the last header in the header course, a quarter bat is used to complete the fin of brickwork.

Setting out: setting out is governed by the stretcher courses, so that, as in stretcher bond, the overall length of a wall and the widths of openings and piers within it should all be dimensioned to multiples of one brick.

There are four variations of the English bond:

English garden wall bond (Fig. 25a)
This consists of three courses of stretchers alternating with one course of

25 Variations of English bond:
(a) English garden wall bond;
(b) English cross bond; (c) Dutch bond

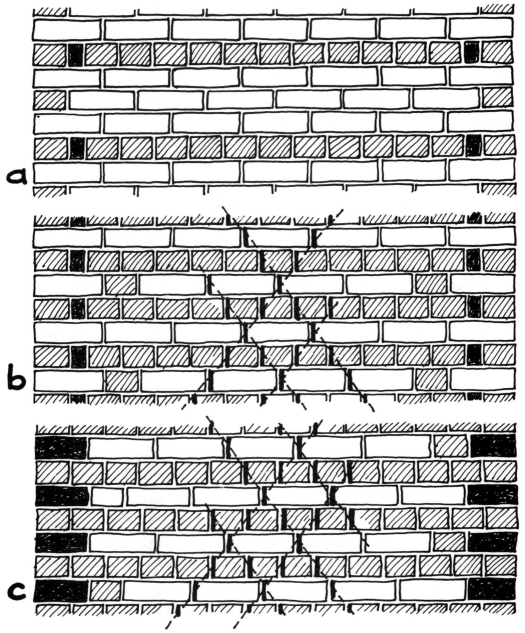

headers. This bond economises on the selected better-quality bricks appearing in the face of the work, and is commonly used for minor buildings as well as for garden walls. The visual effect of the bond, which may sometimes have been the reason for its choice, is of thin, well spaced horizontal bands.

American bond
This is the name given to variants of English garden wall bond with four, five or even six courses of stretchers in succession.

English cross bond (Fig. 25b)
This consists of courses of headers and courses of stretchers alternating, as in English bond, but with the difference that every second stretcher course is displaced by half a brick. This creates a regular diagonal pattern. The bond is designed to achieve an artistic effect and offers no practical advantages.

Dutch bond (Fig. 25c)
This is similar to English cross bond and displays the same regular pattern of diagonals. The difference lies in the manner of setting out the quoins and reveals. In both English bond and English cross bond the setting out is based on the stretcher courses, but in Dutch bond it is based on the header courses.

Flemish bond (Fig. 24d)

In the main area of brickwork (disregarding edges at corners and openings) all courses consist of headers and stretchers alternately. Each header is centred over a stretcher in the course beneath and vice versa.

Flemish bond lacks the strength of English bond, but in several respects it has a better appearance. Its effect is more even-textured and it lends itself better to work in a combination of bricks of two qualities. If selected bricks are set aside for facing positions, or if more expensive facing bricks are obtained, Flemish bond uses them more sparingly than English.

Flemish bond came into favour in the seventeenth century at a time in architectural history when an ostentatious use of materials was giving way to an appreciation of architectural form. The earliest example is Kew Palace, built in 1631. The new taste emphasised the proportions of façades and the relations of voids and solids, and materials were required not to be visually distracting. The striped effect created by brickwork in the old-fashioned English bond was no longer favoured. The name given to the new bond reflects the influence of the Low Countries on London architecture of the time. Flemish bond became almost universal until brickwork came again to be used as a patterned material in the nineteenth century.

Quoins and reveals: quoins and plain reveals in Flemish bond terminate with a header and an adjacent queen-closer in every second course. With recessed reveals the detail is different: as the timber frame is placed beside the last header in one course, a quarter bat is used to complete the fin of brickwork.

Setting out: as Flemish bond was regarded as suitable for work of high

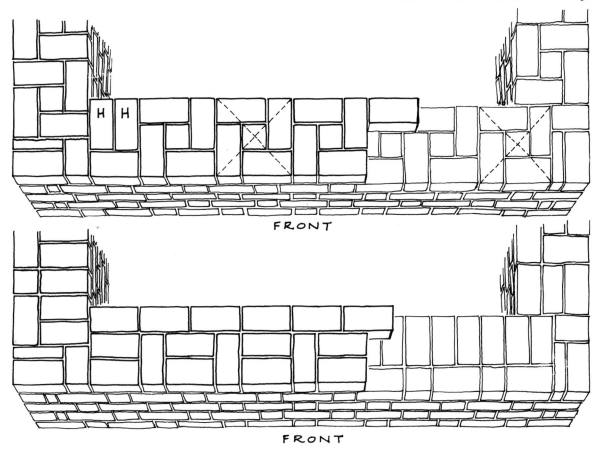

FRONT

FRONT

FRONT

quality, a strict rule is often followed in setting out, requiring careful calculation of opening and pier widths. To preserve full symmetry, an overall width from quoin to quoin should be a multiple of $1\frac{1}{2}$ bricks minus a half, and, where openings are formed with a similar queen-closer detail, the widths of piers between them should follow the same rule. The width of an opening should be a multiple of $1\frac{1}{2}$ bricks plus a half. In common work this exacting rule is breached. Dimensioning is made much easier if the builder allows queen-closers to occur in different courses on either side of an opening, ignoring symmetry. Faulty versions of Flemish bond are very common indeed.

Flemish bond walls of $1\frac{1}{2}$ or more bricks in thickness are of two types, according to whether they are Flemish on both faces or only on one. If Flemish on both faces, the bond is called *double Flemish bond*. Walls of one brick in thickness, the usual thickness of walls in minor buildings, are necessarily Flemish on both faces. It is usual, however, for Flemish bond walls of greater thickness to be single, because if the rear face is to be plastered there is nothing to be gained by retaining Flemish appearance on both sides, and a stronger wall results if the bond reverts to English on the hidden side. The resulting hybrid is called *single Flemish bond*. To appreciate the difference it is necessary to consider the plan view of a typical course, although this is not a view usually accessible to the investigator (*Fig. 26*). A

26 Double Flemish bond (above) and single Flemish bond (below). The double form consists of a sequence of $1\frac{1}{2}$-brick squares (some shown crossed for emphasis). At some point on the rear face two headers come together (HH) as a backing to the additional stretcher on the front face. The two forms are not distinguishable if only the front face is seen.

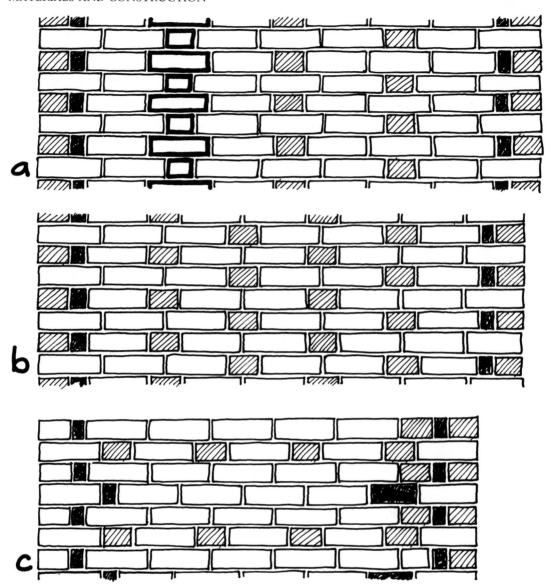

27 Variations of Flemish bond:
(a) Flemish garden wall bond;
(b) monk bond; (c) old English
bond

typical course in a double Flemish bond wall consists of a succession of $1\frac{1}{2}$ by $1\frac{1}{2}$ brick squares with a half-bat in the centre. (There is a minor insoluble problem with this bond: a wall length must be a multiple of $1\frac{1}{2}$ bricks because of the arrangement of squares, but this contradicts the rule stated before that for symmetry overall a wall length must be a multiple of $1\frac{1}{2}$ bricks minus a half.)

There are three variations of the Flemish bond:

Flemish garden wall bond (Fig. 27a)
This is alternatively known as *Sussex bond* or *Scotch bond*. Each course consists of one header and three or five stretchers alternating, the headers in each course being centred over the middle stretcher of the group in the course beneath. This creates a visual effect of jagged vertical stripes.

Monk bond (Fig. 27b)

Each course consists of one header and two stretchers alternating, the headers in each course being centred over the joint between stretchers in the course beneath. This creates a visual effect of regularly spaced spots.

Old English (Fig. 27c)

This bond does not appear in the textbooks but is often seen in the rear and sides of minor buildings. In this a course of headers and stretchers alternating, as in Flemish, is followed by three courses of stretchers, as in English garden wall. So headers constitute only a twelfth of the wall area, in a very economical but weak bond.

As headers are troublesome in a wall of one-brick thickness (variability of length making it difficult to achieve a fair-face on both sides) and as headers add to the expense where one face is to be carried out in selected good quality bricks, the economy of a bond may be looked at in terms of the fraction of the wall face area (disregarding corners) which consists of headers:

Old English	a twelfth (cheapest)
English garden wall	an eighth
Flemish garden wall	a seventh
Monk	a fifth
Flemish	a third
English	a half (costliest)

STONE

Architecture might be treated as geology, such is the importance of stone in historic buildings.

Where a stone outcrops plentifully under shallow soil it is likely to be seen in field walls as well as in local minor buildings. It may be the local traditional material for road mending. Some of the best stone will be earmarked for building but also for field gateposts, farmyard troughs, pavings and so forth. In the Derbyshire Peak District parish of Litton, the field walls preserve the old field pattern splendidly, the agriculture never having been prosperous enough to make it worthwhile removing them. Here, too, the architecture of the mountain limestone is seen at its best.

Within an area of the Peak bounded approximately by Buxton, Bakewell, Matlock, Tissington and Hartington occurs a large outcrop of this limestone. Surrounding this white limestone on all sides, except for a short stretch near Mayfield, is the outcrop of a type of coarse brown sandstone known as millstone grit, the latter being the dominant type of stone of the southern Pennines.

Practically, though perhaps not aesthetically, the millstone grit is much superior to the mountain limestone. Its best beds provide an excellent freestone capable of use for lintels spanning over quite wide openings. Although large blocks can also be obtained from the limestone, it tends, as a weaker stone, to be used in small blocks, the only use found for big stones being as posts for field gates. The millstone grit can be brought to a fine plain finish, though this brings problems of toxic dust; much of the limestone, on the other hand, is probably apt to shatter.

Even in the most high-lying and inaccessible villages of the Peak it is usual to see the mountain limestone used with some admixture of other materials. Usually this means that the masonry consists of some combination of limestone and gritstone, or perhaps, in some nineteenth-century buildings, the imported material might be brick or one of the types of Mansfield stone.

The evidence from old buildings of trade in stone across the geological border of the mountain limestone seems to show that it was entirely inwards. The superior materials from outside were brought in, but the inferior materials were not brought out. Detailed observation would show if there is any tendency for the limestone to be used outside its natural area for hidden situations such as foundations or the backings of walls. The only obvious form in which the mountain limestone was sent out into the surrounding country was as a rich type of lime for agriculture or for plastering.

Limestone quarries and the extensive use of the stone in minor positions are seen along the road from Monyash to Bakewell, a road running from the heart of the limestone district to its fringe. Nearer to Monyash all the gatepost stones are selected blocks of the best limestone; nearer to Bakewell they change to imported gritstone, standing in openings in what are otherwise completely limestone walls. Much of the common material of field walls is evidently surface scatter cleared from the fields they surround, rough blocks from 2in (50mm) in thickness upwards.

The same combination of limestone rubble with imported gritstone in the most critical positions in buildings – particularly lintels – can be seen at various places at the fringe of the limestone area. At Foolow this combination is found, but not at neighbouring Eyam, lying astride the boundary line, where the usual visible construction is entirely of gritstone. The combination of limestone generally with gritstone in the critical positions is seen at Hope, north of Bakewell, but the masonry of neighbouring Edale consists entirely of an inferior quality of gritstone. The combination of materials is also seen at Youlgreave.

Arkwright Square in Bakewell (originally called Birkett's Buildings) is a group of 13 cottages built in a mixture of limestone and gritstone shortly before 1811. Here the walling material is the mountain limestone, used as random rubble. It is generally used in small pieces, but in some parts of the walling the stones are of a size that would require two hands to lift them. There is a cart-sized entry into the central court, with an arched head turned in gritstone blocks. The windows, many of them 'Yorkshire casements', have lintels and sills of gritstone. All the later buildings in the vicinity are constructed apparently entirely in gritstone.

The gritstone used at Monyash, well within the limestone area, is better material than that of some entirely gritstone towns such as Chapel en le Frith. Having to import gritstone, the builders went to a good source: the best gritstone is seen around Matlock, where freestone is available in large, sound blocks. The gritstone in the west parts of the county and continuing into Cheshire tends to be a poor tilestone. The buildings of Matlock commonly use gritstone in about 8in (200mm) courses through the whole height; at Chapel en le Frith a poor stone is sorted into sizes and graded courses are used.

In its turn the gritstone of the southern Pennines around Ashbourne and Belper gives way to the brick of the Derby area, and here too materials cross their natural boundaries. Stone lintels and sills are found in the brick area, but in the later buildings brick penetrates into the stone area for cheap parts such as side and rear walls. At Belper, gritstone lintels are common in otherwise brickwork walls. In some of the property of the Strutts' cotton mill company there, built early in the nineteenth century, there are wedge-shaped lintels, the builders having decided to lay sloping courses of brickwork to conform to the slope of the land, and the lintels being designed to agree with this odd feature.

Any geological boundary, or the boundary where the economical use of a local stone gives way to that of timber or brick, presents a problem for the architectural investigator to tackle.

Most types of stone may be cut readily into blocks suitable for building, though they vary widely in the extent to which they can be brought to a finish. Colour and texture, carving and weathering qualities and resistance to air pollution may be very variable. Different types of stone vary in the extent to which they can be obtained in large blocks for use as doorsteps, landings, flags, sills, lintels, or bond-stones. For larger buildings the choice of a type of stone may also depend on its ability to bear heavy loads.

The characteristics required in a stone also vary according to the position in the building in which it is to be used. Stones suitable for use in the backing of a wall or a rubble core may not be suitable for facing. Those suited to the less vulnerable parts of a wall face may not be durable enough for use at corners. It has, therefore, always been necessary for the mason to select from the material delivered to site for each task as it arises. Hence also the mixing of materials, such as the use of a stone facing to a brickwork wall, which can be the cause of dire troubles to the conservationist trying to prolong the life of old buildings.

Pennine gritstone is usually left rough because of the health problems caused by breathing its dust when trying to bring it to a smooth finish. With Cornish granite the splitting of stones is difficult, so the builder tends to use the largest size of block which he can handle. Flint occurs in sizes too small for effective bonding, and the builder introduces other materials to reinforce his work. In masonry, far more than brickwork, the craftsman has to put careful thought into the fitting of every piece. Stones, furthermore, usually have a 'right way up' to which the cutting should conform.

The conspicuous use of stone as a walling material is only part of the picture. There is generally plenty of stone to be found in the construction of an 'entirely timber-framed' building: stone paving, stone plinths beneath timber sill beams, stone padstones hidden in the ground beneath main post positions, rubblestone or cobble foundations beneath these; the panels of the timber structure are probably plastered with material derived from burned stones. Then the roof may be completed in stone tiles.

In most parts of the country the scope for choosing between different types of stone is considerable, as may be judged from the intricacy of the Geological Survey map. England and Wales abound in stone-bearing formations of very limited surface extent, many of which have had a profound influence on the older local architecture. The tendency is for most geological formations, as they appear at the surface, to be elongated in the south-west to north-east direction: the oolitic limestone, for example, which provides much of the best carving stone in the country, runs from Portland in Dorset through Bath, Cirencester, Stamford and Lincoln, to end on the North Yorkshire Moors. A journey at right angles to this trend, from Holyhead to London, would bring one with great rapidity through the succession of geological formations from the oldest to the youngest. Probably every parish in the main stone districts such as the Cotswolds formerly had its own quarry.

The Geological Survey publishes maps through the HMSO at several scales, including an overall map of Great Britain in two sheets at 10 inches to the mile. There is also a series of paperback handbooks, the *British Regional Geology*, which explains the local landscapes and introduces the geologist's perspective on any building stones mentioned. What a Geological map cannot indicate is the quality of stone for building purposes. A formation may produce excellent material from one quarry and useless material from another; but for the majority of types used in modest buildings the Geological map is a fair guide to local architecture.

Outsiders may try to select a stone with great care, but still be at the mercy of the quarry firm; thus, inferior stone was used for the Houses of Parliament, with disastrous results, though the quarries had been chosen by a Royal Commission appointed for the purpose. It may require the most intimate knowledge of a quarry to know from which strata the most durable stones are to be had. An outsider is also liable to be sold stone which has been allowed to dry for an insufficient time, so that the moisture leads to frost damage, or for an excessive time, so that a hardened skin has formed preventing proper cutting and carving.

Limestone and marble

Limestones are those stones in which the majority of the material is calcium carbonate. This may take the form of fossil shells, usually in a cementing medium of the same chemical composition. They are generally readily carved when freshly quarried, but later develop a hard outer layer.

Limestones may be divided into classes according to the fineness of the grains: compact limestones, such as the lias, may seem quite dense and uniform; granular ones have rounded grains from the size of the eggs in cod roe (*roestones* or *oolites*, such as Bath stone) to pea size (*pisolites*); and shelly ones, in which the form of the shells is apparent, such as Purbeck. Outside this classification the main limestone types are marble (any limestone capable of taking a fine polish), and magnesian limestone (with over 15 per cent magnesium carbonate). A highly magnesian limestone is called *dolomite*.

Serpentine (Cornwall and Anglesea) is known loosely as a type of marble, though it is not derived from limestone. It is generally a rich green or red, with white veins; its use is for interior ornament.

Sandstone and gritstone

Sandstones consist of grains of quartz surrounded by a cementing material, and their durability depends on the latter. They exist in a great variety of colours from white to black, but generally the colour is yellow, red or brown caused by the presence of iron. They are sedimentary or metamorphic, and classified scientifically by the nature of the cementing material. As there may be a proportion of lime present in the cementing material, sandstones merge into limestones.

The practical classification of sandstones is into grits, freestones other than grits, flagstones and tilestones. The classes merge into each other, as grit is a description based on the particles and the other classes refer to the manner in which the stone breaks. Grit, notably the Pennine millstone grit, is, at its best, a coarse grained and very strong stone used throughout the country for millstones and civil engineering purposes and locally for building. Finer grained stones which work readily in all directions with mallet and chisel are called freestones. Other types of sandstone split into sheets: those cleaving readily into thick slabs suitable for paving are called flagstones or landings, and those capable of being split into sheets thin enough for roofing are called tilestones.

Granite and other igneous types

In true granite, commonly seen in Cornwall and Devon, there are crystals of quartz or felspar mixed with particles of mica. Syenitic granite from Leicestershire is similar, but contains hornblende also. It is darker than true granite and is used more for paving rather than in masonry.

Granite is quarried by wedging or now by blasting. It was generally cut into blocks for building at the quarry, because it is a type of stone not liable to damage in transit.

Other types of igneous stone are not much used in masonry except in the vicinity of the quarries producing them. Porphyry is virtually indestructible and is polished for use in ornaments. Elvan (Devon and Cornwall), like granite, is very durable. Gneiss is like granite, but it splits in layers. Mica schist breaks in thin slabs and is suitable for flagstones. Hornblende schist breaks into thick slabs, suitable for very durable flagstones. Trap (greenstone), e.g. Penmaenmawr stone, and basalt, e.g. Rowley rag (Staffordshire), are suitable for paving setts.

Slate

The term slate may be loosely applied to any stone capable of being cleft into thin sheets suitable for roofing or similar purposes. In the strict sense, however, slate is a sedimentary argillaceous rock which has been partly crystallised by great pressure. At right angles to the direction of pressure it develops a plane of 'slaty cleavage'.

True slate (clay slate) is seen at its best in the vicinity of Ffestiniog, where it is of grey or blue colour. This slate from the Silurian formation is capable of being cleft very thinly and was used extensively as a roofing material throughout the country in the nineteenth century. A poorer slate of more varied colour occurs in the Cambrian formation in the vicinity of Caernarvon, and thicker and coarser slates are found in Westmorland and Cornwall. The use of slate as a general walling material tends to be purely local because of its weight and problems of transport.

Stones popularly called slate, but not in a strict geological sense, include several types of Jurassic limestone: Collyweston; Stonesfield (rich in fossils, found near Oxford); Cotswold and Purbeck stones. Several formations of sandstone also produce so-called slates: particularly the coal measures and the millstone grit in the Pennine regions. These non-clay-slate types would be better called tilestones or stone tiles.

There has always been a movement of material from quarry to site regardless of geological boundaries, and the higher the status of a building the wider the territory within which materials are likely to have been sought. It hardly troubles the purist to observe that some English churches are built of Caen stone from Normandy. Alien materials are also less jarring in urban buildings, where the observer is not conscious of any sense of natural landscape. It must be a personal decision at what point the use of alien materials becomes objectionable. The development of modern transport has led to a promiscuity in the use of materials which some regard as very regrettable, particularly if local skills in the proper selection and use of a material are forgotten or ignored as it falls into new hands.

Stonework in detail

Masons' marks
Several types of worker have left their marks, in one sense or another, on old stonework. The stonecutter at the quarry hewed the stone and cut it to rough shape; but the signs of his drills and wedges are likely to be obliterated by the dressing of stones on site. There the work was divided between two classes of mason, known respectively as *bankers* and *fixers*, the former selecting the stones and cutting them to fit in their intended positions, the latter raising them into place and laying them. Bankers might also be *carvers* producing mouldings and ornaments. The workmanship usually visible on built masonry is entirely that of the banker mason.

Banker marks
Personal marks appearing on the face of built masonry, identifying work for payment, are properly called banker marks. Individual masons working as bankers acquired their personal marks at the end of apprenticeship, which they retained through their careers. A master mason visiting a quarry to select stone might still use his mark to identify what he had chosen, or use it in lieu of a signature in written accounts or contracts.[32] Early medieval banker marks tend to be deeply cut – later medieval ones only shallowly; in post-medieval times these marks are generally cut on the bed face of the stone, to be hidden in the finished work. A very late instance of banker marks appearing profusely on the face of stonework is seen at the aqueduct, dated 1789, in the village of the same name in Telford in Shropshire.

Tooling marks
The finish to stonework may be more or less fortuitous, showing the

methods of getting and squaring the stones most expeditiously; or a special finish may be called for. If stones are left as they were split in the quarry they are said to be 'quarry pitched'. Otherwise they have one or other of the various types of tooled finish, depending on the nature of the stone.

Softer types of stone were often brought to a smooth 'plain' finish. The tool likely to have been used is the *drag*, a semi-circular steel plate with teeth which is drawn across the face in random directions. The chisel marks from the preliminary dressing would be removed.

Coarser stones were often brought to a finish exploiting the textural effect of the tool used. They may be hammer-dressed, flakes being removed to leave a pattern of spalled hollows: the tool used is the scappling hammer, and the finish is often called *scabbled* or *scappled*. Otherwise stones may be chiselled. The finest chisel is the *point*, with a tip of $\frac{1}{4}$in (6mm) or less, which can produce a finely pitted texture. A wide chisel with a tip of $1\frac{1}{2}$in (3.8cm) or more is a *boaster*. Parallel marks cut with the boaster produce a *droved* finish.

The tooling marks produced by the point, the ordinary chisel or the boaster tend naturally to be parallel; but if special efforts have been made to keep them accurately parallel and regular, the stone would be described as *fair tooled*. If the grooves are deep and regularly sized and spaced the finish is *furrowed*.

The mason may alternatively seek to produce artificial irregularity, a frequent feature of the basement storeys of monumental buildings. A *vermiculated* finish is where contrived irregularities are carefully marked out on the stone and deeply carved around.

Margins and joints

The distinction between *ashlar* and *rubble* stonework is essentially a matter of jointing: ashlar stones are carefully squared to be laid with thin, regular joints, while rubble is brought to size with the axe or hammer and wide irregular joints accepted. Rubble stonework may be laid either in regular courses; in graded courses, from large stones at the bottom of a wall to small ones at the top; in a random manner, but brought to a regular level every 12 or 18in (300 or 450mm) or so ('rubble brought to courses'); or totally randomly. For rubble the stones are of random sizes, for ashlar they are regularly sized and often arranged so that vertical joints in alternate courses are in line. Any surface finish may be used with ashlar; it is identified rather by its regular size and its fine joints.

The terms used to describe brickwork bond are of very little relevance to masonry. Most walls are independently faced on either side, and the main issue is the use of bond stones – *thorough bands* going through from face to face, or *headers* penetrating two thirds through the thickness. Some minor walls and partitions consist of *parpends*: stones appearing on both faces. Quoin stones at an opening are distinguished into *inbands* (penetrating into the wall thickness) and *outbands* (penetrating along the face).

A *chisel draughted margin*, perhaps 1in (25mm) in width, is often seen around the face of a large stone. In origin this is a practical feature making the squaring of the stone easier. It also allows some economy of labour if a stone does not have to be dressed back to a regular plane over the whole of its face. It need not be thought a pretentious feature: the lintels of the cottages at Wirksworth (*see Fig. 49*) were given neat chisel draughted margins.

If the edges of the face of a stone are cut back or chamfered to emphasise the joints, the stonework is called *rusticated*.

Stones are usually laid so that the line of pressure is at right angles to the natural bed; for most stones the bed should be horizontal. This is especially crucial with columns. It is often impossible to see the bed plane of a stone, though wetting might reveal it. Stones in an arch or vault are usually laid so that the bed is at right angles to the thrust. Stones in a cornice are laid with bed plane vertical and perpendicular to the face, so as not to leave a weakness allowing undercut parts to fall off.

IRON

As materials for construction, there are striking differences between wrought iron and cast iron. The three basic commercial forms of the element iron are these two and steel; mild steel, the specification used for structural purposes, is chemically very similar to wrought iron and also has the lowest practicable admixture of other elements, but not the slag which gives wrought iron special properties. Mild steel came into general use as a structurally very versatile building material in the late nineteenth century, rather too late for consideration here, but the other two call for understanding by the investigator of old buildings. It should be appreciated how the use and form of wrought iron and cast iron are determined by how they are produced.[33] The differences between them are evident in their appearance, how they corrode, and how they behave under structural stress.

Wrought iron can be hammered into practically any shape. Its malleable and ductile properties are brought about by the comparative absence of carbon and by the small admixture of slag. In the process of production, wrought iron acquires a fibrous texture. In hand-craft methods of construction, rod-like shapes were the most convenient, as they were easy for the smith to grasp with the tongs while heating the part to be worked or while hammering it on the anvil. Two pieces of wrought iron, sufficiently heated, would fuse together under the hammer; this fusion was known as *welding*, in the original sense of the word. By welding pieces of wrought iron together the size of articles for use in building was virtually unlimited.

Cast iron has a greater content of carbon, which renders the material crystalline and brittle. It cannot be forged, but is brought to a molten state and cast in moulds to the required finished form. Some additional work may be done to a cast iron article – such as machining to produce a smooth bearing surface or boring to produce accurate holes – but these processes merely remove surplus metal, they do not alter the form by distortion. If a fractured piece of cast iron is examined closely it will be seen to consist of grains of crystalline metal. Near the surface in contact with the mould, and especially near the surface in contact with the air, the grains tend to show a finer texture and to line up to create a slight skin to the metal. In inferior quality castings there may be pockets of air called *blowholes*. The colour of cast iron seen in a fresh fracture is important as an indication of the type:

grey cast iron is the sort required for columns and girders, whilst white cast iron might be used for wear-resistant parts, because of its hardness, or for non-structural items such as window sash counterweights. Other considerations, requiring particular chemical specifications, might be the ability of the iron to flow more readily and to fill the intricacies of a complicated mould. Because of its great resistance to corrosion, cast iron is the material used for rainwater and drainage goods.

Early wrought iron made by the direct process could only be produced in very small quantities at a time: perhaps a bloom the size of a fist as the result of several hours of labour. As the iron was 'reduced' chemically from oxide to metallic state, some of the unwanted constituents passed into a liquefied 'slag' mixed up in the pasty bloom, and the ironmaker had to hammer vigorously to expel it. The slag would only be partially expelled; much remained trapped within the metal, which it helped to preserve from corrosion. The ironmaker most readily produced bars of wrought iron, and it was in bar form that the material was usually stored ready for making up into useful articles.

The earliest substantial uses of wrought iron in construction were for articles like grilles, based on the welding and shaping of bars. When, in 1294, the smith Thomas of Leighton made a screen of wrought iron to guard the tomb of Queen Eleanor in Westminster Abbey, he was using techniques essentially unchanged from prehistoric times. Blooms of iron were heated and hammer-welded to form the long rods of which the screen was to be made. In detail the techniques are simple: metal was cut by chisel on an anvil, or perhaps by hammering it while resting it on a *hardie*. Some joints, where bars cross, were formed with rivets (a technique known since the Bronze Age); other junctions were formed in the manner of a carpenter's housed joint, the end of one bar being inserted into a socket or hole in the other. The joint would be tightened by 'upsetting' to expand the end of the inserted bar slightly.

The delicate details of leaves were probably formed over the beak of an anvil or by *repoussé* technique on a sand-filled leather bag. A facsimile of this screen is displayed in the Museum of Iron at Coalbrookdale in Shropshire. This museum, part of the Ironbridge Gorge Museum, contains an extensive and recently formed collection of items of importance in the history of iron.

Medieval screens guarding tombs in important churches are perhaps the nearest thing to structural ironwork in early building history, but such work is very much out of the ordinary. More common was the use of wrought iron as elaborately decorative strap hinges on doors, and many examples are illustrated in Brandon's *Gothic Architecture (Fig. 28)*.[34] In ordinary buildings the early uses of iron were for nails and similar simple ironmongery: hooks, staples, straps, hinges, but also locks and keys. The medieval smith and carpenter worked in very close conjunction, but there may be reasons of site organisation why carpenters were very sparing in the use of iron accessories. The smith, though in constant contact with the carpenter for the repair and sharpening of tools, was not present on site. The cost of a metal so laboriously produced, its corrosion in damp positions and the carpenter's reluctance to spoil his work with crude fixings will also have inhibited the early use of iron.

Iron scroll-work from doors in Chester Cathedral.   *details one half full size*

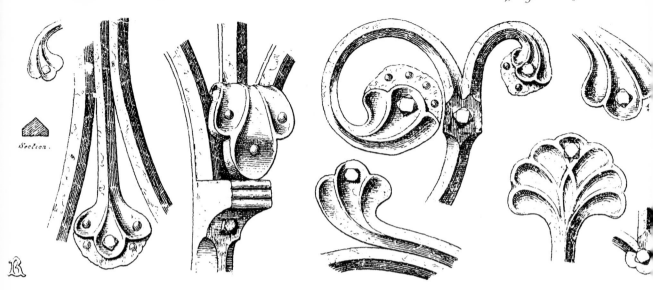

Section.

28 Details of wrought iron from doors of Chester Cathedral (half full size) (R. and J. A. Brandon, *Analysis of Gothic Architecture*, 1847, vol. 1, section 2, Metalwork, plate 4)

Cast iron

The technical advances which led to the wider use of iron in building were hastened by the importance of the metal in warfare. By the mid-thirteenth century the Moors were using simple wrought iron cannon in the form of bucket-like vessels of stout construction with a touch-hole. In 1350 Petrarch wrote that 'these instruments were a few years ago very rare, but now they are become as common and familiar as any other kind of arms, so quick and ingenious are the minds of men in learning the most pernicious arts'. Output of iron became crucial. The effect of increasing the temperature of furnaces and differences in the manner in which they were managed was to bring about a new metallurgical process, called *smelting*, in which the iron reached its melting point, liquefied, took up carbon from the furnace fuel, and might be 'tapped' to set as a dense crystalline mass as it cooled. The new process originated in *c.*1400 in what is now Belgium. The new, developed form of furnace needed to be continuously blown, for which purpose water-powered bellows were used. Because of the relatively powerful blowing required, the new type is known as the *blast furnace*.

An early blast furnace is portrayed on a cast iron fireback made by Richard Lenard of Brode in Sussex, showing Lenard with many of the tools of his trade; at the left is a small view of his furnace. A copy of this is displayed in the Coalbrookdale Museum of Iron. Nearby is the site where the remains, somewhat altered, of Coalbrookdale Old Furnace stand. This was an important charcoal-fired blast furnace, bearing the date 1638, where, in 1709, the first known successful experiment in smelting with coke as a fuel instead of charcoal was tried. The change of fuel was sought for reasons of scarcity of wood for charcoal burning, but, later in the eighteenth century, the new fuel led to a more important consequence – the economic mass-production of iron.

The introduction of the blast furnace led to important changes in the production of wrought iron also. In place of the old method of producing wrought iron directly from the ore, it was found better to use the cheaply and plentifully produced smelted iron and convert it to wrought iron. This required a subsidiary furnace designed to burn out the carbon.

In the new era of the blast furnace the final stages of the production of iron artefacts, including structural ironwork and ironmongery for building, were divided broadly into two departments: the *foundry*, closely related to the first stage of production at the blast furnace, dealt with the casting of articles either directly from the furnace or after a remelting; and the *forge* dealt with the conversion of cast iron into wrought iron, and with the following processes of hammering, rolling, slitting, or otherwise preparing the metal for sale to the smith. (Confusion arises from the fact that a smithy is often also called a 'forge': the word was used in this sense, for example by Chaucer, long before the era of the blast furnace and its attachment to a department of an ironworks. But as a synonym for 'smithy' it is now frowned upon, and is indeed quite unnecessary.)

Early castings were almost always produced directly from the furnace, but in time it was found better to remelt previously smelted iron. Iron cast into a convenient form for storage was called *pig iron* and the individual pieces *pigs*.

Builder's cast iron ware was part of the business of the foundry. The simplest technique was to cast in open moulds: metal was tapped directly from the furnace and conducted into depressions specially shaped in a sand floor. Even the simplest articles show the need to economise on the time and expertise of the foundry. A fireback decorated with a number of fleur-de-lys motifs, displayed at Coalbrookdale, is evidently a very early specimen. It was cast in an open mould, and, to obtain the repeated motifs, a single pattern for the fleur-de-lys was carved and impressed a number of times into the sand bed, as is clear from the slight overlap of some of the impressions.

For all but the simplest cast iron wares a pattern had to be made. Pattern making involved a thorough knowledge of both foundry craft and woodworking. Types of wood used for pattern making in recent centuries included American yellow pine and Baltic yellow deal, types which are straight grained, have few knots, can be obtained in large logs, and to which glue and putty will adhere well. Practical pattern-making places an important constraint on the detailing of cast iron articles. Early castings often show tapering shapes facilitating the removal of the pattern from the sand.

For complex articles closed moulds were used, consisting of two or more parts. Each part had to be designed so that the pattern could be freed from it, and with careful positioning of the joints it was possible to produce castings of great intricacy with projections or hollows on any face. The skill of the pattern-maker working in conjunction with the moulder was crucial in solving the difficulties of pattern assembly and withdrawal, deciding where the parting lines should be, designing any lateral extensions to the pattern to be fitted into the main part but to be withdrawn in a different direction, and constructing and positioning *cores* to occupy any hollow part of the casting. Circular cast iron columns, for example, were usually hollow tubes, the space of the inside cavity being filled by a core during casting. Cores were often held in position in relation to the outside part of the mould by means of iron spacers called *chaplets* which were merged into the metal of the casting. Sometimes traces of these can be seen on the finished article.

Cast iron was especially suited for use in columns. It is at its best in compression and under low stresses generally, as in the posts of railings. It was ideal for forming into cylindrical shapes with integral mouldings. In 1714 Wren was pressured by the commissioners for the rebuilding of St Paul's to use cast iron for the churchyard railings, despite his preference for wrought iron. The posts and rails were reputedly cast at the Gloucester Furnace, Lamberhurst, Kent.

Cast iron columns in the full sense are first reported at the Monastery of Alcobaca in Portugal in 1752, where eight columns supported a gigantic hood over the kitchen hearth.[35] Their height was about 9ft (2.7m). This early instance of cast iron columns used in a minor structural situation was increasingly followed in the eighteenth century. Cast iron, like wrought iron, was evidently thought of as a carpenter's accessory, a prefabricated and fireproof substitute for timber posts; in time it came to be an alternative for stone and was treated to traditional stone ornamental detailing. With the architectural emphasis on column mouldings, it was easier to form these once in the pattern-maker's workshop than many times at the carpenter's or mason's bench. As Gothic detailing came into architectural fashion through the pattern books of such writers as Batty Langley, its thin columns with mouldings and vertical ribs also called for cast iron, and the material was found to be ideal for a new thin type of Gothic window tracery as well. The earliest dated cast iron columns in England are those of St Anne's Church, Liverpool, in 1770–72. The ironmaster John Wilkinson built a Wesleyan chapel in 1790 for his workers at Bilston in Staffordshire, with iron columns, window frames and pulpit.

The first substantial use of cast iron as a structural material was in the bridge spanning the Severn near the works of the Coalbrookdale Company in Shropshire. The bridge was erected in 1779. It consists of iron ribs in a semi-circular arch with a span of over 100ft (30m), linked by cross-pieces; the detailing of the structure is often described as following a carpentry technique, but it would be more accurate to say it follows the precedent of wrought iron detailing. This revolutionary structure was frequently illustrated and very widely known, but its technique was not much copied. A number of bridges were built in cast iron in the 1790s, but they are more reminiscent of masonry construction, using small units fitted together in the manner of voussoirs.

In buildings where a high risk of fire was anticipated, cast iron beams and columns were increasingly adopted from the 1790s on the theory that this would render them more fireproof. At a time when there was considerable interest amongst Parisian architects in the possibility of wrought iron as a substitute for timber in the construction of roof trusses, news of such thinking seems to have reached England and prompted several leading mill owners to consider how iron might improve the construction of large industrial buildings. A solution to the fire problem was reached when, late in 1792, William Strutt of Derby commenced the building of his calico mill

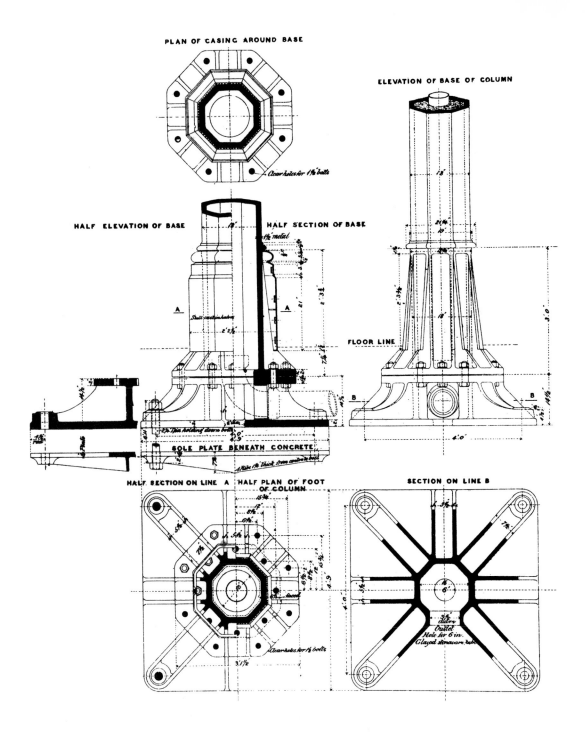

29 Cast iron detailing: base of column from Carlisle Market. The column is a flanged tube bolted to a base plate. The plinth mouldings are thinner castings in two halves. The base plate is bolted at each corner through the concrete foundation to a sole plate. Down the centre of the column runs a stoneware drainpipe. (A. T. Walmisley, *Iron Roofs*, 2nd edn., 1888, plate 40)

on a site off Tennant Street. The building no longer survives, but from a study of the evidence as it appeared in 1950 Turpin Bannister wrote:

'In plan it was 30 feet [9m] wide and 150 feet [46m] long, and it rose six storeys high. It was "remarkable for the floors being all constructed on brick arches and paved with brick" and it was "rendered absolutely indestructable by fire". These brick arches were actually segmental vaults running across the thirty foot [9m] width and supported by . . . beams running in the same direction. The thrusts of adjoining vaults thus counteracted each other, except in the end bays where probably pilasters braced the wall or wrought iron rods tied the wall to the last transverse beam. The . . . beams transmitted their loads to cast iron columns. It is probable that cast iron window sashes and gutters were employed to eliminate the last vestiges of wood.'[36]

It now appears, however, that the beams were of timber with iron sheathing on the vault springing faces. There only remained the small step of substituting cast iron girders for the main beams to produce an entirely iron-framed 'fireproof' building.[37] In 1796–7 Bage's Flax Mill at Ditherington on the outskirts of Shrewsbury was built on the fireproof principle with cast iron girders as well as columns. This building survives. Many other textile mills followed this pattern, and the form of construction occasionally finds its way into domestic building. Strutt's Moscow farm near Belper has its upper floor similarly constructed with brick vaults and cast iron girders, the sides of which are shaped to act as springing surfaces. The roof consists of huge groin vaults in brickwork. Iron girders and brick vaults are also seen in the toll house attached to the previously mentioned iron bridge near Coalbrookdale.

From about 1860 onwards the role of wrought iron was taken over completely by mild steel, and the latter material also took over much of the role of cast iron. The disadvantage of steel is its high susceptibility to softening and collapse in fire and to corrosion, so it has invariably been used in carefully protected situations. Much of the architectural interest of iron buildings derives from their very individual detailing and their exposed 'anatomy', and both characteristics are less possible with steel. So the Victorian use of structural iron, lending itself well to vigorous and innovative Gothic detailing, fell out of use, its decline coinciding with a return to more conservative architectural styles.

Wrought iron

The general term for wrought iron goods in building is *ironmongery*. Iron for this purpose starts as pig iron, and is converted into its almost carbon-free state in the department of an ironworks called the *forge*. In the earlier process this involved two types of hearth known as the *finery* and the *chafery*; in the later process introduced at the end of the eighteenth century *puddling furnaces* were used for the same purpose. The purified iron was hammered into a dense mass under a power hammer. At the end of the forge process came the initial rolling of the iron into bar form. The second ironworks department was the *mill*: here the iron was re-rolled and slit as necessary to produce the bar iron required by the smith, or the sections increasingly required by builders for immediate use on site, such as angles, tees, flats, hoop-iron (for strapping carpentry to brickwork, or for cross-tongues in 'fireproof' floorboarding) and so forth.

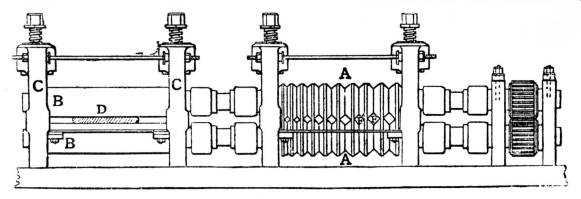

Wrought iron was first rolled between plain rolls. An important innovation was the slitting mill, which, like the blast furnace, was a Belgian invention. Rolls with engaging projections were made, which acted as shears, cutting the iron as it was fed through. In 1588 a patent was granted to Bevis Bulmer for a slitting mill, and in 1628 Richard Foley built one in the Midlands. From the mid-seventeenth century slitting mills were common. From the viewpoint of the smith producing builder's ironmongery, the introduction of the slitting mill completed the revolution in the supply of his 'raw' material which had started with the introduction of the blast furnace.

The next major step in the supply of material was the invention of grooved rolls. Grooves serve to control the sectional shape of the iron as it emerges from the rolls. They were introduced by Henry Cort, the owner of a forge at Fontley in Hampshire, in the late eighteenth century, in order to roll bars of circular cross-section. The principle of using grooves was readily adapted for rolling other desired cross-sectional shapes such as angles and tees. I-shaped sections designed to serve as joists did not appear until the mid-nineteenth century. (The I shape is excellent for joists because the maximum amount of material is concentrated at the top and the bottom, giving a high moment of inertia about the horizontal axis.) Sizes were severely limited with wrought iron, but, as steel was introduced, the range of structural sections increased dramatically, to transform the structural design of buildings.

In the nineteenth century wrought iron was classified for sale according to the number of times it had been piled and re-rolled. After the initial hammering the bloom of iron from the puddling furnace was rolled into a bar of about 4×1 in (100 × 25 mm) and about 10–15 ft (3–4.5 m) long. This initial form of iron was called *puddled bar*, and was not yet considered fit for sale. It was then cut into short lengths and the pieces stacked in a *pile*, the grain of the metal being arranged parallel or crosswise according to the intended final use. Piles were reheated and re-rolled to produce the lowest commercial quality: *crown* or *merchant* iron. For higher commercial qualities the crown iron was then re-piled and re-rolled, up to three times, to be sold as *best*, *best best* and *best best best* iron (abbreviated to B, BB and BBB).

The early developments in the structural use of wrought iron in building

30 Mills for rolling iron into sheets or bars: two shafts are connected through pinions (at the right). Each mill consists of two rolls, either plain (BB) for rolling sheets and plates (D) or grooved (AA) for rolling rods through a progressively smaller series of openings (FF). Each is held in a pair of housings (CC). In front of the lower roll in each case is a 'cramp bar' to hold the guides for feeding the iron into the mill. Beneath (not shown) there would be a pit to collect cooling water and mill scale. Some mills consisted of three rolls, so that the iron would pass between rolls on its return also. (*Encyclopaedia Britannica*, 11th edn., vol. 14, p. 831, fig. 35)

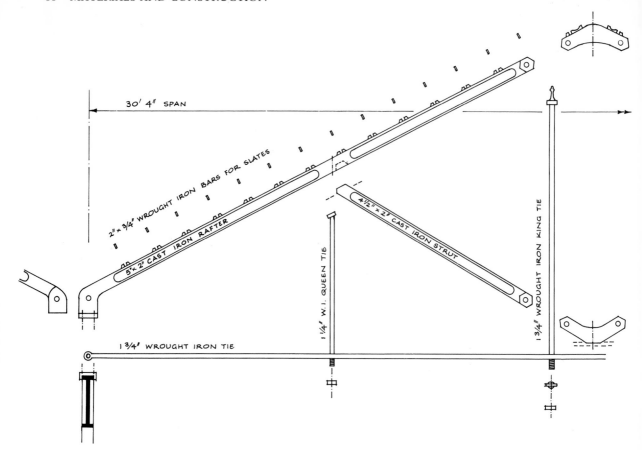

30' 4" SPAN

2" × 3/4" WROUGHT IRON BARS FOR SLATES

5" × 2" CAST IRON RAFTER

4½" × 2" CAST IRON STRUT

1¼" W.I. QUEEN TIE

1¾" WROUGHT IRON KING TIE

1¾" WROUGHT IRON TIE

31 Trusses with cast iron compressive members and wrought iron tensile members from the Woolwich Smithery roof, by John Rennie, engineer, and Edward Hall, architect, 1816

occurred in Paris, where J-G Sufflot planned a wrought iron roof to span the 52ft (16m) square stair hall leading to the Salon Carré and the Grande Galerie of the Louvre in 1779. The roof consisted of forged bars assembled with collar joints. Because of the good tensile strength of wrought iron, it came to be used selectively for members under tension. Wren had used wrought iron chains around the base of the dome of St Paul's to prevent it from bursting outwards; wrought iron had also been used for chain suspension bridges, notably the footbridge over the Wear at Winch, County Durham, in 1741. The logical place to exploit wrought iron in ordinary construction was for the tensile members of roof trusses. In 1810 William Murdoch designed a composite truss with its compressive members in cast iron and its tensile members in wrought iron, and similar trusses (*Fig. 31*) were amongst those designed by John Rennie and Edward Hall for the Woolwich Smithery in 1816. These trusses can be seen reconstructed at Blists Hill Open Air Museum in Shropshire.

Wrought iron was much used decoratively in the Regency period and later, but the main exploitation of wrought iron in building lay rather with civil engineering structures. Thomas Telford used the chain link type of wrought iron bridge for the Menai Straits in 1819 and Conway in 1822. Stephenson used wrought iron tubular bridges at Conway and Menai in 1845 and 1850. The last of the great wrought iron bridges was Brunel's magnificent bridge over the Tamar in 1859.

In the construction of larger buildings at the end of the nineteenth century, rolled sections and plate were often rivetted together to build up stancheons and girders, but large rolled sections did not become available until mild steel had taken over this structural role.

The techniques of the smithy, unlike those of the ironworks forge, are not usefully described in terms of historical development. Much of the work of a modern smithy could have been performed in Roman or medieval times; only the scale of operations has varied with the availability of the 'raw' material. The smith's hearth consisted of a slab large enough to rest the work and tools on. A layer of fuel lay on it and air was delivered to it by bellows through a *tuyere*, the tip of which was several inches above the level of the slab. The hottest part of the fire, where the iron was put to heat, was immediately in front of and above the tip. In recent centuries the usual fuel was bituminous coal. Also in recent times, particularly since about 1800, a water-jacketed type of tuyere has been in use. For managing the fire the smith used a variety of hooked pokers, spade-like slices, and rakes.

Anvils have been of standardised form for many centuries. The usual material was wrought iron, with a carbon steel face fire-welded on. A non-faced part called the *table* was used with tools which would be blunted on the hardened face. In a common type of anvil there is a *beak* at one end for bending metal over, and at the other end two holes, one square to serve as a tool holder, the other round for punching through.

Hammers and tongs were of a range of sizes according to the nature of the work. Hammering on the end of a heated rod was called *upsetting*. This would be done to form a head on a bolt. For cutting a rod, a chisel was held against it and hammered. For cold metal the cutting edge was angled to about 30°, for hot metal to about 60°. Alternatively a *hardie* was used. This was similar to a chisel but pointing upwards. It stood on the face of the anvil with a square projection engaged with the square hole, known for this reason as the hardie hole. The metal would be hammered down on the hardie until weak enough to break.

For bringing metal to a round shape a hollow die called a *swage* was held against it and hammered. In most smithies there would also be a large iron block called a *swage block*, used like a portable anvil. Around its edges were a number of hollows to act as swages of various curvatures. Other types of die were readily invented for special purposes such as forming the leaves of decorative ironwork.

Nuts and bolts could be hand-forged, and the cutting of screwthreads on the ends of rods is still an everyday requirement in building. The method was to use a *tap*, a male pattern cutting screw, and a *die*, a female pattern cutting screw, of carbon steel. Early nuts were usually square, that being the easiest shape to cut from iron flats. From about 1850 nuts and bolts made in the smithy tended to be superseded by mass-produced hexagonal nuts and bolts (first used by Nasmyth in 1830).

LIME

The advantage of lime over clay as a mouldable building material is that, while it dries, it undergoes a chemical change causing it to set permanently.

One wonders under what circumstances the discovery was first made that burned limestone produced a powder with such variable qualities.

Lime is the name for calcium in any of its ordinary chemical combinations, especially its oxide CaO; gypsum (plaster of Paris) and cement are special forms of lime with additional setting and hardening qualities. Lime is found naturally as calcium carbonate in chalk and limestone. Remains of the simple kilns where these materials used to be burned at about 1000°C to convert them to quicklime (calcium oxide, otherwise called caustic lime) are frequently seen at old quarries. Lime might also be burned in clamps.

The building trades were an important market for quicklime. Builders *slaked* it to produce hydrate of lime. This was done by forming a heap of quicklime on the ground and pouring water on to it. They then prepared the hydrate in various ways, depending on the purity of the lime and the purpose for which it was intended to be used. Lime and sand were used by bricklayers or masons as *mortar*. Other compositions of lime were used by plasterers. *Stucco* commonly refers to the composition used for facing external walls; *plaster* usually refers particularly to that for internal walls and ceilings. In the best internal work plaster was applied in three coats, known as *render, float and set*, each of a different specification. *Parging* or *pargetting*, finally, was the composition used to give a smooth lining to flues; though in the sixteenth and seventeenth centuries this word covered any type of plastering. Eventually, as better cements were introduced from the eighteenth century onwards, concrete, a third major application of lime, came into widespread use. The factor determining whether a type of lime was suitable for mortar or plaster was its *hydraulicity*.

Before the researches of Smeaton in the eighteenth century and Vicat in the early nineteenth, it seems to have been supposed that the hardness and durability of a mortar would depend simply on the physical hardness of the limestone etc. from which it was derived. The scientific basis of the subject had hardly advanced since antiquity. The new research showed that the crucial thing was the presence of impurities, especially clay, in the chemical composition of the lime. Smeaton first noticed this in 1756 in the course of his experiments to find a suitable mortar for the masonry of the Eddystone lighthouse, leading to his choice of Aberthaw blue lias lime with pozzolana.[38]

A hydraulic lime, cement or concrete will set in contact with water and in the absence of air. This is a crucial property in engineering works and a valuable one in building. Regardless of Smeaton's observations, experimental chemists at the time thought manganese to be more probably the essential constituent of a hydraulic lime, until in 1818 Vicat published the definitive account of hydraulic limes.[39] Hydraulic qualities are needed in the mortar of any large masonry where air cannot readily percolate into the interior of the mass. If the larger examples of medieval stonework were jointed in non-hydraulic lime mortar, the joints may have taken decades to set. This may explain the slowness of construction and even perhaps the occurrence of some collapses. Some English limestones do, however, produce a hydraulic type of lime suitable for building.

Before the introduction of Parker's cement in 1796 the only way of obtaining a highly hydraulic mortar for docks and similar work was by adding pozzolana, a volcanic ash imported from Pozzuoli in Italy, or trass, a similar material found at Andernach on the Rhine and milled to powder at Dordrecht.

During the nineteenth century use was made of English natural cement under the general name of Parker's or Roman cement. This was patented by Parker in 1796 and given the latter name in about 1800. It was made by grinding the nodules (*septaria*) of clayey limestone found in the London clay of the Isle of Sheppey in Kent and at Harwich in Essex. The cement was very hydraulic. Another term for material of this type was *water cement*. Other varieties were Medina cement (Hampshire) and Whitby, Mulgrave's or Atkinson's cement (Yorkshire). Common mortar was made with sand and Roman cement in equal parts. From the mid-nineteenth century the place of these natural varieties was taken by artificial compositions of chalk and clay under the general name of Portland cement. This was invented in 1824 by Joseph Aspdin, a Leeds bricklayer, and was named from a fanciful claim that coarse stucco in it resembled Portland stone.

In ordinary construction, down to the mid-nineteenth century, lime mortars were in very general use, and they continued to be widely used well into the present century. A lime mortar is easily distinguished from a modern Portland cement mortar by its whitish colour and its soft, dry, crumbly texture compared with the hard, slimy appearance of the latter. Sand constituted the main bulk of a mortar, as it was cheaper than lime. Additives such as crushed brick, tile, coal or bones might be present for additional bulk or as colouring matter. Differences in mortar colour and texture may give clues to alterations in brickwork and masonry, so when repointing is carried out during restorations useful evidence may be lost.

A great number of proprietary plasters were also marketed during the late nineteenth century, many based on gypsum or on lias lime.

Types of lime

For practical purposes, limes are mainly classified by purity, the purest being called 'fat' or 'rich' and the others 'lean', 'poor' or 'water' limes. The mountain limestone of Buxton and Crich in Derbyshire produced a very fat lime. Other fat limes were those from Dorking in Surrey and those from the oolitic limestone. An extremely pure, fat lime could be produced by burning oystershells, as in Holland. Broadly, the fat limes were chosen for plaster and the lean ones for mortar. (Fat limes were also preferred for agriculture and for furnace flux.)

Lean limes are then further classified according to the activity or inertia of their impurities, those with active impurities being the hydraulic ones. Most lean limes from grey chalk or limestone sources are poorly hydraulic. The principal limes used in London for mortar, called 'stone' limes, were those of Dorking in Surrey and Rochester in Kent, both only moderately hydraulic. With these, three parts of sand were mixed to one part of lime for common plastering. The most valued hydraulic lean limes were those of the blue lias, including those from Lyme Regis in Dorset, Barrow-on-Soar in Leicestershire, Keynsham and Watchet in Somerset, Whitby in Yorkshire and Shipston and Rugby in Warwickshire. Other important lean limes were those from the Sussex grey chalk, Berwick in Northumberland, Aberthaw near Cardiff, the magnesian limestone of Bolsover in Derbyshire, and the Halkin mountain limestone from Holywell in Flintshire. In the Vale of Belvoir, it was common to use equal parts of sand and blue lias lime for internal plastering and one part of sand to two parts of lime for stucco. In hydraulic lime mortars, crystals of hydrated calcium silicate and hydrated calcium aluminate form throughout the mass during setting to create considerable strength.

Slaking

Builders received quicklime from the quarry in lump form in bags or barrels. In dry conditions this could be stored, but if damp air penetrated to it there was risk of the less hydraulic types *air-slaking*. This type of uncontrolled slaking was to be avoided.

A builder's first task was to slake the quicklime by adding a third or a half of its weight in water, so converting it to hydrate of lime. The slaking behaviour of fat limes is very rapid. That of lean limes depends on whether they are feebly, ordinarily or eminently hydraulic (as classified by Vicat).

Feebly hydraulic limes (with 5 to 12 per cent of clay) are easiest to slake. After a few minutes pause, the lumps of quicklime slake by crackling and breaking up into powder with considerable heat and vapour. Ordinarily hydraulic limes (12 to 20 per cent) show no sign of activity for an hour or so, then the lumps of quicklime crack all over giving off slight heat and fumes. Eminently hydraulic limes (20 to 30 per cent) are very difficult to slake; after a long inert period there is a slight heat noticeable to the touch, but hardly any tendency for the lumps of quicklime to break up.

The slaked lime was then stored until required. Why, then, it may be asked, was air-slaking to be avoided, since lime had to be slaked for use and slaked lime could be stored? Controlled slaking resulted in hydrate of lime. Uncontrolled slaking due to contact with the air caused only part of the lime to change its hydrate, part changing back to the unwanted original calcium carbonate.

Lime in mortars

A builder might be tempted to use a fat lime in mortar for its ease of slaking and working. Fat limes sold in London were sometimes coloured with a little iron oxide to give them the characteristic buff colour of leaner lime, and marketed fraudulently under the assumed names of Dorking, Halling or Merstham lime. Mortar made from a fat lime such as chalk would be of little value, setting very slowly or not at all.

Lime was slaked and mixed with sand in one operation. On a suitable floor the sand was placed in a ring and the proportion of lime put in the centre; the heap was watered through a rose and the sand from the edges shovelled up to cover the lime. After a day or two to slake, the whole mass was thoroughly mixed. An ordinary lime mortar was then covered with sacking to 'temper' before use; a hydraulic mortar, like modern cement mortar, had to be used immediately.

For some purposes a bricklayer would require a fine mixture with a

clean, white colour, and would use plasterer's lime putty (see below). This included the thin joints of arches built in *rubbed bricks* and the thin false-joints set into *tuck pointing*.

Lime in plasters

Fat lime for internal plastering was slaked into a pure hydrate of lime and then sieved or ground as necessary to remove any unslaked material. The hydrate was then allowed to mature for several weeks, or for a much longer time, depending on the intended use, and mixed in various ways with other materials:

1 Sand and cow dung were added to make material for parging the flues of chimneys.

2 Sand and ox or cow hair from the tanner's yard were added to create material for the first coat of wall and ceiling plaster, called *coarse stuff*.

3 For the finer uses the hydrate had to be further matured in a lime pit. This was a pit or a bin lined with plaster and covered with sacking or straw. Any excess of water was run off and the hydrate placed in the pit to mature for three or more months to ensure that the slaking process was absolutely finished. At the end of this period the deteriorated top skin was discarded. The result was *lime putty*. This could be used by bricklayers for fine joints or for decorative false jointing. The main uses of lime putty were in plastering: (a) lime putty could be mixed with sand and hair for a better quality coarse stuff for the initial coat of plastering, known as *render*; (b) it

32 Making mortar: from Cruikshank's cartoon 'London going out of Town – or – The March of Bricks and Mortar'. Mr Goth and his workmen, in the form of hods and other tools, at work: in the centre three workers are 'running' slaked lime through sieves to remove unslaked lumps; in the distance is a brick clamp, evidently blazing out of control. (Print of cartoon in Ironbridge Gorge Museum Trust Library, ref. AE 185.504) could be mixed with a little sand to make *fine stuff* for the second coat, known as the *float* coat; and (c) it could be mixed with plaster of Paris to make a fine *gauged stuff* for the final or *set* coat.

For stucco, for external use, a hydraulic lime was similarly prepared and mixed with sand.

Plastering

The lathing of partitions and ceilings was a plasterer's responsibility. On laths the first coat of plaster was called *pricking up*, on brickwork and similar surfaces it was called *render*. The simplest plastering, called *laid work* stopped at one coat. In two-coat work the first coat would be roughened with a brush and then given a final set coat. For the best three-coat work the render would be scored and given float and set coats. In this, floating was the important stage for getting the wall surface true. Strips of plaster called *screeds* were laid and checked for trueness, to divide the wall into convenient sized panels. A similar technique was used to achieve a true ceiling.

When the floating was semi-dry, the finishing coat would be laid on with a smoothing trowel, sprinkled with water and re-worked until a fine surface was obtained.

Ornamental plaster was one of the priorities of building owners wishing to show off their expenditure, and one of the priorities of innovative builders wishing to cheapen and simplify their work. Ordinary plaster is not suitable for heavy ornamental mouldings, so for any projection beyond a couple of inches a false backing had to be constructed in lathwork or carpentry. For a smooth, non-enriched cornice a mould faced in brass or zinc was used to apply the plaster to its built-out backing. Corners and small breaks would be finished by hand. Some ornaments were cast in plaster of Paris and either screwed or cemented into place. Papier mâché offered a cheap substitute for ornate plaster features. Another cheap expedient patented in 1856 was to use canvas, stretched on a light framework, washed over with gauged stuff. This was called *stick and rag* or more properly *fibrous plaster*.

Plaster might be made to resemble marble by adding pigments and bringing it to a fine surface. *Scagliola*, used in the seventeenth and eighteenth centuries, consisted of plaster of Paris mixed with colouring matters in a solution of glue or isinglass. When thoroughly hardened, the surface was wetted and rubbed with pumice stone, then rubbed with tripoli (a scouring powder) and charcoal and finished with an oiled felt rubber.

The common decorative finish for plaster was called limewash or whitewash, a milky liquid made of rich lime and water. It might be coloured with ochre or other matter. The addition of size created a jelly-like substance called distemper, used for the same purpose.

THREE

Fieldwork

The camera is by far the best tool of recording, and it is not sensible to draw anything which can be photographed adequately.[40] The other options to be considered before embarking on measuring and drawing are formal questionnaires and straightforward, 'open-ended' verbal descriptions.

Because of the difficulty of combining any two or more of these options in a coherent presentation of results, the recorder is tempted to draw more than is warranted. Since no building can be adequately interpreted without its plan being drawn, drawing comes into all but the most superficial work. It is far easier to relate the form and appearance of a building to its plan by means of plan and elevations to be read together in one drawing than by means of a plan and a disconnected set of photographic views. A verbal description is also difficult to integrate: it may be directly produced in the field or reconstructed from a questionnaire, the information in which may have been temporarily reduced to code. One should decide which option is likely to be at the forefront in the final presentation. The end result might be an annotated drawing or a verbal text with accompanying illustrations. Perhaps the best record of a building is a thorough verbal description accompanied by one or two photographic views, a drawn plan, and analytical drawings of important features.

The economic use of time and resources is one consideration; the other is the need to work progressively. There is a natural self-educational progress from the simple to the detailed, and the same progression suits practical fieldwork moving from a wide-ranging reconnaissance survey to the close examination of typical examples and special points of interest. This chapter will make suggestions for tackling fieldwork at several progressive levels of intensity.

The most open approach to owners of buildings is the best. There is no point in introducing oneself to all and sundry if one is merely carrying out wide-ranging observations of old buildings as seen from the public road, but as soon as one's interest is intensive enough to penetrate to the backs of private buildings, some introduction will be necessary. Owners generally respond well to students and amateurs, but less well to anyone they think might be from the rates department, so some reassurance may be necessary.

Fieldwork kit

Depending on the preferred level of work, the following items may be useful for practical fieldwork:

Photographic equipment

The ideal is an architectural camera with a 'rising front', by means of which vertical lines in the subject may be kept parallel as seen on the image. This avoids the leaning-back illusion so common in photographs of buildings. The minimum requirement is any good camera capable of producing a black and white print of about half-plate size without disagreeable fuzziness. A wide-angle lens is very useful. A tripod is essential for indoor views and it is a good practice to use it all the time. Flash is also needed for indoor work and sometimes out of doors. It is useful to have some blackboard chalk for marking measured 'targets' when photographs are used as an aid in a difficult survey. Other items which may be included in a formal record photograph are a scale rod and an identification board with movable white letters on a black background, to give such information as the number of the photograph or building, compass point of orientation of the view, date, etc.

Measuring equipment

A 2m/6ft folding measuring rod is essential. One can be obtained with metric on one side and imperial measure on the other. The same rod might be painted with enamel paint to serve as the photographic scale, provided the clarity of the numbers and divisions is not obscured. Virtually all necessary measurements can be taken with a rod, but for longer running dimensions it is helpful to have a 20m/60ft plastic or Fibron tape. A steel tape may be cheaper but it is awkward to use and liable to be damaged. The greater accuracy of a steel tape is most unlikely to be needed in record surveying. Tapes are manufactured with a hook at the end for attachment to the corner of a building. A useful accessory which one can make for oneself out of the stout wire of a coathanger is a brick-hook: a wire bent into an L shape with a hook at each extremity and a loop at the corner, of the size necessary to grip a corner brick in a wall. This is very useful to attach the end of a tape to for taking measurements across a yard.

Other measuring accessories include string, preferably white string cheap enough to abandon and thin enough for breaking or cutting. Builder's line is not really suitable. A line-level is useful; this is a small spirit-level with two hooks by which it may be suspended from a horizontal string to check that it is really level. These can be obtained in any hardware shop. When using a line-level, it should be placed exactly at the mid-point of the string between supports. A plumb-bob is necessary, preferably with enough string attached to extend down one storey. On a windy site a plum-bob may be steadied by letting the weight hang in a tin or bucket of water. A hammer and nails are necessary – 40mm round nails do not cause conspicuous damage to timbers, and can be cleanly removed. A kitchen knife is useful for feeling into carpentry joints, and a joiner's *contour gauge* is useful for recording moulding profiles. A torch is invaluable, and a brush useful.

Drawing equipment

Some may prefer to use a clip-board or a small drawing-board on site. Miniature drawing-boards with parallel motion are available, but a simple wooden board is sufficient. It would be as light as possible. Others may prefer to use bound notebooks with stiff covers, known as manuscript books. If a method with loose paper is preferred, one can, in wet conditions, change to drawing on tracing film. This material is expensive, but is waterproof and takes pencil perfectly under all conditions. A bound book has the advantage that one's notes will not get lost so easily. The best compromise seems to be to use a bound manuscript book for most work, changing to clip-board and tracing film in wet conditions, and sticking the sheets of film into the book for permanent filing.

Beginners are tempted to put a sheet of squared paper under the paper on which they are sketching to assist in getting their dimensions and right angles approximately correct. This is a hinderance to the development of drawing skill, and should be resisted.

For tracing film or tracing paper, pencil is suitable. The best grade is usually 2H. A clutch-pencil with integral sharpener is ideal. The chosen grade of pencil should be suitable for shading as well as line-drawing, because no effort should be spared to make site sketches attractive and intelligible. On ordinary detail or cartridge paper, such as the paper of a manuscript book, ballpoint is ideal. It is very helpful to work in different colours. One might draw the lines of the fabric in black and the dimensions in red. In this way lines of alignment or dimension lines will not be mistaken as walls. Indian ink in a technical drawing pen is not suitable in strong sunlight and out of doors: the spirit base dries too quickly so that the pen clogs up.

An alternative to drawing is the use of a 'pocket memo' dictation recorder. In cold weather, when the fingers are not very flexible, this is attractive, but it is only suitable for purely descriptive notes or for recording measurements where the procedure is very carefully planned at a clerical level. The recorded information should be transcribed at the first possible moment, while the visual memory is still fresh.

Preserving notes

As research progresses, the investigator will also accumulate copious information from sources other than the building itself. Much of this evidence will be fragmentary. From the outset it is sensible to create a card index to make it easy for information to be retrieved. The smallest size of card, 5 × 3in (127 × 76mm), is sufficient. The heading line might be divided into boxes, for county, town or parish name, local address, and reference number (e.g. National Grid reference or County Sites and Monuments record number). It is easiest to index buildings in sequence of postal address.

Cards are ideal for storing the isolated bits of information that arise from conversation or reading. In time, files of photocopies of published articles, copies of plans, collections of old postcards, pages of one's own notes and many other classes of materials will be accumulated, and the set of cards will serve as a central index. Cards, however, are not suitable for extensive notes on one topic or for raw site notes; these should be in bound form, with cards to index them.

The plague of research is the tendency for records to be split up in a large number of fragmentary and incomplete collections. Fieldworkers creating new records, of whatever nature, cannot go to the expense of contributing copies of their work to large numbers of separate collections. It is fortunate, therefore, that centralised repositories for architectural records exist at county and national level. At county level there is the County Sites and Monuments record under the local authority, usually within the museum service or the planning department. At national level there is the National Monuments Record at Fortress House, 23 Savile Row, London W1X 1AB. All architectural records should be deposited with these organisations, where they will be open to inspection by the bona fide researcher. It is quite pointless to create records as a contribution to research in architecture without depositing copies in one, or preferably both, of these repositories. Both are collectors of photographs and drawings and, though contributors should try to give them work of a professional standard, even the poorest records are unlikely to be refused.

When producing drawings or photographs for an academic thesis or for publication, one naturally wishes to keep them private for a period; but eventually even these records ought to find their way into a public collection.

RECONNAISSANCE

A checklist of things to observe during reconnaissance could be:

1 The present use of the building and any obvious sign of change of use, such as a house having been a retail shop or an inn.

2 The structural walling material. This is usually timber, brick or stone, though occasionally cob. If walls are rendered they should be so described, with the investigator's guess as to what structural material lies beneath. Brick walls in older buildings may in fact conceal timber framing. Sometimes what at first glance seems to be a brick wall proves to be *mathematical* tiles; once one or two specimens of the sham have been looked at, there should be little further difficulty in distinguishing tile from brick.

3 Whether the structure should be regarded as consisting of more than one *build*, i.e. whether different blocks or wings were constructed at different times. There might be a main timber range with brick wings, or different parts in timber framing of different appearance. Minor alterations such as reconstructed windows, altered partitioning or a new roof would not amount to a new build.

No useful observations will be made about the original intentions of the builder or first owner unless different builds are distinguished. Distinguishing builds is similar to the archaeologist's task of distinguishing phases in an excavated site. A new build introduces a new overall state of affairs leading the occupants to reconsider their manner of using the building. It is always better to make too many rather than too few distinctions in what is observed.

The number of storeys must be noted, distinguishing different blocks of the structure if necessary. An attic wholly or largely within the roof space is regarded as half a storey, but a loft for storage reached by ladder would not rank as a storey. A sagging roof line or other clues may also reveal the number of structural bays. Extra storeys are often added to buildings, so different builds may be distinguished horizontally as well as vertically.

33 Perspective view of Hill Farm, Tanworth

4 The probable date of the original and any additional build. At reconnaissance stage the dating guess need not be of a high degree of accuracy. A few errors will hardly have statistical significance, and any important buildings discovered will call for closer study at a later time. Often there is a date written on the building, though dates before the eighteenth century are sometimes unreliable.

5 Any identification of present or past occupiers.

6 The most important thing is to take time to stand back from the building, ignoring detail, to try to appreciate the overall form. The proportions of the structure, the positions of chimneys and main doors, taken together with one's impression of the position of the site relative to town, village or farm, may be clues to important discoveries. Classic house plans such as the hall with cross-wing or the type with a *baffle-entry* adjacent to a central chimney stack may be revealed by this, even if the building has been completely encased in new brickwork.

Hill Farm in the Parish of Tamworth in Arden, Warwickshire, was examined before it had to be destroyed to make way for the M42 motorway. Following the pattern suggested, reconnaissance notes on this farmhouse (*Fig. 33*) might be:

Warwickshire/Tamworth/Hill Fm/SP 147757
(1) Farmhouse
(2) Brick front; stucco dressings? Part of rear is timber framed.

33 Perspective view of Hill Farm, Tanworth

34 Closer (rear) view of Hill Farm

(3) & (4) 2 or 3 builds? Front range $2\frac{1}{2}$ storeys is 19thC or perhaps early 20thC.

Rear extention $1\frac{1}{2}$ storeys evidently older. Part brick and part timber framed.

(5) Recently Mr Goode, owner/occ. Now vacated?

(6) Farmhouse with 18/19thC farm buildings around adjacent yard. Farm 50–100 acres? May be quite an old site: perhaps goes with the enclosure of the parish at early date. Front range is typical symmetrical double fronted in debased Georgian style of cheap construction one room deep.

Insufficient of older parts at rear visible to guess at plan. Worth closer look.

If a closer look is taken (*Fig. 34*) and if one is in possession of the outline of the building shown on the Ordnance Survey plan, it is possible with very little time and effort to produce a roof plan showing all the roof slopes, chimney positions and dormers. This might be a thumbnail sketch in one's field notebook (*Fig. 35*). Once lettered, this plan provides an unambiguous way to refer to any range or wing of the building or any main wall, and the task of compiling it turns one's mind to the plan and its organisation, starting the process of analysis.

The roof slopes can be shaded or hatched to give the three-dimensional

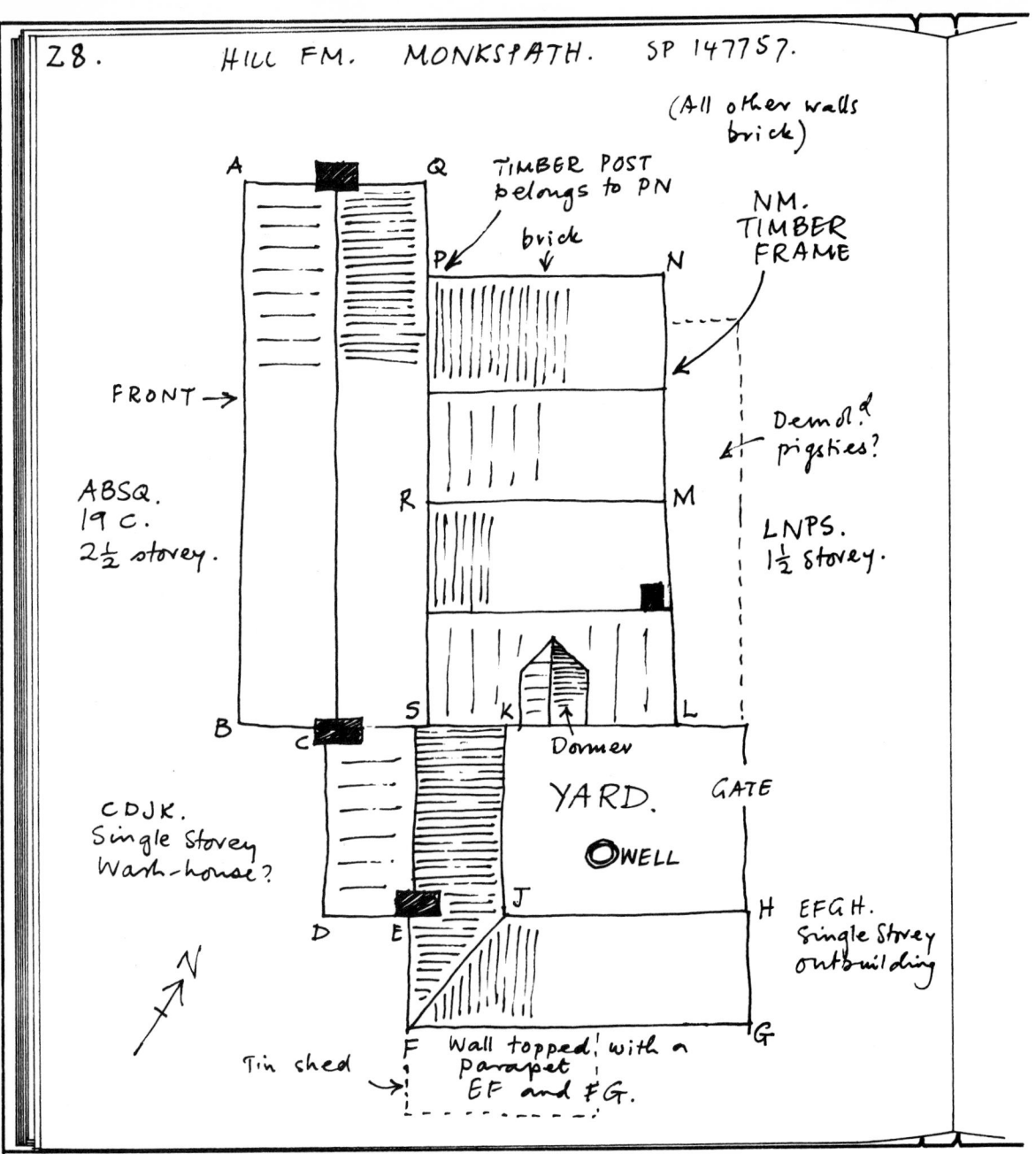

Z8. HILL FM. MONKSPATH. SP 147757.

(All other walls brick)

A   Q   TIMBER POST belongs to PN

brick

NM. TIMBER FRAME

P

N

FRONT →

ABSQ. 19 c. 2½ storey.

R

Demol.ᵈ pigsties?

M

LNPS. 1½ storey.

B

S   K   L

C

Dormer

CDJK. Single Storey Wash-house?

YARD.   GATE

WELL

D   E

J

H   EFGH. Single Storey outbuilding

N

G

Tin shed →

F   Wall topped with a Parapet EF and FG.

35 Roof plan thumbnail sketch in field notebook

effect, and chimneys are marked here as black rectangles. There is no need to take measurements for this plan. In the case of Hill Farm, the pair of roofs at the rear marked by the letters LNPS is completely below the eaves line QS at the rear of the front range. Had the ridges of the two rear extensions been higher than the eaves there would have been dents in the outline ABSQ. It is also clear that the roof of the outhouse at the front of the drawing is a single slope facing the yard, and that it turns a corner to merge with the yard-facing slope of the wash-house roof. This creates a valley collecting rainwater at J. The type of dormer is also clear: it is high enough to have its own eaves, and its front is a continuation of the external wall. With a note where each outside door is and how many storeys there are to each part, we have an informative plan.

The expense of photography may be daunting if a survey territory is extensive, but at reconnaissance stage it should be worthwhile taking at least views of groups of buildings. If 35mm photographs are taken, a contact print can be pasted on to an index card and kept in the same general index as reconnaissance notes and thumbnail plans. Groupings of buildings and street perspectives are views of considerable importance which can easily be forgotten in the haste to concentrate on building elevations and details.

At reconnaissance stage very little can be done with only small-scale maps. For rural fieldwork the 6 inch to 1 mile Ordnance Survey (now reissued at 1:10,000) is essential, and for fieldwork in built-up areas the 25 inch to 1 mile scale is much to be preferred. For some urban areas a 1:500 scale survey exists. Maps are so expensive that it is far more sensible as well as far more historically informative to obtain photocopies of the out-of-copyright early editions of the Ordnance Survey plans from the local reference library. The local County Sites and Monuments may be able to provide serious fieldworkers with copies of the 6 inch or 1:10,000 maps overprinted with their site reference numbers. These maps remain Crown copyright, though this does not hinder their use for purposes of private research.

Maps also provide the first clue to dating, or at least to identifying which are the newest parts of a rambling building. For nineteenth-century buildings it is useful to compare what is shown on the early editions of the Ordnance Survey, in order to find the span of time in which various buildings and parts of buildings were put up. From map evidence and reconnaissance a colour-coded plan of a village can be produced to show the antiquity of various structures.

The local Electoral Roll is another useful source, helping the investigator to become familiar with people's names and to get the addresses of buildings correct. In conversation with local residents much helpful information about the histories of buildings may be forthcoming; but local people will naturally refer to buildings by the present occupier's name. Names are very important also if the chain of occupation is to be traced back with the help of such sources as local trade directories and census returns. A regular practice should be followed of referring to buildings by postal address in one's own notes. Grid references, though useful to confirm a location, are much too abstract.

QUESTIONNAIRE SURVEY

In an ideal questionnaire every term used would be backed up with a precise definition and there would be a fully-anticipated range of possible responses, all mutually exclusive. If the investigator allows the abstract problem of data-processing to become an end in itself, he may be tempted to forget that in a subject as complex as building some allowance must be made for the impossibility of watertight definitions and for the necessity of open-ended responses. The *ignis fatuus* of the ideal questionnaire may be brightened by the hope of computerising results.

A fieldworker aiming to feed his discoveries back to central deposit in the County Sites and Monuments Record of his county should note the questions posed on the standardised record card. The Primary Record Card particulars are equivalent to a questionnaire. Amateur contributors would not be expected to fill up the Record's own cards, or at least certainly not any computer-coded parts. For the maintenance of uniform standards this can only be done by the paid staff. The private researcher may be guided by a form of report issued for field use.

When dealing with the exterior of a building the Shropshire Sites and Monuments Record calls for the investigator to notice the general classification of the building in terms conceived by Professor Cordingley, its relationship to adjacent buildings in terms of group layout, and both external and internal features of construction and ornament. The more detailed external points include:

Walling material: not just whether brick, stone etc., but which specific type, if identifiable – e.g. sandstone, hand-made brick, timber frame, stucco on unknown material, etc.

Walling technique: e.g. whether stones laid randomly or in courses, whether timber frame includes close-studding or small square panels, etc.

Walling special features: e.g. wattle and daub infill panels, a jetty, decorative brickwork courses, etc.

Roof materials: i.e. the material of the covering, e.g. tiles, shingles, iron sheets.

Roof shape: e.g. hipped, gabled, Mansard etc.

Roof special features: e.g. decorative barge-boards, finials, bellcote etc.

Chimney: the material, position of the stack, plan-shape of the stack above ridge level, and any special features such as cast iron pots.

Windows – shape of opening: not just the shape, e.g. lancet, but the features and arrangement of the openings.

Window frames: the material of the frame and the movement of any opening lights.

Windows, special features: tracery, type of glass, presence of shutters, etc. Bricked-up windows should be noted here.

Doorways: the features of the surround to the door, the frame, the door itself and any additional points such as doorscrapers.

Other special (external) features.

Where internal survey is possible, the more detailed points include:

Plan form: for domestic buildings, a number of suggestions are possible, according to whether the house is large, small or of cottage status.

Sectional form: particularly the number of storeys.

Roof type: i.e. the structure rather than the covering. This is the place to record truss type.

Main beam mouldings: the underside arrises of main beams in floors over important rooms are often chamfered, hollowed, or more elaborately moulded. The sectional shape should be recorded.

Stops: the detail by which a moulding on the underside of a main beam terminates should be noted.

Fireplaces: the features of the fireplace and its surround, any hood, any kitchen range etc.

Internal decorative features: e.g. moulded or decorative doorways, but including major features such as a gallery or a spere truss.

Miscellaneous features: anything else worth remark, such as a date-stone. The presence of carpenter's marks should be noted.

A quite different method of recording by questionnaire is that of the Manchester School of Architecture, which has been made the basis of large surveys in several other countries (notably Canada, Norway and Scotland) although it was devised with English pre-Industrial Revolution domestic architecture in mind.[41] Thus the Vale Royal planning department produced record cards for 2000 houses in a six-months Manpower Services sponsored survey. The method involves a booklet of standardised thumbnail illustrations of architectural features from which the recorder has to select those which describe the building under scrutiny. For each case the recorder has to look at 13 pages of illustrations, and choose one of nine options from each of five rows. Each option is represented by a figure from one to nine. A full description of a building is thus coded in a row of 65 figures, and entered on a 5×8in (127×203mm) record card together with a photograph. The choice of which 13 pages to examine depends on the identification of the main walling material, and nine alternative walling options are given.

The method permits, in effect, 2,394 yes/no responses. The price paid for this highly-developed system is the loss of any open-endedness because of the inflexibility of replies in number-code, and the unintelligibility of results until processed and interpreted. The full system as developed by Dr Brunskill in succession to Professor Cordingley is described in R. W. Brunskill 'A Systematic Procedure for recording English Vernacular Architecture' in the Transactions of the Ancient Monuments Society XIII (1965–6).[42] As the offprint edition of this article, though giving the full set of illustrations, does not carry quite such a clear introduction, the reader is advised to refer to the original. The system is not to be confused with a simpler type of record card illustrated in Dr Brunskill's *Handbook of Vernacular Architecture* (1970).

This system is not suited to buildings bearing the signs of the Industrial Revolution, for which a more suitable standardised record card would be the one sponsored by the Council of British Archaeology and illustrated in K. Hudson *Handbook for Industrial Archaeologists* (1967).

MEASURED SURVEY

The most important rule is to be unhurried. One should be able to spend time assessing the problem before starting with the tape measure. It is important to have time to take more information than one thinks will be necessary for the survey. Above all, the task should be enjoyable and free of anxiety.

Work should be comfortable: the better the sketches the better the end result so a firm board or book to draw on and clear pens or pencils are essential. The surveyor's pockets should be well organised and everything returned to its proper place when finished with.

In assessing the problems of the survey before starting, one should decide on the probable scale of the intended result and the dimensional tolerance appropriate to it. It is useful to spend time to obtain diagrammatic plans and sections at about 1:200 scale (but freehand, not measured), with walls represented as single solid lines, in order to give names or letters to the various rooms or parts of the structure and to serve as a key to the measured sketches.

If a reconnaissance as previously suggested has been carried out, one may already have produced a key roof plan. One may then start by checking this for correctness, and noting from the roof features what appears to be the original core of the building; then the floor plans are sketched. From this it should be clear which sectional views are desirable, and these may then be sketched.

There are two possible standards of survey, corresponding to the building in *carcase* state on the one hand or in *finished* state on the other. For an overall survey, especially if the survey is intended only for record purposes, the carcase standard is usually the only one possible. It is practically impossible to represent a building in finished state satisfactorily at a scale smaller than 1:20 or $\frac{1}{2}$in to 1ft; only details or very small buildings can be represented at this scale.

The system of taking dimensions depends on whether the survey is of carcase state or of finished state, and on the chosen tolerance. For normal purposes a record survey would be of the carcase state with a dimensional tolerance of $\frac{1}{2}$in or 10mm; but any details requiring larger-scale drawing, for which the finished state and greater accuracy is required, would have to be remeasured. For example, a half-brick wall thickness in a survey to carcase standard would be given as $4\frac{1}{2}$in (115mm); in a survey to finished standard it might be as much as $5\frac{1}{2}$in (140mm) or even more to include plaster thickness. The former dimension is appropriate to setting out the building plan overall, the latter to recording the joinery detail of a door frame. Carcase dimensions should be the norm for the recorder, finished dimensions being the exception.

The measuring sequence should be systematic, proceeding regularly from left to right along walls (or right to left if preferred) in every case without exception, so that the starting point of any dimension will be obvious. Vertical measurement proceeds more logically upwards than downwards, but whichever way is preferred it should start from a good datum. Estimated dimensions should be carefully distinguished from measured ones.

If time and circumstances permit, the first draft of a survey to scale should be drawn out whilst still on site.

The plan of Hill Farm starts with setting out lines sketched in pencil (*Fig. 36*). These pencil lines are then altered and adjusted until the

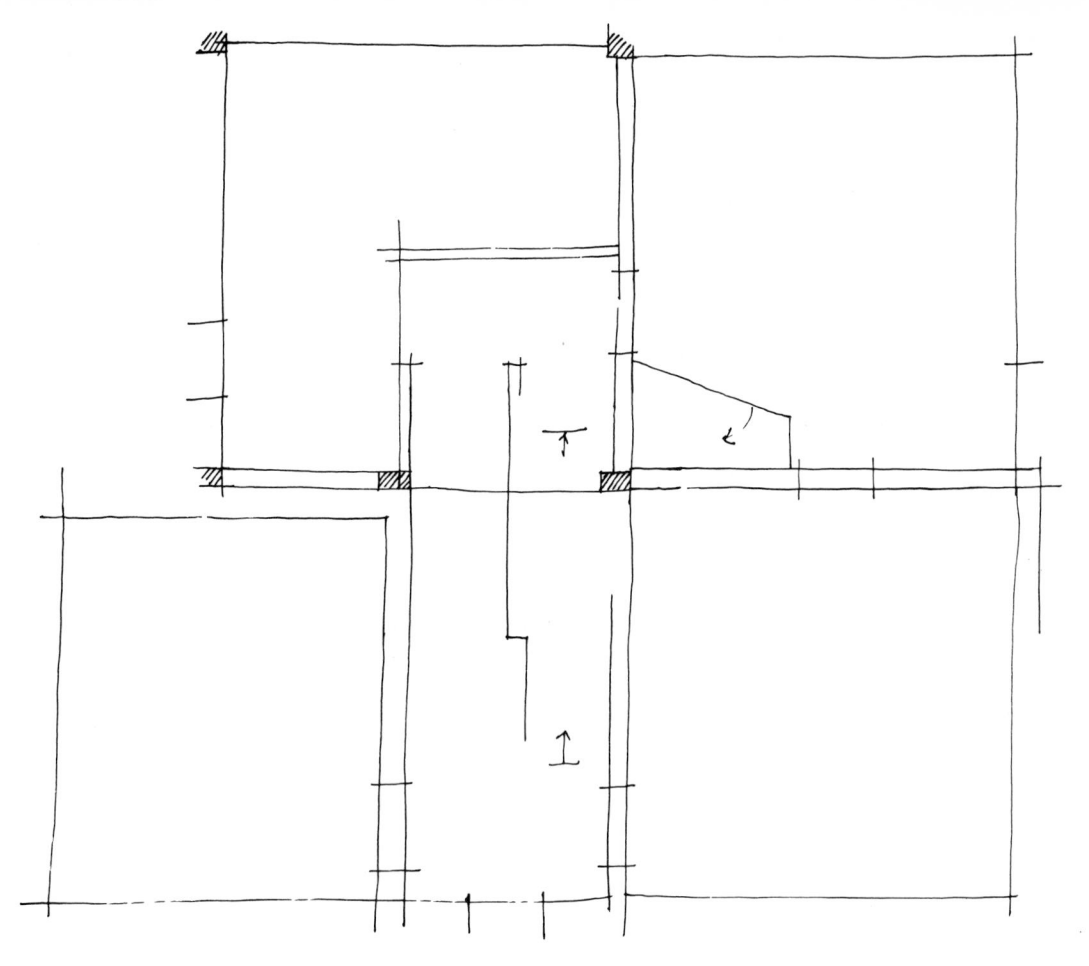

36 Hill Farm Plan, 1st state

arrangement sets out the room shapes in acceptable proportions. Partitions and the post positions of timber-framed walls are added, taking care to continue preserving realistic proportions. Simple though the first sketch of the Hill Farm plan appears, it takes care and patience to get it right. Rough measurements should be paced out for this purpose.

The plan is then inked-in over the pencil draft (*Fig. 37*) and the pencil lines, if obtrusive, are rubbed out. At this stage the positions of window openings are added and it may be necessary to show window or door frame details in a manner appropriate to the intended final scale. A plan is, by convention, usually taken at just above window-sill level, but the level may be varied locally as commonsense dictates to make the most of the information. There is no sense, for example, in showing an oblique cut through a roof slope when drawing an attic floor plan. A good surveyor avoids nonsensical views and details.

In fieldwork drawings, structural timbers can be distinguished from secondary carpentry or joinery by means of pencil shading. The frames of doors and windows are usually shown on an overall plan to carcase standard as little rectangles, without any attempt to follow the intricacies of mouldings and rebates. Frames should be realistically proportioned to the walls in which they occur. Except for a very small-scale survey, care should be taken to show whether the end of a wall abutting a frame is square or is recessed to receive it. In a survey to carcase standard, no attempt should be made to show wall joinery other than door and window frames. The aim is to show the building as if there were no plaster on the walls, no skirtings, architraves, dadoes, cover mouldings, or any other items of construction belonging to the finish rather than the carcase of the building.

Details within rooms follow. The quarter-circle of door swing lines should be shown. Stairs may be indicated by the first few lines representing the vertical faces of the individual steps with an arrow to indicate the rising direction. The arrow makes it plain whether the staircase goes up from or rises up to the floor in question. Important overhead features such as roof-lights, dormer windows etc., or, as in this example, the visible main beams of the floor above, should be shown in dotted lines. The architectural convention of showing the beam overhead, rather than the engineering convention of showing the beam underfoot, should be followed.

The draughtsmanship of the site sketch should anticipate that of the final

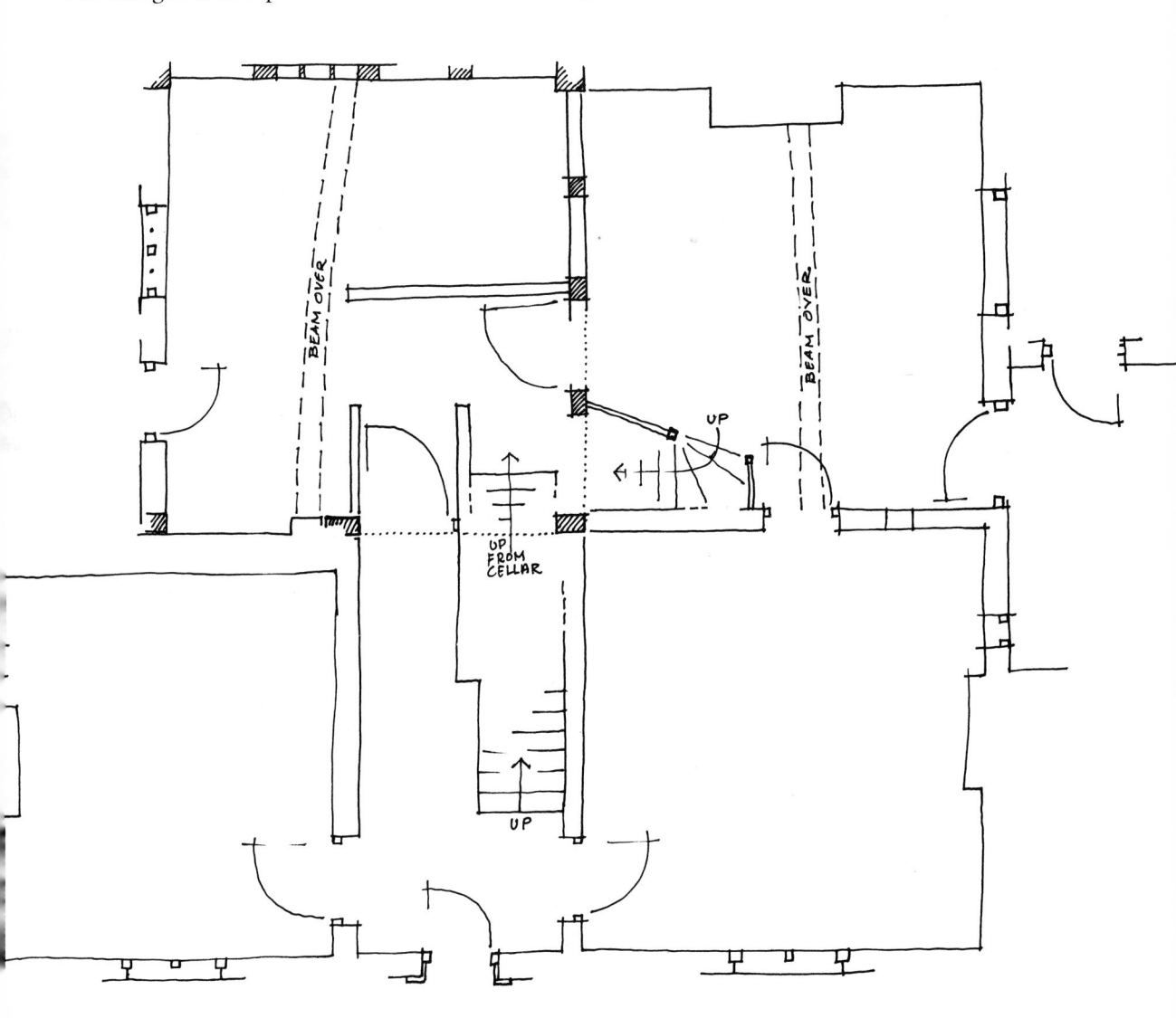

37 Hill Farm Plan, 2nd state

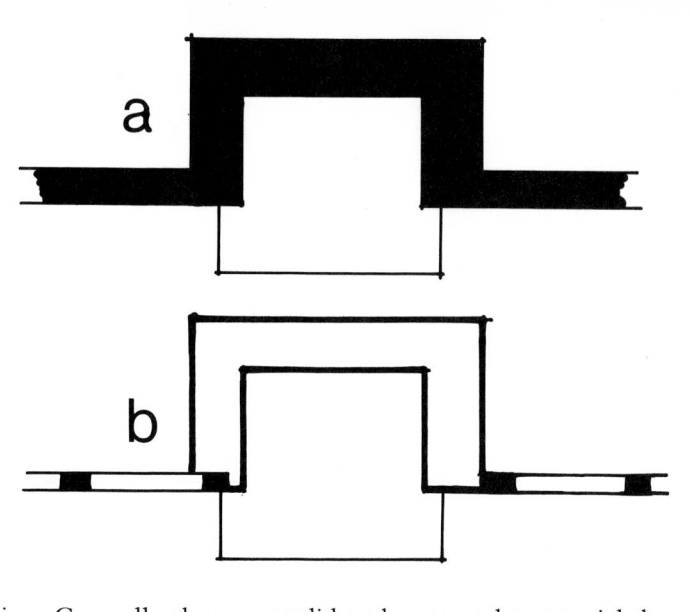

38 Solid masonry problem

fair version. Generally the more solid and structural a material the more dominant it should appear on the finished drawing. It is not possible to have a uniform convention to cover both timber-framed buildings and those of masonry (or brickwork).

In the drawing of a timber-framed building, each timber cut through in the chosen view should normally be inked in as a solid black rectangle, if structural, or shown in heavy outline, if non-structural, provided the distinction is obvious. Where timber framing is brick-filled or enclosed in more substantial masonry, the framing must take precedence over the masonry etc., so that the latter must be shown in heavy outline.

In a building entirely of masonry structure, on the other hand, it is often convenient to show the masonry in solid black. There are three conveniently distinguished types of outline: solidly filled, heavily outlined, and lightly outlined. The last is reserved for features seen beyond the plane at which the view is taken, such as a doorway threshold or the edge of a hearth. Masonry might be shown as solidly shaded, if primary, or in a heavy outline, if secondary to a timber-framed structure (*Fig. 38*).

When a satisfactory plan has been drawn, it is ready to be dimensioned (*Fig. 39*). This is the stage at which a survey sketch is apt to get into a tangle. For clarity, dimension marks and figures should be in a colour of ink or ballpoint contrasting with the colour of the lines representing material. When working in imperial measure, a figure on its own is taken to be so many inches; there is no need to write 'in' or use the symbol for inches. A six or a nine should be underlined. When working in metric, the convention is strictly to use only millimetres. If the measuring tolerance is merely to the nearest 10mm, measurements should still be given in millimetres but there should be a note on the survey sketch to state the tolerance accepted.

Some isolated dimensions are necessary in every survey, but generally it is far better to take *running* dimensions. This means taking a series of measurements from a common starting point. Work usually proceeds regularly clockwise around the room or anticlockwise around the

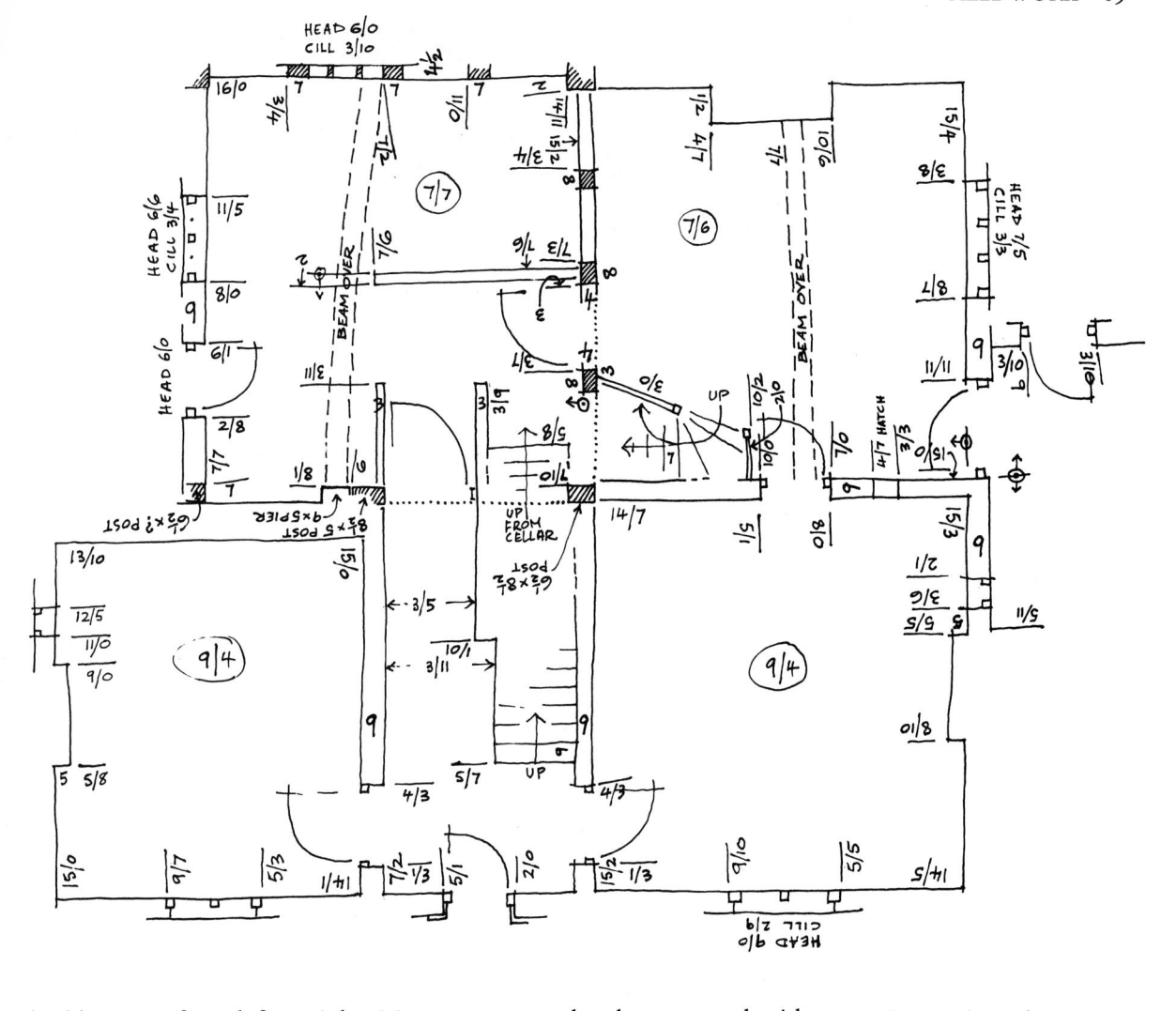

39 Hill Farm Plan, 3rd state

building, i.e. from left to right. Most rooms can thus be measured with only four positions of the tape, preferably by three or two people working together. When the origin of each set of dimensions is the room corner, there is no need to indicate the fact as it will be obvious when drawing out the survey. The point identified as the corner may be ringed if there would be any doubt. When surveying at carcase level, the person holding the zero end of the tape in the room corner has to allow for the probable thickness of plaster. As each run of dimensions progresses, the person drawing the plan marks a dash at each feature and writes the dimension against it. It is clearest if the heads of the figures are close to the dash and if the orientation of the figures on the paper indicates the direction of progress of the run of dimensions.

Finally one should work systematically through the plan trying to estimate all wall thicknesses.

When surveying at carcase level, the person reading the tape must see through the construction to a certain extent. When measuring along a wall to the position of a door or a window in a plastered brickwork wall, for instance, the crucial point to be measured is the one where the brickwork abuts the timber frame, and this point will be hidden as seen from the inside of the building though usually visible externally. The position of the point internally may be hidden by a return of the wall plaster into the opening, by timber cover-moulds or architraves or even by more elaborate construction such as wall-panelling or boxes to take window shutters. A recorder not familiar with building construction should take every opportunity to examine such details in buildings being demolished to gain an instinctive ability to estimate the position of the face of the structural opening hidden behind the finishing work. In simple building the position of the structural opening is merely hidden behind a moulding known as an architrave, nailed to the frame and overlapping the plastered face by about $\frac{1}{2}$in (12mm).

It helps clarity if the central area of a room on a plan is kept fairly free of writing. A dimension written in the centre of a room and ringed represents the floor to ceiling height. When working to carcase standard, the ceiling thickness would be allowed for, so that the recorded dimension would be an estimate of the distance from the surface of the floorboards to the underside of the common joists above. A separate note is made of the floor thickness. Other useful vertical dimensions to relate to floor level in a room are the sill and head heights of windows and doors. As with horizontal dimensions, the position of the structural opening should be estimated even if not directly visible.

The procedure described is suitable for most types of building, but, where machinery dominates the building, it may be better to use the axes of main shafts or the centrelines of bedplates as datums from which to measure, rather than corners of rooms. (The convention for representing an axis or centreline is a line consisting of alternate dots and dashes.) The choice depends on how substantial the machinery is: an engine house for a large steam engine would be measured from the axes of the cylinder and the flywheel, but a machine shop with several small items of machinery would be measured in the usual way, and the setting-out lines of each item then tied into the building survey.

In all but the simplest surveying, the lengths of room diagonals should be measured as a check on how out-of-square the room is. (If the diagonal dimension between two corners of a room seemingly square is 1 per cent greater than expected, e.g. by Pythagoras' theorem, the angle of the other corners of the room is likely to be 1° (or more exactly 1.15°) more than a right angle.) It is important to measure two diagonals rather than just one; because of the uncertainty of estimating plaster thickness in the corners of rooms, the triangle of two sides and a diagonal is likely to be inaccurately measured. If two diagonals are measured, the errors are likely to be similar and a good compromise fit can be achieved.

Elevations are more difficult to draw than plans, because the significant detail exists at several scales. It is convenient, therefore, to sketch at more than one scale. The overall sketch can be confined to the essentials of setting out, and detailed features shown in separate sketches to larger scale. The overall sketch of an elevation can be used for indicating the lines where one material gives way to another: it becomes an analytical diagram. It is the diagram of measured lines on which an artistically polished elevation

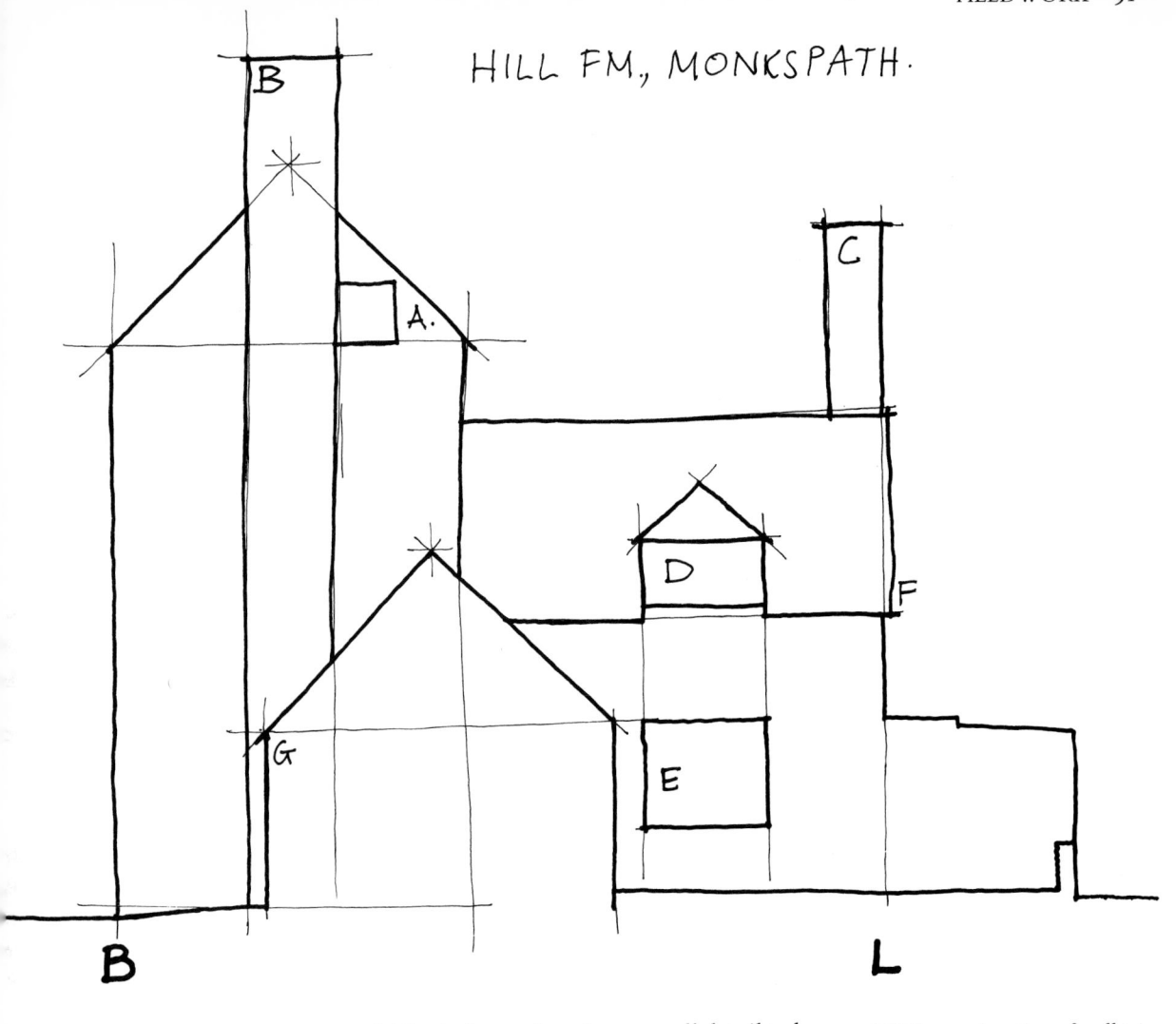

HILL FM., MONKSPATH.

B

L

drawing may later be constructed. The information about small detail to be added in the final drawn version does not necessarily all have to be measured, as long as the essential lines are correct. The surveyor might be content to rely on photography to supply the details.

To produce the overall sketch it is crucial that the meaning of each line added to it should be clear and unambiguous. Each should represent the position of an edge or of a change of material. Decorative architraves and consoles to windows and doors, string-courses and cornices, barge-boards, etc., may have to be shown in the final drawing if the appearance is not to be misrepresented; but they get in the way of taking the important dimensions. Where a clearly definable part of the elevation is occupied by decorative features, it should be outlined as part of the skeleton of essential lines. Their inclusion helps the surveyor to produce a sketch in which realistic proportions are achieved.

The elevation of the wall which runs from the point marked B to the point marked L on the key plan may serve for an example. This wall is shown (*Fig. 40*) as it would appear in the field notebook, resolved into its

40 Hill Farm: elevation of wall B L

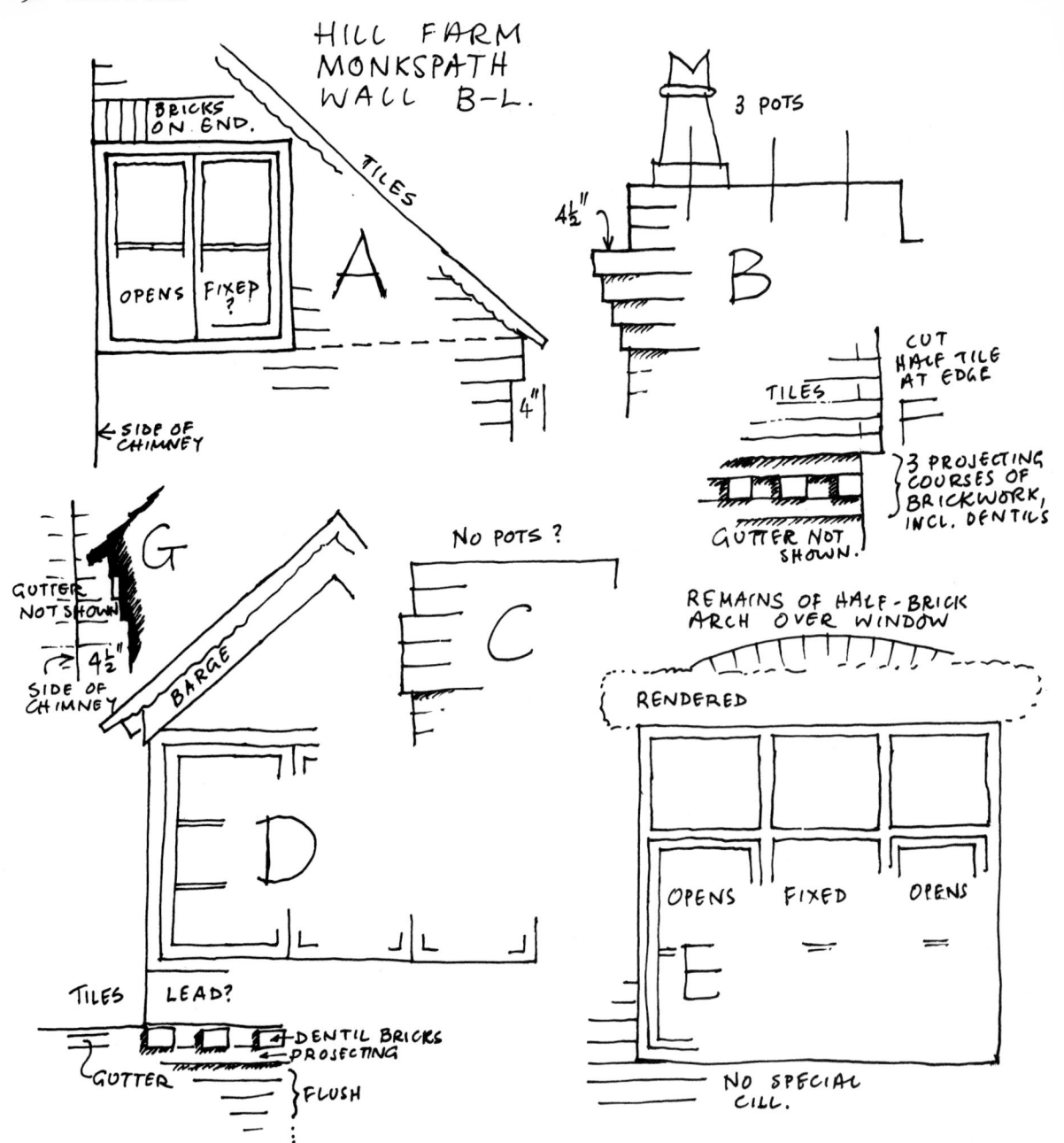

HILL FARM
MONKSPATH
WALL B-L.

3 POTS

BRICKS ON END.

TILES

A

OPENS FIXED?

← SIDE OF CHIMNEY

4"

4½"

B

TILES

CUT HALF TILE AT EDGE

3 PROJECTING COURSES OF BRICKWORK, INCL. DENTILS

GUTTER NOT SHOWN.

G

GUTTER NOT SHOWN

4½"

SIDE OF CHIMNEY

BARGE

NO POTS ?

C

REMAINS OF HALF-BRICK ARCH OVER WINDOW

RENDERED

D

OPENS FIXED OPENS

TILES LEAD?

DENTIL BRICKS PROJECTING

GUTTER

FLUSH

E

NO SPECIAL CILL.

41 Supplementary large-scale details

essential lines. These are initially set out in pencil by trial and error and then inked in. When sketching one should try to get the overall proportions right and then divide the drawing into its smaller parts, still attending, above all, to achieving realistic proportions. Each element of the drawing, whether a chimney, roof, door, wall or window appears in this diagrammatic sketch in its simple geometrical form, usually as a rectangle. Larger-scale details are then produced in the margin of the drawing or on an adjacent page (*Fig. 41*).

It is no less important with timber-framed walls to concentrate on

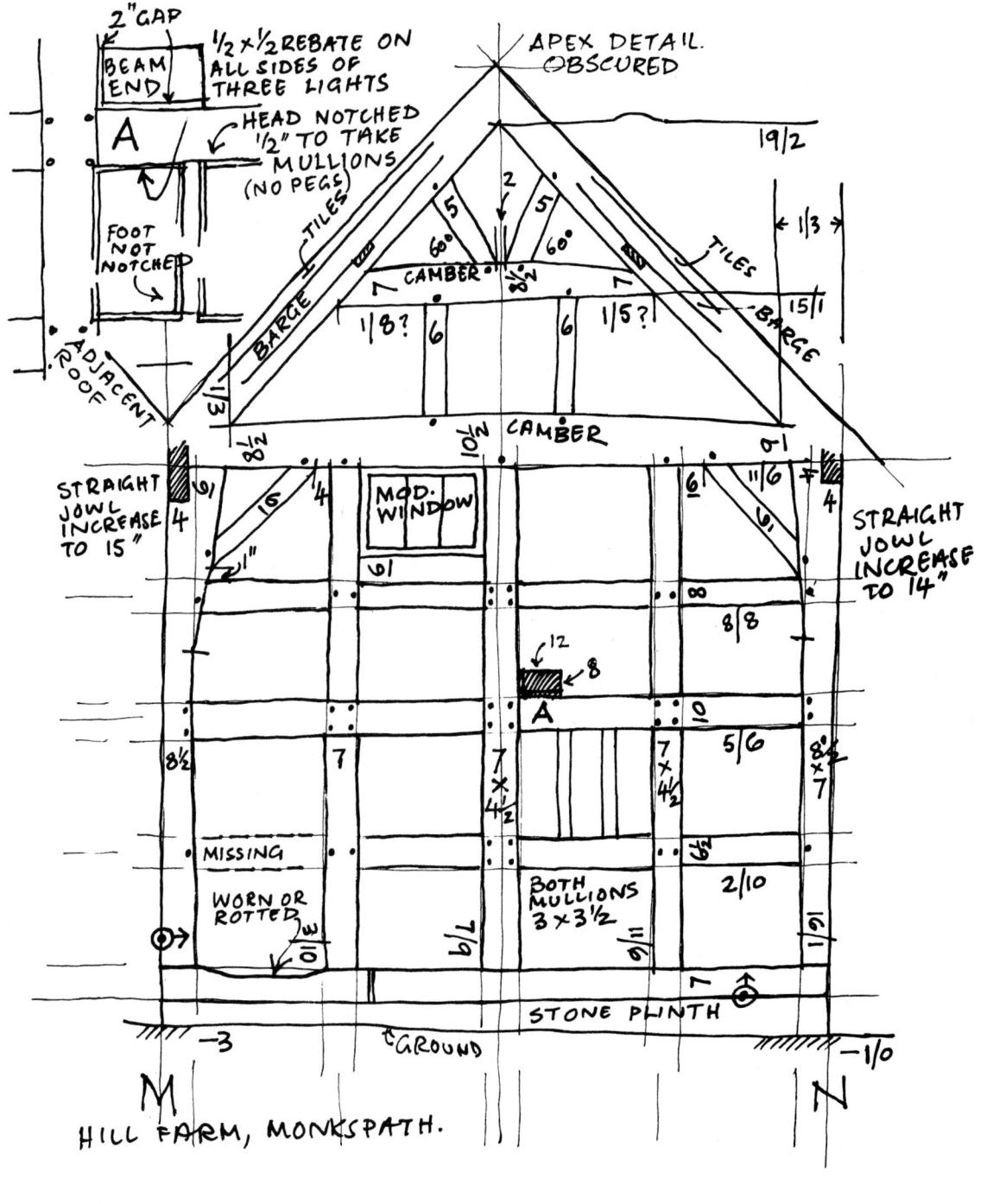

2" GAP

BEAM END

½ x ½ REBATE ON ALL SIDES OF THREE LIGHTS

APEX DETAIL. OBSCURED

A

HEAD NOTCHED ½" TO TAKE MULLIONS (NO PEGS)

FOOT NOT NOTCHED

TILES

BARGE

19/2

1/3

TILES

BARGE

5   2   5

60°   60°

CAMBER

15/1

ADJACENT ROOF

1/3

1/8?   6   6   1/5?

10N CAMBER

STRAIGHT JOWL INCREASE TO 15"

6/   4   16/   4

MOD. WINDOW

6/   "/6   4

STRAIGHT JOWL INCREASE TO 14"

21"

6/

8/8

12   8

A

10/

7 x 4½

5/6

8½ x 7

8½

7

7 x 4½

MISSING

WORN OR ROTTED

3/   10/

6/7

BOTH MULLIONS 3 x 3½   6/   11

6/2   2/10

6/1

7   ↑

STONE PLINTH

-3   GROUND

-1/0

M   N

HILL FARM, MONKSPATH.

getting the proportions of every part of the drawing right. It is unlikely to be satisfactory to reduce timber framing to single lines in the manner of a child's matchstick drawing, so all timbers will appear as two lines from the outset. A drawing of a timber-framed wall should be at a large enough scale to show pegholes, at least as dots. When inking in the lines the distortions may be suggested (*Fig. 42*).

42 Field drawing of timber-framed wall

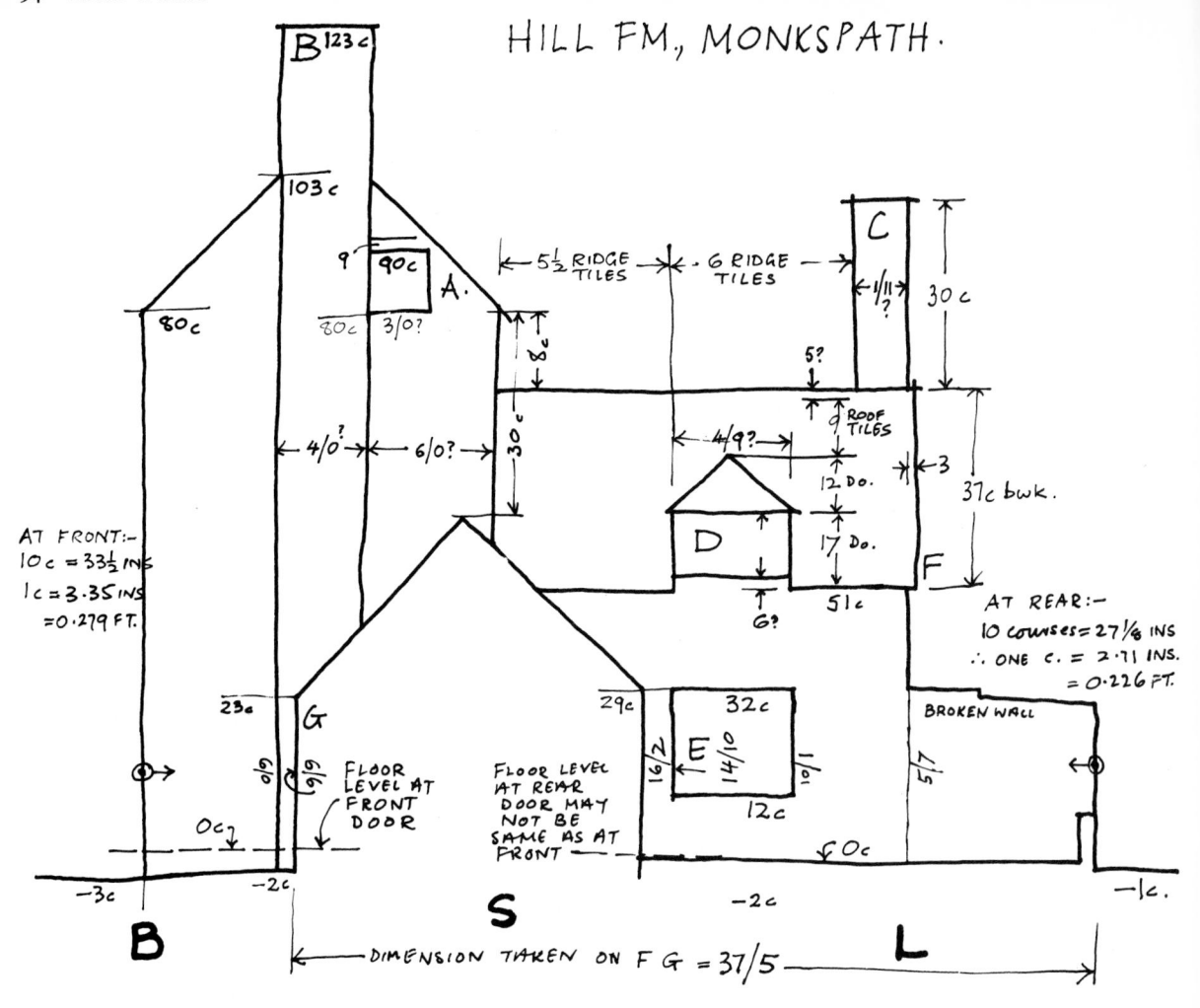

HILL FM., MONKSPATH.

43 Hill Farm: elevation of wall B L, dimensioned

The eaves of a roof overhanging a wall may consist of several lines – the line of the bottom edge of the tiles or other roof covering; the top and bottom edges of a rainwater gutter and the top and bottom edges of the board on which it is fixed; the top and bottom edges of the timber (the wall-plate) on which the rafters bear, and finally the lines of an indefinite number of courses of a decorative brickwork cornice. In addition there may be the added complication of projecting rafter ends. For the purposes of a diagrammatic sketch, however, only one line is indispensable: the line where roof and wall meet. In the case of a stone or brickwork wall this line is the bottom line of the timber wall-plate. In the case of a timber-framed wall, the top of the wall framing is the crucial line, though both edges of each timber would be shown. Whatever appears on the finished drawing, there should be one dominant line treated as a local datum for any measurements of detail.

When a roof appears eaves-on in a sketch, it normally takes the form of a simple rectangle, perspective being suppressed. Where a roof appears gable-on, unless there is a parapet at the verge, the significant lines to include in the fieldbook sketch are those representing the plane of the surface of the tiles, thatch etc., and the outer and inner planes of the rafters, if visible. Alternatively there may be barge-boards, the upper and lower edges of which would be indicated.

The wall BL of Hill Farm is also shown (*Fig. 43*) as it would appear in the field notebook after dimensioning and other explanatory comments have been added. Dimensions in a brickwork wall which are out of reach may be estimated by counting brick courses or lengths and measuring a similar number somewhere else within reach. This only presents any difficulty if the type of brick changes or there are irregular-sized or cut bricks. Any estimated dimension should be distinguished with a question mark. As a check on estimated vertical dimensions it is useful to remember that rainwater pipes are usually in 6ft (1.828m) lengths. It may be convenient to take all vertical dimensions in numbers of courses, leaving all the arithmetic to be done later. A specimen ten courses should be carefully measured and noted.

Because of the presence of a locked outhouse, the dimension SL is impossible to obtain directly. An estimate is obtained by counting the ridge tiles and working out their probable length from other known dimensions. Another problem is to place the dormer window correctly. It is noted that there are 38 courses of tiles from ridge to eaves, nine above the dormer apex and 21 above the dormer eaves, and these counts are easily converted into measurements. There is now sufficient information to set the elevation out in measured draft and to trace a fair copy (*Fig. 44*).

It is sometimes better to take vertical dimensions downwards using eaves level as datum; but it may be more practical to make the main floor level at the main entrance the datum and measure upwards. Working upwards, levels are noted on the drawing with the same convention as in the dimensioning of a plan, placing the heads of the figures against the lines to which they refer. A continuous run of dimensions from datum to the apex of the roof and the tops of chimneys is the optimum, but if the wall face is broken by jetties, this may not be possible.

Doors and windows

Much of the complex detail in an elevation is found in the surrounds of doors and windows, and an unpracticed surveyor may find it confusing. There are too many lines, and an idea of priority is needed. The guiding rule is to prefer lines where a *change of material* occurs. Inessentials are to be left until a detailed sketch of the feature is drawn. To show how to distinguish what is essential for an overall elevation the following examples may be worth study (*Fig. 46*):

A In this simple instance the outline to be distinguished is the edge of the structural opening as seen externally: the top of the brick sill and the brick reveals. An extra measurement at the top gives the arch rise. The sill and arch are both part of the wall. When these lines, three straight and one curved, have been drawn to scale, the additional lines for the sashes and the arch are added unmeasured.

B This window resolves itself into four small rectangles and one larger enclosing rectangle. As there are no appreciable window frames inserted in

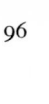

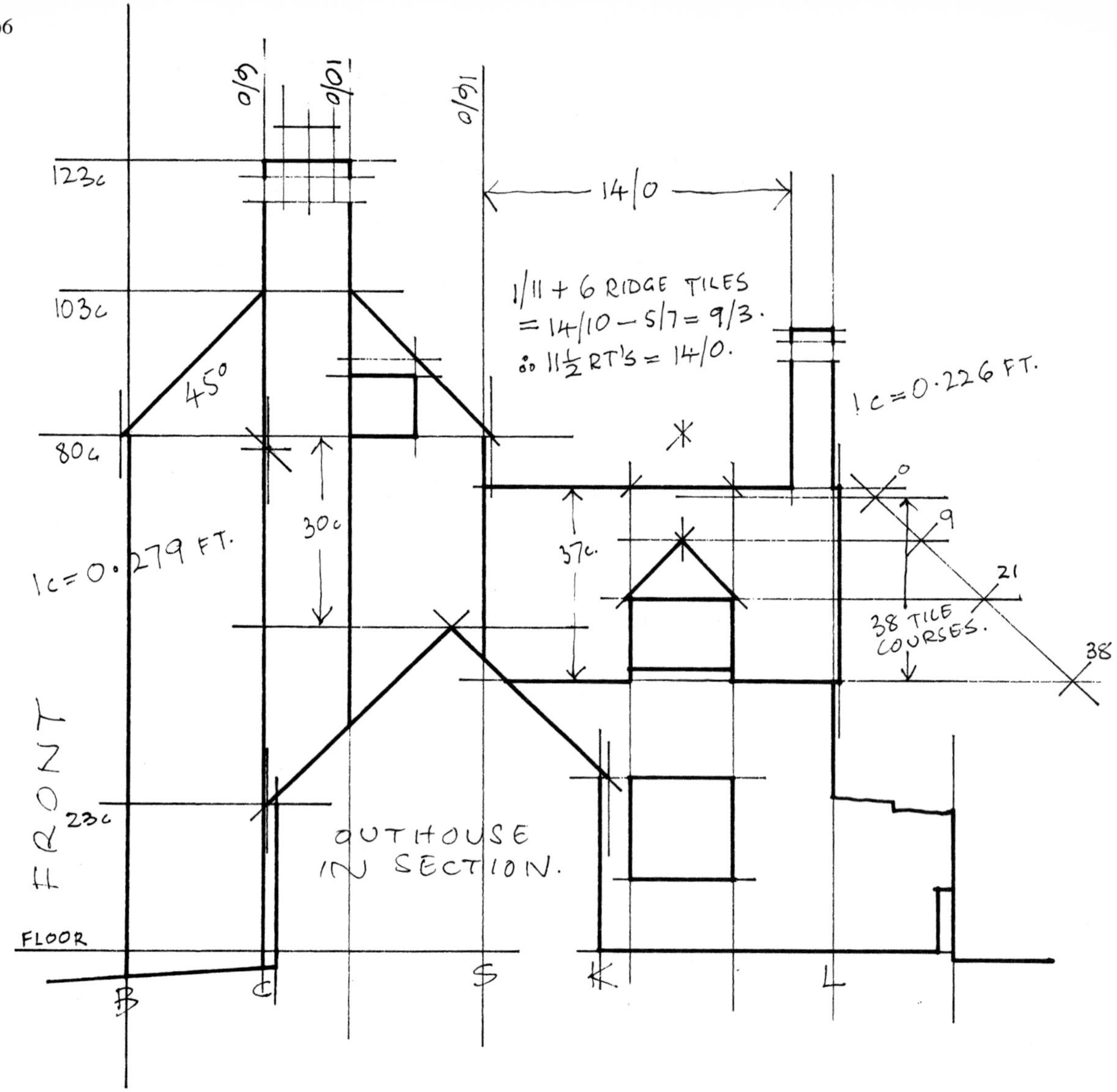

The figure (elevation drawing) contains the following annotations:

- 9/0
- 10/0
- 19/0
- 14/0
- 123c
- 103c
- 80c
- 45°
- 1c = 0.279 FT.
- 30c
- 37c.
- 23c
- 1/11 + 6 RIDGE TILES
- = 14/10 − 5/7 = 9/3.
- ∴ 11½ RT'S = 14/0.
- 1c = 0.226 FT.
- 0
- 9
- 21
- 38
- 38 TILE COURSES.
- FRONT 11
- FLOOR
- OUTHOUSE IN SECTION.
- B C S K L

44 Hill Farm: finalised elevation of wall B L

the four openings, no detail will be shown within them. In this case there is another change of material where the stone dressings abut the brickwork; this should be measured also.

C This modern window differs from that at A in that the sill is part of the window joinery, so the measurement would be taken to its underside.

D If the design of a window or door includes an outer 'order' or recess as well as the aperture proper, whether there is a change of material or not, the outer outline should be represented in the overall drawing of the elevation.

E Likewise where a door is inserted into a former window position the lines of both features, including what remains of the earlier one, should be measured to. This example would call for annotation.

F It may not be possible to see the edges of a structural opening (the important change of material) because they are hidden behind a decorative surround, such as the pilasters and entablature of a doorway. In this instance the measurements would naturally be taken to either side of the pilasters

and to the top and bottom of the entablature whether they are of stone or a timber sham.

G If a door frame (or window frame) is of such massiveness that it is practically part of the structure, it might be treated as in effect a timber-framed piece of wall, and both sides of each member measured to.

H This dormer window is assembled in the manner of post-and-truss timber framing, and the lines selected for dimensioning are those of the structural frame and the outline of the window frame inserted into it. The sizes of the timber members would be noted separately.

J Compare this simpler example of a cottage dormer window in which the window frame doubles in function as the dormer structure.

In all these examples the guiding principle is to look generally for the important change of material. Explanatory notes should be at a minimum. The essential lines will be drawn out to scale, and inessentials estimated.

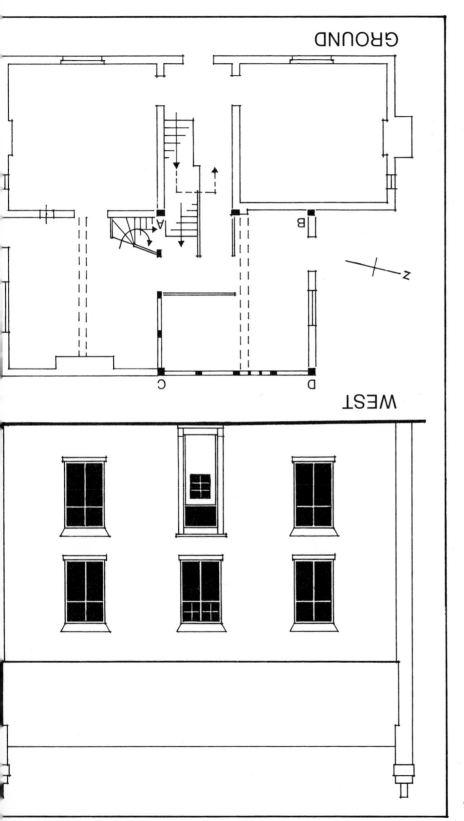

GROUND

N

A
B
C
D

WEST

45

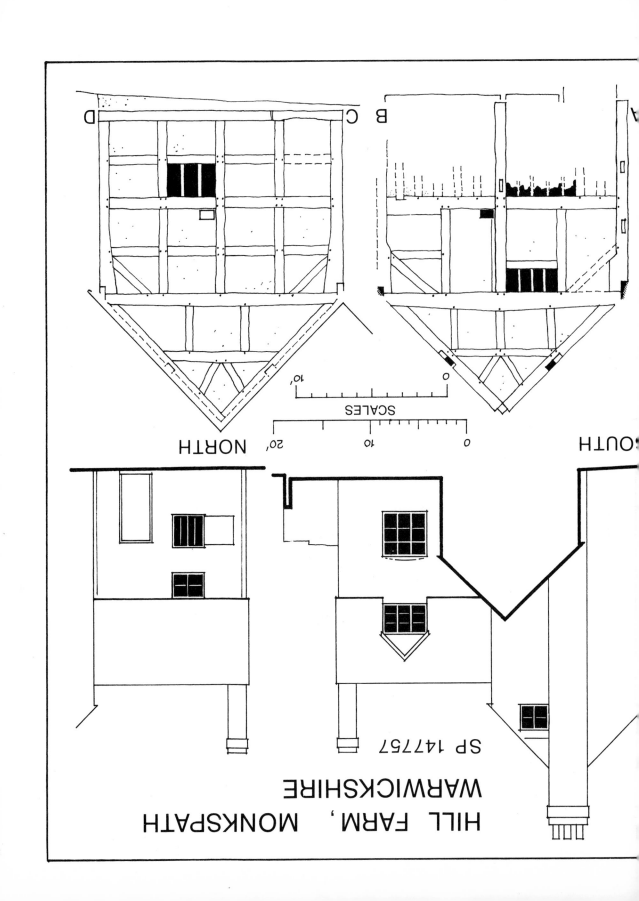

HILL FARM, MONKSPATH
WARWICKSHIRE

SP 147757

NORTH

SOUTH

SCALES

HILL FARM, MONKSPATH, WARWICKSHIRE

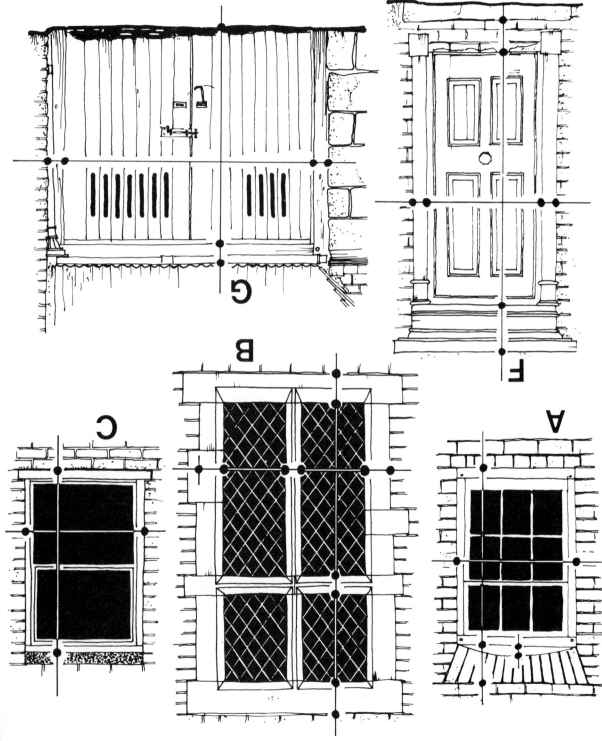

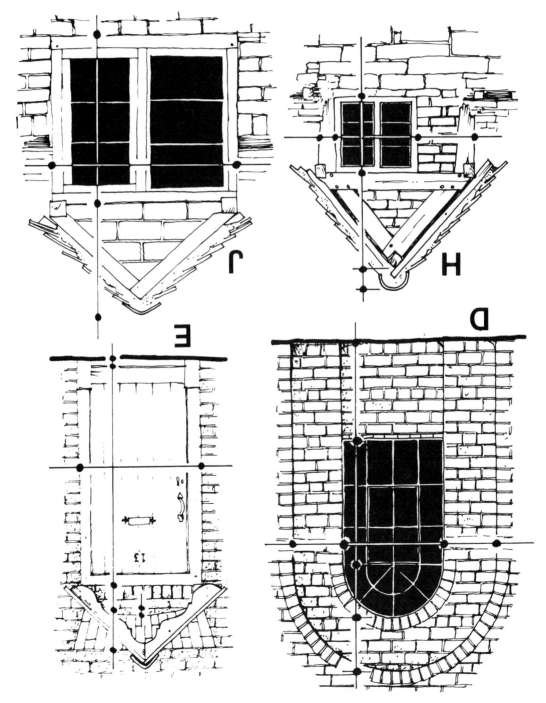

ARCHAEOLOGICAL SURVEY

When an exact survey of a specimen of construction needs to be drawn it can be produced in several ways:

1 By photogrammetry. A specialist firm, equipped with the sort of photographic apparatus used in the production of maps by aerial photography, takes two or more photographs of the elevation or building sufficient to locate every point in three dimensions. Points are projected to reconstruct the information in the form of a correct orthographic elevation. Naturally this is an expensive method of surveying, but it may be appropriate for inaccessible work, such as producing elevations of bridges. Accuracy is ensured by fixing 'targets' on the structure to be surveyed, which are located precisely by theodolite survey: these are the fixed points for ensuring that all other detail is shown in correct location.

2 By drawing in perspective from ordinary photography. Tracings from photographs can be produced directly from printed enlargements, though this is expensive. A far cheaper method is to work from a photographic slide. It is awkward to trace an image projected from a transparency unless the projector is on the other side of the paper from the draughtsman; it is therefore advisable to use a light-box – a large wooden box with a glass worktop and a mirror beneath at an angle to project the image up to the underside of the worktop. Provided everything is firm this is a very easy and comfortable way of working. The glass can be plain rather than ground, as the tracing paper or film acts as ground glass. It is desirable to take several photographs of the view to be drawn, from the same viewpoint exactly, with different exposures so as to ensure that detail in the shadows is visible as well as detail in sunlight.

3 Gridded measuring. In ordinary archaeology, plans are often drawn with the help of a frame measuring 1m square with strings across at 20cm intervals. This is placed on the ground and detail within the string squares is transferred visually to its position on graph paper, usually at the scale of 1:20. When drawing upstanding architectural details, a frame is inconvenient, but, if permissible, marks at suitable intervals horizontally and vertically can be chalked on the wall and the positions of all details can be ascertained by two measurements within the square in which they occur. If it is not permissible to make marks on the face of the wall, it may be possible to fix a vertical plumb-line and a horizontal datum line of string and take measurements from these. The drawing should be done directly on to graph paper and a fair copy finally traced.

The photogrammetry and gridded measuring methods produce drawings in true elevation with points set out where they can be measured from the drawing. But before deciding on these rather than on perspective drawing from slides with the help of a light-box, one should consider the purpose of the drawing. Is it necessary to record geometrical positions? The object of archaeology is to record the relationship between parts, not their positions in space. The drawing should be a basis for analysis, a medium for annotation and for marking discoveries and distinctions between 'contexts'. Drawing in elevation is traditional because it is easy; but it may be less informative and is certainly less 'real' than perspective. If some details need to be located geometrically, as a basis for starting further measuring, their co-ordinates can be noted on a version of the drawing as any other factual notes would be.

Recording for removal

If recording is being done as a preliminary to a building being dismantled for exact rebuilding at another site, such as a museum, work must be governed by the need to label everything and pack it for transport and delivery to site in the sequence required. The object is not to replace everything to the millimetre, but to maintain exact relationships and appearance. Certain rules should be followed:

1 Measurements, numbering and datums. The drawings should not be cluttered with dimensions which the craftsmen will not be able to use; as long as the material to be reconstructed is assembled in order, it will find its own dimensions. Datum lines (usually a brick course easily identified all round the building, if possible a plinth) must be marked on drawings. Overall dimensions horizontally and aperture sizes should be given as a control on joint width, but dimensions to openings are less important. All joinery items should be numbered.

2 Numbering timbers. Give a numeral to every truss from one gable end to the other in sequence and a piece number to each timber, to be marked as drawn. An embossed plastic label can be tacked on. A code such as 'IV-9' would be read as the timber numbered 9 on the drawing of truss IV. As timber is not injured by small nails, the numbering can be on face. The original carpenter's marks should not be relied on, but if there is anything odd about their sequence it should be noted on the drawings. Other timbers are to be numbered without truss numeral, as marked on the drawing. Any numbers which might be read upside down should be underlined.

3 Numbering tiles. This is not normally done, but tiles can be numbered in chalk if required. If numbered in paint, the overlap face should be used.

4 Marking bricks or stones. Each brick etc. should be numbered individually. The simple system is to letter each face of the building (e.g. N, S, E and W); make datum zero, then number the courses up from datum, and letter each brick or cut brick in sequence from left to right. A code such as W 23 F will signify the west face, 23rd course, sixth brick along. To make the method foolproof there should be an elevation drawing fully annotated with the codes. The bricks can be marked on face with chalk by the surveyor as a preliminary to permanent marking on a hidden face during dismantling.

5 Coursing of brickwork or stonework. This has to be carefully controlled if appearance is to be correctly maintained and joinery re-fitted without difficulty. From datum take a note of the exact (to the millimetre) level of every fourth brick bedjoint or every stone course. (When measuring to a bedjoint the top of the brick beneath is taken to be the representative point.) If there is doubt about horizontality, the run of vertical dimensions should be repeated beside each window, and certainly at every corner. The bricklayer or mason will make a marked 'rod' to control his dimensions vertically.

6 Levels. Ceiling levels are not important if they are simply the underside of a floor; but all floor levels and the top ceiling soffit should be related carefully to brick course levels or to absolute datum.

7 Record drawings and photographs. The drawings should be completed and the photographs safely developed before dismantling work on site starts. The dismantlers should have a set of the drawings on site on which to mark any observations of their own.

Work on site

8 If bricks or stones have been marked in chalk by the surveyor, the dismantlers then have to clean the mortar from each course in turn and mark the top face of each brick with the same number in Decaplex plastic paint. A rear brick in the same course can be given the same number in brackets if necessary.

9 While the marking paint is drying the supervisor has time to make a sketch or description of the course in his notebook.

10 Bricks should be cleaned with a scutch, not a brick hammer. Bricks can be got down from a scaffolding through a 6in (150mm) plastic pipe discharging into a wheelbarrow with a folded old mattress to cushion the impact. Crates and pallets should be very clearly marked with what courses they contain.

11 Face bricks or stones should be palletted or crated exactly in sequence as numbered.

12 When dismantling reaches datum, the course should be levelled with a dumpy level, if this has not been done before.

It is not necessary to comment on site security and safety here; demolition and building sites are governed by the Factory Acts and the Health and Safety Acts.

DATING

From the dating of buildings by primary evidence emerges the empirical recognition of various principles of construction or various 'types' of architectural feature – structural system, plan, design of window, carpentry joint, moulding and so forth – which stand out as stages in the development of practical or aesthetic ideas and to which a dating range appropriate to a locality might be given. To identify 'types' of feature soundly calls for familiarity with the pragmatic way in which builders think. Any temptation to look for systematic abstract classification of types should be resisted, since builders do not think in such terms. A 'type' of building or feature ought to be, above all, something which was common enough to be recognised and probably distinctly named by contemporaries, even if its original name is now lost.

Sometimes a new principle or type of feature starts with some datable technical innovation or with an important building which comes to be widely imitated. Such was the beginning of iron-framed mill buildings with the work of William Strutt and Charles Bage; Strutt's calico mill near Tennant Street in Derby in 1792 having been a structure with brick vaults, timber beams and cast iron columns, and Bage's flax mill at Ditherington in Shrewsbury four years later achieving full fire-proofing by substituting cast iron girders.[43]

The gradual adaptation of a feature or principle within the time of its popularity may stand out; thus it may be considered that from the seventeenth to eighteenth century, the proportion of window to wall area tends to reduce in the façades of brick town houses, or that from the fifteenth to seventeenth century, boldly projecting jetties tend to be earlier than modestly projecting ones. So when taking notes about the dating of a 'type' of feature one should note its definition, its date range in different localities, with the date of its peak of popularity, and its adaptation over the date range given.

In architecture, dating evidence is often of a very uncertain nature, consisting of the placing of fashionable ornament into historical periods. Datable features tend to be the non-functional parts of a building such as mouldings and tracery, though types of plan and developments in the production of materials are increasingly important. A fashion may be of different dates in different places, and the dating of a fashion is only the dating of its main occurrence. The value of any datable fashion has to be taken on its own merits: the simpler the feature the greater the likelihood of its occurrence by chance at other times. The lack of ornament in poorer buildings and in districts with intractable material, such as Cornish granite, also hinders dating. Historical ornament is a subject which tends to be a matter of feel rather than reason; it is worth taking all the ornamental arts of a period into consideration – architecture, furniture, dress and so forth – to judge what would have looked 'right' to a person of the time.

A summary of the date ranges of features visible externally in domestic architecture is given by J. T. Smith and E. M. Yates in their article 'On the Dating of English Houses from External Evidence' in *Field Studies* vol. 2 no. 5 (1968).

Dating buildings

> 'On the question of dating in general, the only method, if it may be called a method, is that of intensive comparison of all features of the buildings of a locality and region, related of course to past experience in examining buildings, as well as to the experience of other researchers in the same field. Indeed, in practice, the search for some dating feature is generally merely to confirm objectively an almost spontaneous intuitive conviction.'[44]

Dating in principle, using documentary and other impeccable evidence to establish the date range of carefully described features, is a different matter to dating as a fieldwork exercise. Of the latter, Mr Charles indicates that judgement is to be exercised in a way which takes all features into its view rather than by blinkered deduction from chosen points of evidence. Dating may not be a matter of simple reasoning from evidence because the available clues are often of a very intangible nature, and every observation has to be taken in context. Well-informed intuitive conviction is the best guide.

As a fieldwork exercise architectural dating must use the same logic as that of archaeology, where firm clues exist. Archaeological reasoning is sometimes the only tool; it has to be used correctly. Archaeological evidence modifying judgement is well illustrated in the case of the Hendre Wen, Llanrwst, barn, moved to the Welsh Folk Museum at St Fagans under the direction of Eurwyn Wiliam. This barn from Denbighshire had been listed as a Grade II building and described in the Schedule as 'probably 16th century; stone and timber with slated roof. Roof has three cruck principals'. Mr Wiliam comments:

> 'The sixteenth century date is presumably derived from the good form of the crucks, which were the only "datable" feature in the building before its demolition.'[45]

On dismantling this building to prepare for moving, crucial dating evidence was discovered which put the building in a new light:

> '... half a shallow dish, glazed on the inside, found as thirty-five sherds scattered under the footing course and at varying heights up to a metre in the wall itself ... The barn could not have been built before this type of dish was manufactured ... The sherds were submitted independently to three experts, all of whom agreed that it was Buckley ware of the late eighteenth century.'

This led to a reconsideration of the history of the construction of the building to accommodate the view that eighteenth- or nineteenth-century masonry supported a re-assembled cruck roof derived from a sixteenth-century building.

The importance of roofs

Roofs have a special value in the dating of buildings, because they are likely to be far less altered than the fabric of the habitable spaces beneath. The size of the timbers, the types of truss, their spacing and orientation, signs of smoke blackening or evidence of the timbers having been formerly open to view have all to be taken into account.

Logic in dating

The history of a building, like that of an archaeological site, calls for division into phases marked by major changes in the manner of occupation, such as the addition or demolition of a wing or a radical change of use. Minor changes within phases, such as a re-roofing or a reconstruction of windows, may be eminently datable also.

It is worth looking at how dating evidence is exploited in archaeology, for a model of the logic involved. Archaeological reasoning from the minutiae of evidence starts with two ideas, the 'feature' and the 'context'. A feature is an item of construction which can be described by what appears to be its purpose: a pit, a sill beam, a threshold, a floor, and so forth. Features are elements of interpretation. A context, on the other hand, is an element of pure evidence: a deposit or layer of material distinguished from what lies above, below or adjacent. Strict archaeological recording calls for all datable objects found (coins, sherds of pottery, etc.) to be scrupulously assigned to their correct contexts, so that the dating evidence they give may be extended up or down the time sequence to draw dating conclusions about other contexts also, and ultimately to give dating to features and thence to phases. It is easier to grasp the principle in terms of excavation work, or even geology, where the evidence is mainly in the form of layers lying one over another; but standing buildings are no less made up of distinguishable contexts formed in sequence and the logic is the same.

In the course of reasoning from dating evidence it is essential to grasp two model arguments: one deals with the date before which something cannot have occurred, called the *terminus post quem*; the other deals with the date after which something cannot have occurred, called the *terminus ante quem*. These established Latin expressions are so ambiguous that it is better to refer to the 'earliest possible' and 'latest possible' datings respectively. The effect of both arguments is to exclude a range of impossible datings of the contexts and hence features and phases concerned.

An example should make the use of the two model arguments plain. Suppose a pitched stone foundation on artificially formed ground carries a rubblestone wall. Beneath the foundation, during repair work, a coin of Edward II is found. In the wall is an ashlar-dressed glazed window opening, with a four-centred arch and of a style which may be dated to the sixteenth or early seventeenth century. Clearly there are five contexts: the ground, the pitched stone, the rubble masonry, the ashlar, and the glass; as four of them happen to be features also, we can refer for simplicity to (1) the ground, (2) the foundation, (3) the wall, (4) the window and (5) its glazing.

These five contexts must have come into existence either in the sequence in which they have just been mentioned, or in the same order but with the wall and window, 3 and 4, built simultaneously. The foundation and wall (2 and 3) may be contemporary, but no matter; they still appeared in that order. So the time sequence is either

```
later
  ↑                           5
  |              5            |
  |              |            4
  |            3 & 4          |
  |              |     or     3
  |              2            |
  |              |            2
  ↓              1            |
earlier                       1
```

The first piece of dating evidence is the coin of Edward II. It may be unclear whether it was in the ground before the foundation trench was dug, or whether it fell in during digging or during the laying of the pitched stone for the foundation. If in doubt between two contexts, a find with dating significance should always be assigned to the later one, and this is therefore regarded as occurring within the foundation. Edward II came to the throne in 1307, so any context containing such a coin cannot have been formed before 1307. (A numismatist might give a later date for the first issue of the particular type of coin.) Likewise any later context cannot have been formed before 1307; for all these contexts – foundation, wall, window and glass – 1307 is the *terminus post quem*, the earliest possible dating.

The second piece of evidence is date range of 'sixteenth to early seventeenth century' given to the type of window. This dates the window and might date the wall and its foundation. As hard evidence, it gives both an earliest possible and a latest possible dating to the window itself, and it gives a *terminus ante quem* to all the contemporary or preceding contexts.

So in strict logic it is shown that

1 The ground underlying the foundation stones was formed not later than 1650.

2 The pitched stone foundation was formed not earlier than 1307 and not later than 1650.

3 The wall was built not earlier than 1307 and not later than 1650.

4 The window was constructed between 1500 and 1650.

5 The cames and glazing in the window must be no earlier than 1500 but of any date thence down to the present.

The conclusion might be set out thus:

Context	Possible date range:			
	Before 1307	1307 1500	1500 1650	After 1650
5	×	×	√	√
4	×	×	√	×
3	×	√	√	×
2	×	√	√	×
1	√	√	√	×

The unreliability of conclusions drawn from archaeological reasoning stems not from any logical weakness but from the impossibility of distinguishing contexts with certainty. If this is a problem with excavation evidence, it is a many times greater problem with contexts which are elements of buildings. One of the manifest aims of people repairing buildings is to disguise their work; part of a wall dismantled and rebuilt may be indistinguishable from the part not tampered with, but it becomes a totally different context.

In such a simple example the reasoning seems too elementary to be worth committing to paper, but, confronted with a tangle of torturously altered construction, it is well worth the effort of tabulating the contexts, trying to identify which may be taken to be contemporary for the sake of simplification, and analysing them in this manner. The most may then be made of whatever dating evidence can be found. Then one may stand back, heed Mr Charles' advice, and try to see the wood as well as the trees.

DRAWINGS

In addition to equipment for use 'in the field' (*see p. 75*), a recorder of old buildings needs to have access to equipment for producing finished drawings. This section concentrates on line draughtsmanship for a straightforward technical purpose, using basic equipment.

The first objectives of record drawings are permanence and an ease of copying. The drawing produced by the recorder's hand may not itself be the ultimate record, so these two aims are to some extent alternatives; as information storage in the future moves increasingly into electronic form, the permanence of the original becomes less important. Whether working for simple record or for publication, the preservation of line quality at changed drawing scale is paramount.

The recording draughtsman produces essentially two quite distinct drawings: the measured survey and the fair copy. In the days before the widespread introduction of tracing paper, these two drawings would appear on the same sheet of paper, the temporary pencil lines of the setting out to scale would be followed by the inked-in lines of the finished drawing. Now it is more convenient to use tracing paper or film for the finished version and to do the setting out separately, perhaps retaining both versions in one's 'archive'. It can hardly be overstressed that no good comes of trying to bypass the first stage in the hope of working directly on the finished version.

Drawing equipment

Basic equipment to produce record drawings of an acceptable standard would include:

1 A drawing board with T-square and set-square; on the board should be a sheet of cartridge paper or other suitable backing to serve as cushioning beneath the drawing.

2 Cartridge paper or similar dimensionally stable paper on which to set out the first measured version of a drawing; scissors to be used for cutting it up to re-arrange the parts of the drawing for the fair tracing to follow.

3 Drawing clips or draughting tape (not ordinary household adhesive tape, and not drawing pins).

4 A 2H pencil and the means to keep it sharp, and a soft rubber eraser.

5 Measuring scales.

6 Stout tracing paper for the finished fair version.

7 Drawing pens, Indian ink, a sharp safety razor-blade and a rag.

With this basic equipment it should be possible to draw out the results of a survey accurately, arrange the various parts of the intended finished drawing to achieve good composition and clarity, and produce a fair tracing with lettering and title, suitable for preservation or for reproduction by commonly available means.

Drawing-board
The crucial thing in a traditionally constructed drawing-board is the ebony edge against which the T-square runs. It should be tested by placing the ebony edge of a new T-square edge to edge with it and looking against the light for any gaps. If it is in good condition it will be just as satisfactory to use as a parallel motion straight-edge or a draughting machine. Small cheap boards are manufactured with a pine edge only. A good quality board consists of rift-sawn battens of knot-free pine glued edge to edge with tongue and groove joints, with 'clamps' of hardwood screwed on the rear through slotted holes. This design of board can stand very hard use indeed. The essential need, however, is merely for a good surface combined with any straight-edge which gives reliable parallel motion.

Normally the size of a board would need to be enough to carry A1-size standard sheets with about 1in (25mm) to spare all round. Boards manufactured before the present standardised 'A' series of paper sizes are generally either 'double elephant' or 'imperial' size. As is clear from the following table, an imperial board is just slightly too small:

Paper size	Drawing-board sizes	
	New	Traditional
A1	A1	Double elephant
841 × 594mm	920 × 650mm	1092 × 737mm
A2	A2	Imperial
594 × 420mm	650 × 470mm	813 × 584mm

Some draughtsmen may prefer to limit drawing size to A3 (420 × 298mm) in order to use ordinary electrostatic copying (Xerox etc.).

The position of a board is important. Some prefer a board set nearly horizontally; others, perhaps equipped with a parallel motion straight-edge or a draughting machine, prefer the board to be close to vertical. A nearly horizontal board is more straining on the back, but otherwise more convenient; its main advantage is that the draughtsman can sit directly facing a window for the best possible light.

A pine drawing-board should be covered with a backing sheet to cushion drawings against the effects of raised wood grain, pinholes etc., and to provide a light coloured background when working with tracing paper. Special plastic backing sheets with a green or cream surface are not too expensive (but are vulnerable to chemical damage, e.g. from solvents). A few sheets of blank dyeline print paper make an acceptable temporary backing.

A T-square consists of two parts, the blade and the stock, made of mahogany and screwed and dowelled together. The strength of the joint is crucial and the moment it shows any sign of weakness it should be opened up, its contact surfaces roughened, and screwed down again in Araldite adhesive, taking care to maintain an exact right angle. The working edge is usually ebony, but a transparent plastic edge may be thought more practical. The underside of a T-square quickly becomes dirty and should be cleaned with turps substitute.

A draughtsman should have at least a 30° set-square, preferably a 45° one also, or better still an adjustable one. Set-squares with the hypotenuse side three times the length of one of the others were formerly popular, for use in conjunction with 'Marquois's Scale'. This was for ruling close parallel hatching lines. The scale was held firmly on the paper while the set-square was advanced along it. Parallel lines could be ruled at a distance apart equal to a third of the calibration of the scale. An adjustable set-square will do this if opened to $19\frac{1}{2}°$. To rule parallel lines at a fifth of the scale calibration, open the set-square to $11\frac{1}{2}°$, for a tenth, to $5\frac{3}{4}°$, etc. (the proportion being the sine of the angle).

Papers

Tracing paper superseded cartridge paper as the everyday drawing medium for technical purposes because of its usefulness when sunprint and blueprint copying came into use; but the surface of modern tracing paper is so good that many professional draughtsmen prefer it regardless of the needs of copying. Its disadvantages are brittleness, especially as it ages, causing it to tear easily, and dimensional instability as it gets damp. There are now three weights of tracing paper sold – 63, 90 and 112 grams per m²; either of the two heavier grades is satisfactory. The thinnest grade is too easy to damage while erasing.

The enemy of Indian ink on tracing paper is grease. While drawing, every care should be taken to rest one's hands on a scrap of masking paper rather than directly on the tracing paper. Pounce or powdered talc can be used to degrease the surface, but the ink tends to adhere less when these are used, and they interfere with dyeline printing. The best way to degrease tracing paper is to rub over the whole surface with a soft rubber, and then to follow the rule of handling the paper as little as possible.

For greater permanence and dimensional stability, polyester drawing film is now very popular, though two to four times more expensive than tracing paper. It is far more abrasive than tracing paper, and special nibs (e.g. tungsten carbide) are needed for technical pens. It is easier to maintain a very even line quality on drawing film, and grease is less of a problem.

The erasing of ink from tracing paper is an art which has to be learned. An electric eraser works well, provided the surface is not allowed to overheat from the friction. An ordinary hand-held pencil rubber is practically useless, and an ink rubber is not much better. A razor-blade makes a very good eraser: it should be almost new, and held tightly at right angles to the paper with the finger tips very close to the paper surface, and scraped gently over the line to be erased. When erasing with a blade, it is very important to ensure that the drawing lies directly on a very hard surface, not a padded one. After erasing, the paper roughened by the blade should be 'boned' smooth again, by polishing with a hard rubber, a knife handle or the flat of a fingernail. Scraped areas may show in dyeline prints unless carefully boned.

'Impregnated' erasers are sold for use with Indian ink on tracing film. An ordinary pencil rubber can erase surprisingly well on film if slightly wetted. Delicate erasing can be done in a congested part of a drawing with the wetted butt end of a matchstick.

To erase lines from dyeline prints on paper is practically impossible. To erase them from dyeline prints on polyester film is not difficult; this can be done with an ink eraser (working on the back of the sheet, where the pigment is incorporated in a lacquered surface), with a razor-blade or with solvent (such as acetone). After the use of a solvent the liquid should be blotted up quickly before it dries or it may allow the pigment to be re-deposited on the surface. If solvent is used great care should be taken not to inhale the fumes.

Pencils

Traditional pencil 'lead' as known since the eighteenth century is a mixture of graphite and clay and is ideally suited to work on paper. For polyester film, polymer leads are preferable, to give a denser, smudge-free line; polymer leads are only available in loose form for use in clutch pencils or draughting pencils.

The fullest range of grades is available for the traditional wood-cased type of pencil, ranging from 9H (the hardest and faintest) to EEB (the softest and blackest). 2H is best for normal line drawing on paper where a clear line is to be obtained with a reasonable interval between sharpenings.

The loose graphite leads used in clutch pencils are 2mm in diameter, and have to be sharpened. Draughting pencils take leads designed to give the intended line width without sharpening: these are made in the size range of 0.9, 0.7, 0.5 and 0.3mm.

For pencil drawing on polyester film, polymer leads are available for use in clutch pencils and draughting pencils. The range of grades is restricted to 7H to HB for clutch pencils and 5H to 2B for draughting pencils.

A sharpened pencil should have a conical point. To maintain even line quality from end to end of a ruled line the pencil should be slightly rotated in the fingers as it is moved along. This is far better than relying on the crude 'chisel' or 'wedge' point which is sometimes advocated.

Different types of eraser are sold for use with graphite and polymer leads.

Pens

For freehand ink draughtsmanship the split flexible nib gives the best control of line thickness and variation. Mapping pens or the larger and stronger metal nibs such as the Gillotts type are the ideal for freehand use with Indian ink.

For ruled lines, pens exist on the leaf and tubular principles. Apart from its survival in bow and beam compasses included in boxed sets of instruments, the spring leaf principle is now almost obsolete in the design of pens. The traditional dropper-fed hand-held type, the 'ruling pen', is very liable to blot. With the better examples the head of the screw controlling the distance apart of the leaves is calibrated to indicate the line width. From this type was developed, in 1932, the Graphos pen, which was a great improvement: fed with fresh ink, the Graphos gives a quality of line which has never been bettered even on coarse drawing surfaces. It is also a fountain pen, though because of drying problems some might prefer to ink it from a dropper like a ruling pen. The Graphos nib consists of two leaves, one of which hinges sideways for cleaning. There is a large range of interchangeable nib types and sizes, including some on other than the leaf principle. It is hardly a suitable pen for the occasional draughtsman.

Technical fountain pens on the leaf principle have been almost completely ousted by those on the tubular principle, of which the Rapidograph was the first introduced, in 1952. These pens use a tubular nib with a wire running through the tube and attached to a weight at one end. Ink tending to dry in the tube is dislodged by shaking the pen to agitate the wire up and down. The standard line thicknesses for these pens are now established as 2, 1.4, 1, 0.7, 0.5, 0.35, 0.25, 0.18 and 0.13mm. The occasional draughtsman should use the 0.35 size (colour coded yellow). Smaller sizes are difficult to use and give a line too thin and light for good copying. If the budget rises to two or three pens, the 0.5mm should be obtained also, then the 1mm.

WINDOW IN A HOUSE, WEST ORCHARD,
COVENTRY.

Indian ink has been the universal medium for technical draughtsmanship in ink, but it is notoriously liable to dry and solidify in the nib and calls for great discipline in cleaning pens regularly and emptying them whenever they are to be left unused for a period. If clogging is very troublesome in hot weather, or if a greyer line is wanted, Indian ink can be diluted with rainwater. For permanence, special solvent-based etching ink should also be used when working on tracing film, as ordinary Indian ink tends to lose its adhesion to the film in time.

Indian ink may soon be rendered obsolete by the development of truly opaque dyes which do not have the same solid matter in suspension to cause clogging: the Pentel Ceranomatic pen is available in the same range of nib sizes as other tubular nib pens, but uses dye rather than ink. Whether the dye has a duration comparable to Indian ink, to be satisfactory for archival purposes, remains to be seen.

Scales

White plastic scales are now universal, replacing brass, ivory and boxwood. Each of the faces is calibrated on either side, and each calibration is usually marked to give a different ratio starting at each end: so eight distinct ratios can be provided. A scale of triangular section can give up to 12 distinct ratios. The normal flat scale is slightly lens-shaped in section and slightly

47 Fourteenth-century window of a house in West Orchard, Coventry; woodcut by Orlando Jewitt. Jewitt worked extensively as an illustrator for the writer and publisher J. H. Parker; his work shows a mastery of texture and tone and is worth studying by the draughtsman in pen and ink or pencil also. (J. H. Parker, *Some Account of the Architecture of England from Richard II to Henry VIII*, part 2, 1859, facing p. 240)

DELBURY CHURCH
SHROPSHIRE. BN

48 Delbury Church, Shropshire, by D. A. Gregg, 1906. In contrast to the severe precision of the engraver's technique, this shows what can be achieved in the much freer medium of ink rendering. Tone values are simplified to reveal the shape of the building and to improve composition: the range is white and two grades of grey. Lines of shading are varied in angle but it does not matter that they do not follow stone or tile lines. The corners of the picture are left light and the framing is informal. (*Architecture, Carpentry and Building*, vol. IV (American Technical Society, Chicago, 1925) p. 303)

flexible; it is far more convenient to use than the clumsy, rigid triangular type. A plastic scale can be be melted by friction, and so should never be used as a knife to slice off sheets of paper from a roll.

There are two sorts of calibration, 'engineer's' (fully divided) and 'architect's' (partly divided). The engineer's type starts with zero at one end and both the large and fine divisions are marked for the full length of the scale. In the architect's type one fully divided larger unit precedes the zero, and the remainder of the scale consists of undivided larger units. This type is less tiring to the eyes.

In order to work with imperial units while drawing at one of the standardised ratios introduced with the metric system, a conversion scale may be used: the RIBA conversion scale 'B' gives feet and inches at the scales of $1:5$, $1:10$, $1:20$, $1:50$ and $1:100$.

Aids

Draughtsman's 'instant aids' ought to have a low priority for the recording amateur. Recording calls for unpretentiousness rather than commercial slickness, and draughting aids used without the manual skill which they are supposed to render unnecessary can produce the worst of tawdry effects.

The technique of clear, simple, well-formed hand lettering should be every draughtsman's priority, but there are legitimate uses for substitutes. Instant lettering of very high quality is possible with dry transfer methods,

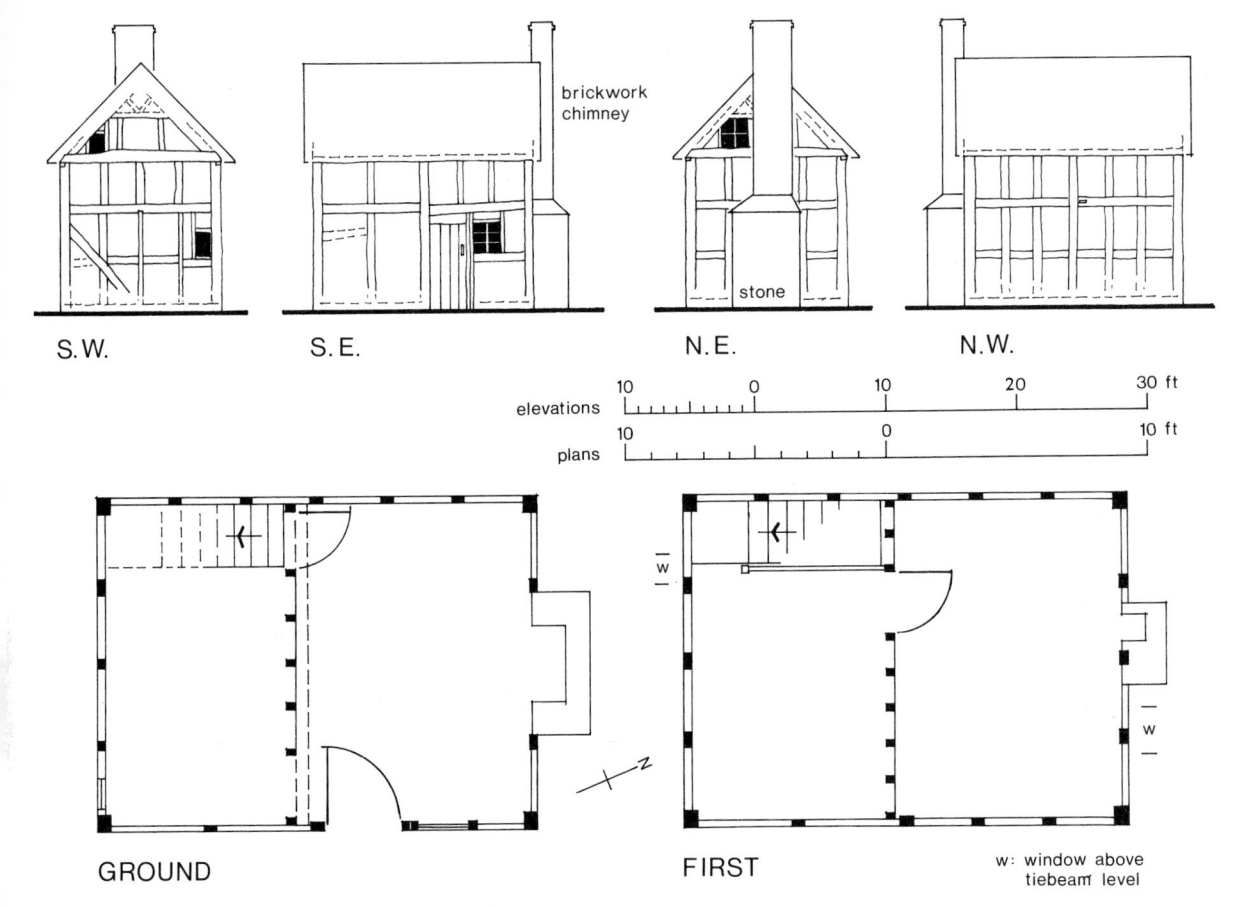

S.W.   S.E.   N.E.   N.W.

brickwork chimney

stone

elevations   10   0   10   20   30 ft

plans   10   0   10 ft

GROUND   FIRST   w: window above tiebeam level

w

w

COTTAGE AT STOCKTON ON TEME, WORCESTERSHIRE

but requires patience and a steady hand. It is also rather expensive. The first trade name in the field was Letraset, but many manufacturers now produce it in a wide variety of typefaces and a large range of sizes. A draughtsman should consider the appearance of the style of hand lettering which he finds most easy and natural, and choose typefaces which are similar in proportions and weight. To use dry transfer lettering successfully, some rules should be followed:

1 Ignore the spacing guide marks printed underneath the letters. It is not possible to achieve correct spacing for display purposes with them; the optimum distance apart of any combination of two letters has to be judged as it arises. The object is to obtain the same visual weight of each group of several adjacent letters, to achieve overall evenness. The word LETTERING shows the problems: T is a lightweight letter, E and R are heavyweights. The combination TT should be close set; the combination TE medium; and the combination ER wide set.

2 Rule a thin line on the rear of the tracing paper or film and place the bottoms of the letters directly on it. If working on opaque paper, draw a faint pencil line on the face which can be gently rubbed off afterwards.

49 Cottage at Stockton, Worcestershire

Lines can also be ruled on a movable backing paper, to be moved around a drawing as required.

3 Remember that letters like E which have a straight top or bottom edge sit exactly on the line, but letters like S, which are curved at the top or bottom, penetrate slightly beyond the top or bottom lines.

4 When a letter is in position ready to be rubbed down, use a blunt spatula to rub with. Rub gently so as not to stretch the backing film (makes differ, and some can be rubbed more vigorously than others). When the letter changes to a greyer colour, the adhesion to the backing film has been broken, and it can be pulled off gently with a rolling movement.

5 As soon as the backing has been taken off, press the letter hard into the paper with a finger tip to ensure that it is completely stuck down.

6 To erase mistakes, lift off the offending letters with Sellotape or with a medium rubber.

Small lettering is better done with stencils, preferably the ones manufactured by the makers of the pens one is using. The nib, at least, should be the correct size; stencilling with a nib which is too small creates a very ugly effect. The pen should be held exactly at right angles to the paper or film surface.

Shading or hatching can be done with special adhesive screens which are put down on the drawing and then cut around the outline of the area to be treated, or with dry transfer screens similar to lettering. It is also possible to have instant colour, brick pattern, tiles, stone effect, trees, human figures, north points, and so on; these things are only mentioned as something best avoided.

Beam compasses and dividers are particularly useful. In drawing out surveys it is often necessary to set out points by triangulation, and long beam compasses provide the quickest method. They do not have to be of instrument-maker's quality. As a substitute for using beam compasses, co-ordinates can be found from triangulated measurements with the aid of a suitable pocket calculator:

1 Set the calculator to work in degrees (rather than radians). Let the base line be called AB, and let the point to be located be called O; note the measurements OA andOB.

2 Calculate $(AB^2 + OB^2 - OC^2) \div (2 \times AB \times OB) = D$

3 Calculate $-(ArcCos.D) + 180 = E$

4 Calculate $(Cos.E \times OB) + AB = X$

5 Calculate $Sin.E \times OB = Y$

X and Y are the two required co-ordinates measured from A. X is the dimension in the direction towards B; Y is the dimension at right angles.

With a microcomputer the following BASIC program converts direct measurements into co-ordinates similarly:

```
10 INPUT"AB = " A: INPUT"OA = "B: INPUT"OB = " C

20 PRINT"X = "A+C*COS(PI–ACS((A*A+C*C–B*B)/(2*A*C)))

30 PRINT"Y = "C*SIN(PI–ACS((A*A+C*C–B*B)/(2*A*C)))
```

Reproduction of drawings

The two common methods of reprographic printing are dyeline (other-wise called Diazo) and electrostatic (such as Xerox). Such services are easy to find in large towns, but in smaller country towns some local inquiry may be necessary; local firms with drawing offices may provide a dyeline printing service for outsiders, without there being any entry in Yellow Pages.

The dyeline process shines light through the original drawing; the electrostatic process reflects light from its surface. Both are inexpensive; both are positive to positive processes. The original drawing is traditionally called the negative (though no black and white reversal is involved in the modern technique), in contrast with the print.

The dyeline process consists of a printing stage and a developing stage. The surface of the print paper is initially yellow; the light bleaches out the parts of the drawing to become white and the remaining yellow is converted in the developing stage to black. The yellow surface of the print paper does not deteriorate in a brief exposure in subdued light, so that it is possible to inspect the intended image on the print paper before development (unlike photography, where a darkroom is needed). The advantage of this is that, if a copy is to be made of part of a drawing, a masking sheet of black paper can be put over the part to be retained and the print paper put through the machine a second time, to lose the remainder of the image, before putting it into the developing stage.

Because the ink line is on the face of the tracing paper or film, there is a slight loss of sharpness by the time its shadow passes through the thickness and across any air gap to fall on the print paper. To maximise sharpness, a sheet or two of (preferably black) cushioning paper beneath the print paper will ensure that the contact is as close as possible. (A line drawn on the rear of the tracing should be in immediate contact with the print paper and will print more sharply.) Another way of achieving a sharp print is to use a film print (a 'copy negative') as an intermediate stage: the exposure of the film print from the negative is done face to face, with good sharpness, and the second print from film print to final print is also face to face.

With dyeline printing, drawings can be produced from two or more overlay transparent sheets; if part of a drawing is standardised, such as the sheet margin line and a title common to a series of drawings, the repeatable part might be drawn on one sheet and the variable parts on another. They have to be fed into the printing machine carefully to maintain alignment, or taped together with invisible tape along the edge to be fed first into the machine. Overlays would make it possible to have different versions of a drawing with different annotation.

Electrostatic copying equipment to handle large drawing sizes is not readily accessible to many people, but sizes up to A3 should not cause problems. A problem is that a slight misadjustment may go undetected, but distort the evenness of scale of the copy: if two halves of a large drawing are copied separately and then taped together, they may not fit properly at the join.

Drawing size and lettering size

Drawing size, lettering height and line thickness are related if it is intended that a drawing should be read as a whole. (This does not apply with technical working drawings, which are read a bit at a time.) If a drawing is to be read as a whole, the paper will naturally be placed at a distance from the reader's eye such that its width fills an angle of about 30°. With normal acuity of vision this means that a certain line thickness and a certain size of lettering are appropriate, in proportion to the drawing width. Obvious though this is, it is a point often forgotten, and drawings in books and periodicals often have faded-out lines and lettering that is far too small because the draughtsman judged their sizes when working on an original filling perhaps 60° of his field of vision.

Clearly, when working on a drawing 900mm wide, a nib size of 0.9mm is needed, to achieve a line thickness of 0.15mm on a copy reduced to 150mm in width. So a rough rule would be that *the line thickness should be no less than one thousandth of the drawing or page width*. Much depends on the quality of reproduction and printing.

For lettering, the simple rule is that *the face-height of the capital E should be no less than one hundredth of the drawing or page width*. An imperial version of this rule of thumb (suggested in *Current Archaeology* no. 72) is that a lettering typeface size measured in points should never be less than the drawing width measured in inches. (Points are the printer's measure of the body-height of a letter, a point being $\frac{1}{72}$in—i.e. six lines of 12-point type to the inch).

So a drawing 900mm or 36in wide must have lettering no less than 9mm high or 36 points size. The lettering may look enormous on the original, but as the rule is based on the facts of human eyesight, it is absolute.

From this there should follow a more severe rule where drawings are to be made into slides for projection. If viewers are expected to read lettering on a projected drawing filling about 10° of their field of vision, as against the 30° normal for hand-held reading, the lettering will have to be three times as large. So a drawing 900mm wide, for making into a slide, should have lettering no less than $9 \times 3 = 27$mm high. In fact, audiences are so used to straining to see tiny lettering on slides that breach of this rule seems to be tolerated.

Line quality

Achieving perfect line evenness is one objective in draughtsmanship, but it is a little stultifying to stop there. The natural irregularities of line can be exploited to add to the liveliness of a drawing. Line weight can be varied to help give a suggestion of different distances, with some parts coming forwards and others receding, leading to a suggestion of three dimensions. The meeting of lines can be adjusted to suggest whether they are in the same plane or not.

Where lines meet in the same plane they should normally do so with a little extra weight at the join and a small overlap. A perfect join with no weight variation is hard to achieve every time, and if there are to be variations some lines will cross and others fail to meet; lines failing to meet at an intended join look weak and sloppy, so the draughtsman should err in favour of crossing his lines. If the lines are in different planes it is helpful to stop the further one slightly short deliberately, to help the front line stand out.

It is often appropriate, having set out a survey or a perspective with geometrical accuracy, to ink-in some or all of it freehand to lose the hard, exact quality of ruled lines. The drawing of timber framing is a case in point: the timbers may really be straight as a die, but if drawn with ruled lines they look more like reinforced concrete framing. Similarly brick or tile courses, where it is tempting to rule the horizontal joints and leave the upright or perpend joints unshown, tend to look like weatherboarding. A freehand technique of interrupted lines can give texture suggestive of brick or tile. It may be appropriate to go further and have some free hatching also, for which random directions and an avoidance of dead straight lines are helpful. If a drawing is textured to any extent in this manner, no part, however strongly lit, should be totally without stipple or some other hint of texture, or it will simply look like a hole cut in the paper. There is a whole art form in the ink rendering of architectural subjects, which influences finishing technique on utilitarian drawings.

Alternatives to perspective

The attractiveness of illustrating a building or a detail in correct perspective is limited by drawbacks both to the draughtsman and to the reader of his drawing. To set up a perspective it is necessary to have vanishing points and measuring points which are often far outside the margins of the finished drawing. Measuring to scale is complicated and inconvenient. Detail which has been carefully measured and drawn in correct position is not readily remeasurable by the reader.

In attempting to achieve an effect of perspective the draughtsman's first possibility is to use shadow effects and the variation of line and texture to bring a sense of depth into what is shown in simple plan, section or elevation. When drawing shadows they may either be projected from a realistic position of the sun or they may be conventional: the source of light is conventionally supposed to be at $45°$ to the vertical and horizontal axes of the picture plane, so that a projecting feature in an elevation casts a shadow downwards to a distance equal to the projection and to one side to the same distance.

Isometric projection is tolerably close to perspective. It enables a reader to measure details which could not be measured in a drawing in true perspective, as the diminution of receding dimensions is ignored. The flattened perspective of a view through a powerful telescope is close to isometric projection. Three related views are chosen – in plan, elevation or section – and redrawn so that their principal axes are made to cross at $120°$ rather than at $90°$. They are then amalgamated into one drawing. The technique was devised early in the nineteenth century for the illustration of complicated machinery. Later it was taken up by architectural illustrators for illustrating complicated three-dimensional structures such as masonry vaulting. The aesthetic drawback of its slight distortion compared with correct perspective is rarely objectionable.

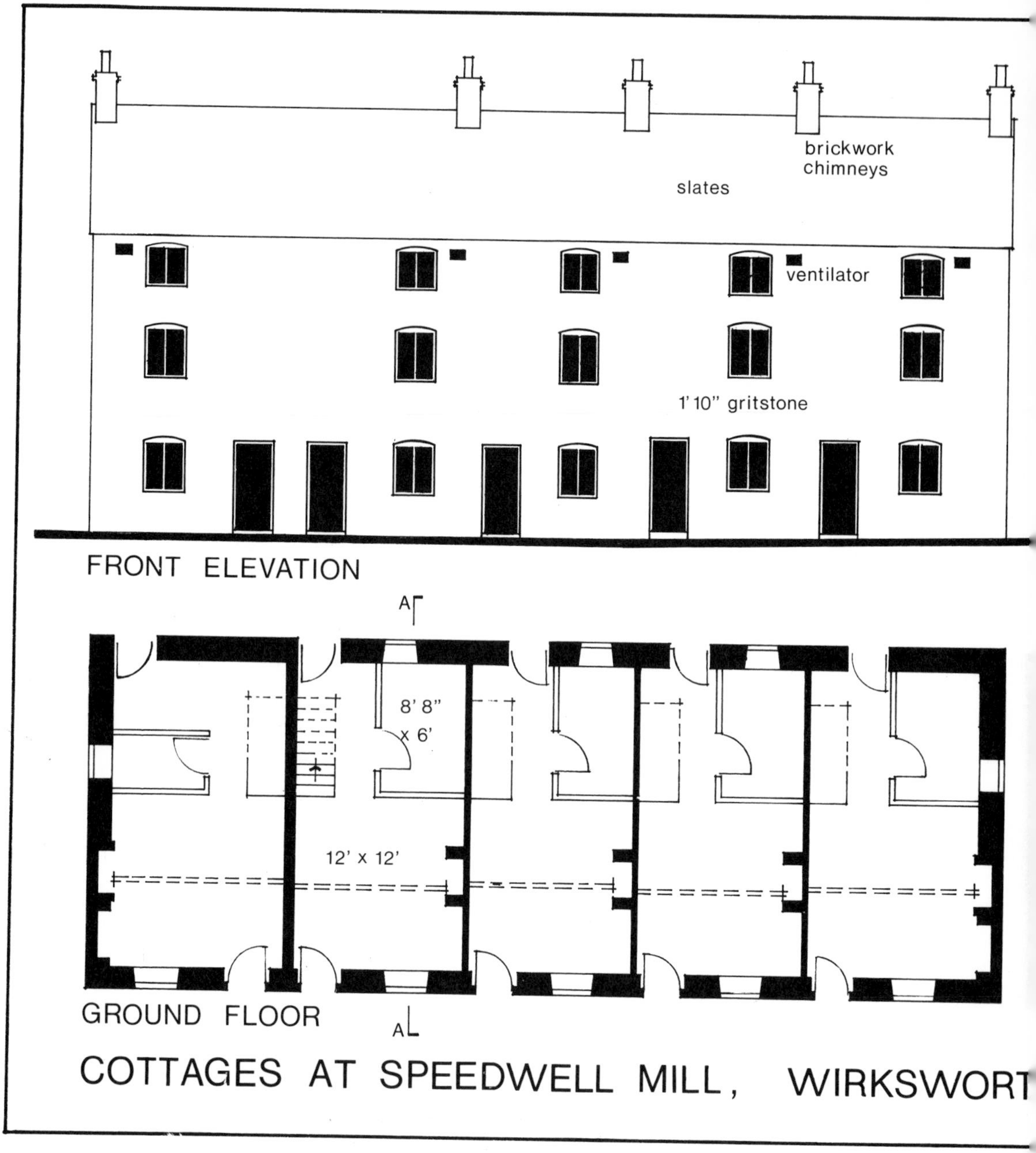

FRONT ELEVATION

brickwork chimneys

slates

ventilator

1' 10" gritstone

GROUND FLOOR

8' 8" x 6'

12' x 12'

COTTAGES AT SPEEDWELL MILL, WIRKSWORT

Usually, but not always, the vertical axis is made vertical on the paper. If this is done, there are eight possible isometric views – upwards and downwards at each of the four corners. Other variations are possible. Angles other than 120° for the crossing of the main axes may be used to lower the eye level or to achieve a view which is not quite corner-on. The example of a complicated rafter-foot detail (*Fig. 51*) in 'exploded' form shows a useful adaptation; one of the horizontals is positioned horizontally on the paper, with the vertical and the other horizontal each at 120° to it.

A special case of the isometric is *axonometric* projection. This is very easy

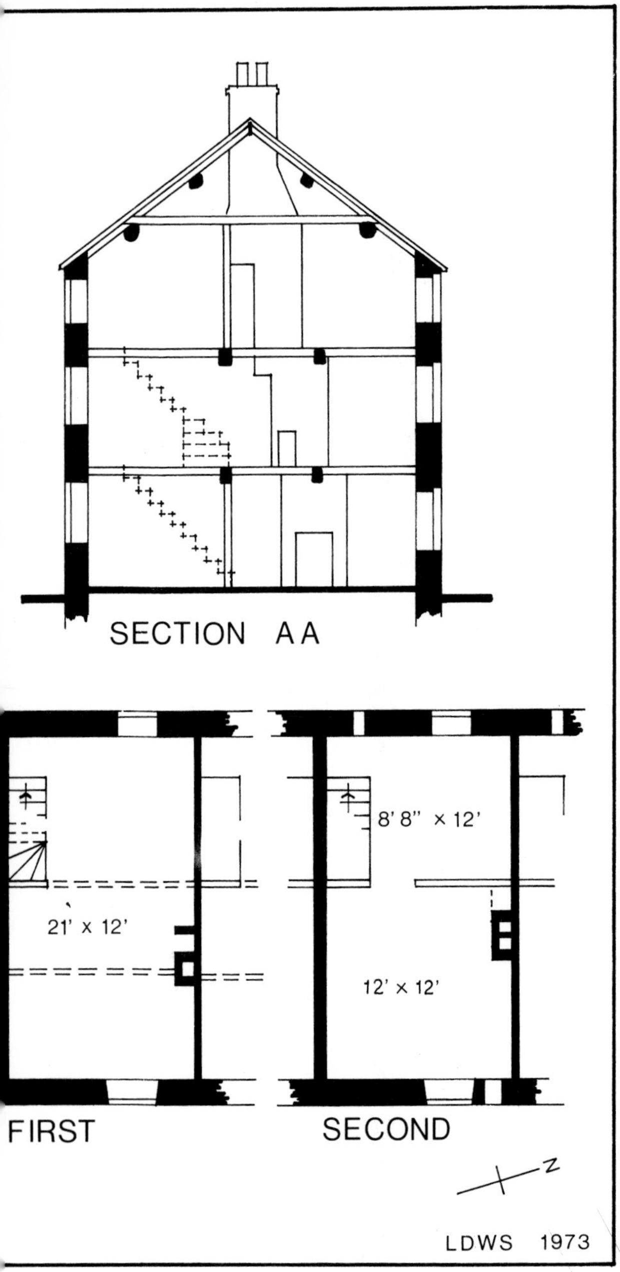

SECTION AA

8' 8" × 12'

21' × 12'

12' × 12'

FIRST   SECOND

LDWS 1973

50 Cottages at Speedwell Mill, Wirksworth, Derbyshire

to draw. Usually the plan is taken as the starting point and drawn with its axes at 45° to the margins of the drawing; vertical dimensions are simply projected upward on the drawing. The result is eminently remeasurable, but the distortion in the overall effect is often disagreeable. This technique may also be varied according to the draughtsman's ingenuity. A particularly fine exponent of isometric and axonometric techniques in draughtsmanship was the French architectural historian Auguste Choisy, whose work on Roman building construction[46] is worth study for its demonstration of the potential of these projections. As the great majority of

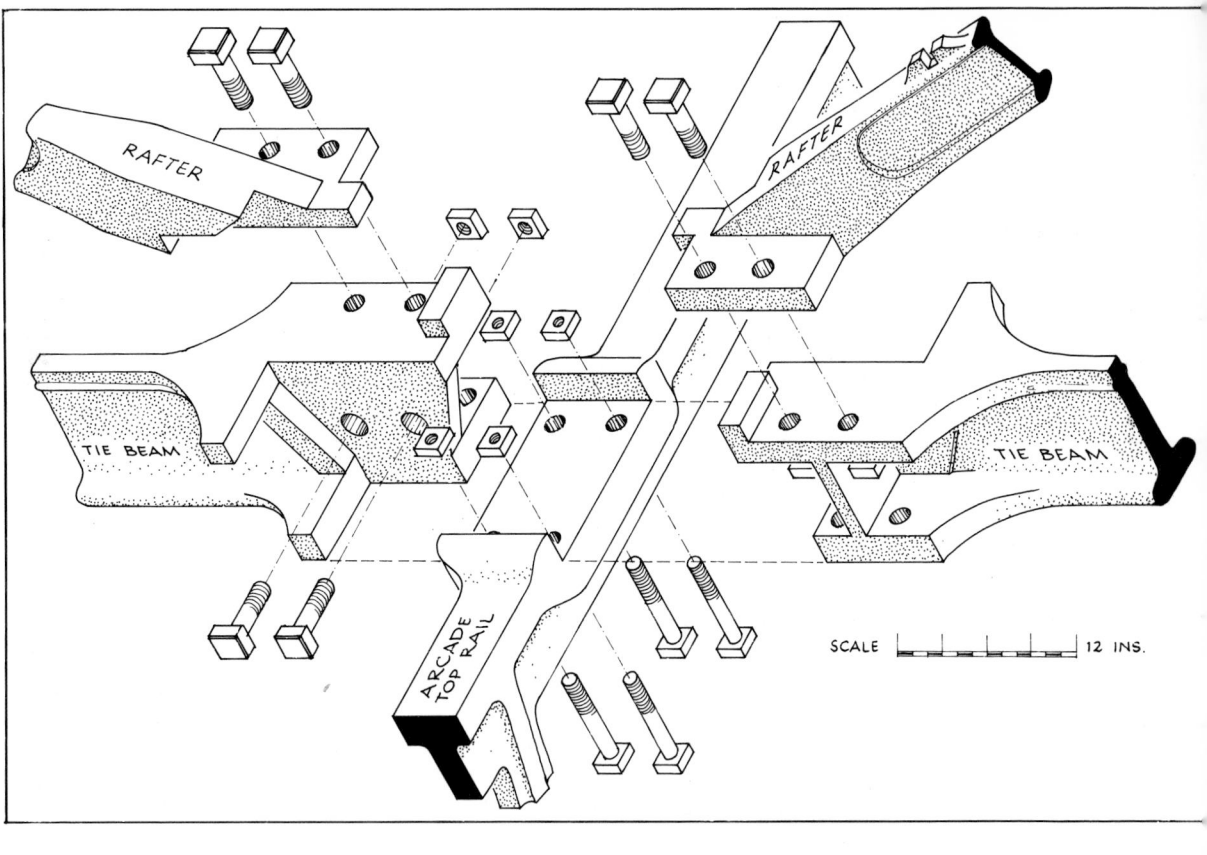

Labels in figure: RAFTER, RAFTER, TIE BEAM, TIE BEAM, ARCADE TOP RAIL, SCALE, 12 INS.

51 Exploded view of the junction
of cast iron rafters, tie-beams and
top rail of arcade in the
Woolwich Smithery roof, by
John Rennie, engineer, and
Edward Hall, architect, 1816

dimensions which a reader may want to remeasure from a drawing are
likely to be parallel to one or other of the three main axes of the building,
normal isometric projection usually remains the best compromise.

When showing a scale in an isometric drawing one must be careful to
show it parallel to one or more of the axes of the drawing. It should not, for
example, be shown parallel to the bottom edge of the drawing, unless one
of the axes is horizontal. Correct scaling is often emphasised by showing the
scale in each of the three axes.

Sectional views presented in isometric projection are a natural choice
where complex structural details within buildings are to be shown. It is well
suited, for example, to showing the junction of floors and columns in early
fireproof mill construction. The draughtsman starts with a plan and
vertical sections rather than elevations, but the principles of setting out the
drawing are the same. It is normal in such cases to show a mass of building
detail projecting along each axis to a point where a cut-away view is best
calculated to give the maximum constructional information. This produces

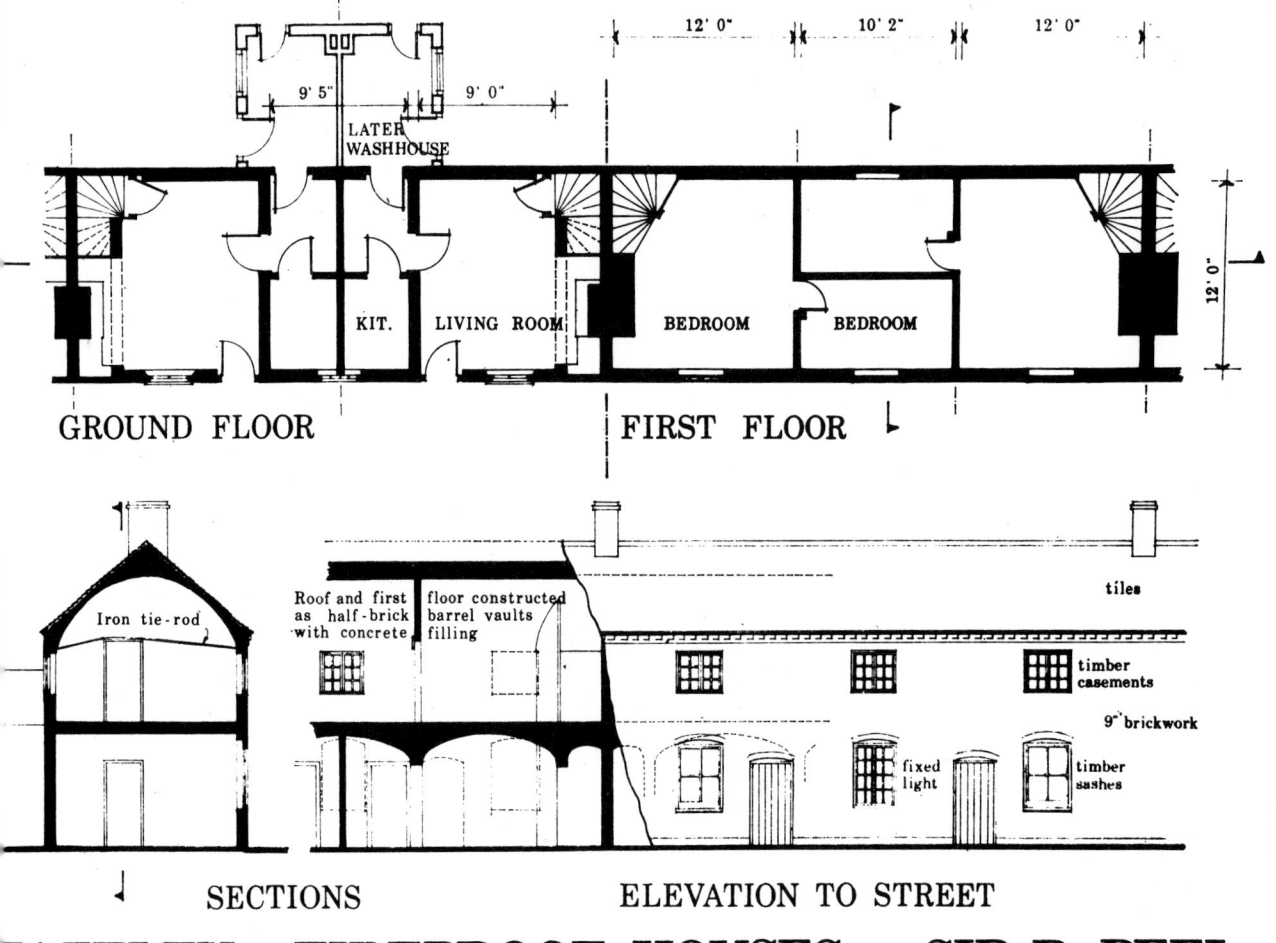

9' 5"   9' 0"

LATER
WASHHOUSE

12' 0"   10' 2"   12' 0"

12' 0"

KIT.   LIVING ROOM   BEDROOM   BEDROOM

GROUND FLOOR   **FIRST FLOOR**

Iron tie-rod

Roof and first floor constructed
as half-brick barrel vaults
with concrete filling

tiles

timber
casements

9" brickwork

fixed
light

timber
sashes

SECTIONS   **ELEVATION TO STREET**

FAZELEY : FIREPROOF HOUSES OF SIR R. PEEL

what appears to be a slice of the building, archaeologically dissected, which the reader visualises as part of a continuous structure.

Two drawings showing the unusual construction of a terrace of cottages in Mill Street, Fazeley, in Staffordshire, surveyed during demolition, illustrate the value of a dissected isometric detail. These cottages, built in the first years of the nineteenth century by the millowner Sir Robert Peel, revealed an unusual application of the idea of fireproof floor and roof construction in domestic building.

The first drawing, in plan, section and elevation (*Fig. 52*) gives the reader all the information necessary to grasp the features of the brick vaults used for the chamber floor and the roof. Even so, the drawing is not immediately comprehensible. The reader must work at understanding it. In the second drawing (*Fig. 53*) an imaginary slice has been cut from the terrace of cottages at the position most likely to clarify the obscure features. The mind quickly grasps that this is a drawing almost in perspective, and that the eye is looking downwards rather than upwards. The use of shadow

52 Orthographic projection (*Post Medieval Archaeology*, vol. 6, 1972, p. 193, fig. 84, 'Early fireproof housing in a Staffordshire factory village – Fazeley, Mill Lane, plan and elevation')

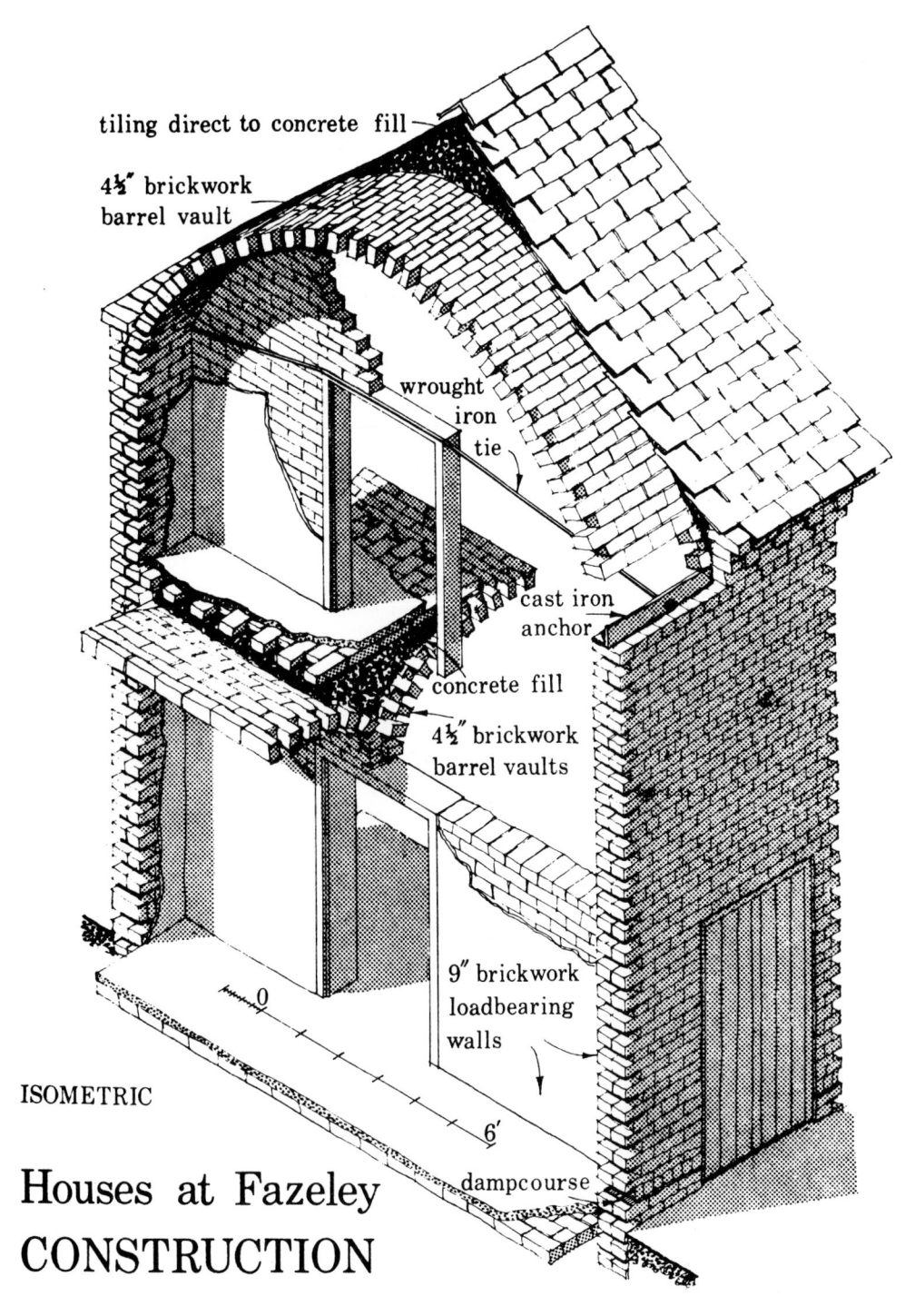

tiling direct to concrete fill

4½″ brickwork
barrel vault

wrought
iron
tie

cast iron
anchor

concrete fill

4½″ brickwork
barrel vaults

9″ brickwork
loadbearing
walls

ISOMETRIC

0

6′

dampcourse

Houses at Fazeley
CONSTRUCTION

53 30° isometric projection (*Post Medieval Archaeology*, vol. 6, 1972, p. 195, fig. 84, 'Early fireproof housing in a Staffordshire factory village – Fazeley, Mill Lane, Isometric') is important in providing the clue. The mind then applies corrections to the evidence of the eye, and can to a certain extent rotate the figure in imagination to obtain the plan or either sectional view. The roof vault, for instance, though drawn as a semi-ellipse on the paper, is seen to be semi-circular in reality. This and the rest of the structure may then be explored visually without effort.

FOUR

Research background

The library and the record office searchroom are the places both for planning a campaign of research and for carrying out documentary research in support of a campaign of recording. The investigation of the history of a building, a building type or the buildings of an area is unlikely to be complete if written evidence is neglected. The researcher needs to start with a bibliographical foray into his subject if he is to plan his time efficiently and make the best use of the splendid archival resources available. This means starting in the library rather than the archive searchroom, building up a picture of what has already been studied and, as one's choice of direction becomes clearer, a picture of what type of original documentary records are likely to be most helpful. Printed editions of important records and works of reference are more readily consulted in the library, and such materials should be tackled before going on to original manuscript sources in archive collections.

BIBLIOGRAPHY

Many historical references to old buildings and their owners or occupiers, in books as in documents, tell of no more than their existence at a particular date. The task of compiling a bibliography of books, articles and manuscript sources may therefore reap a poor return in information, though it is still the best way to commence any serious research. It is especially useful to start with a bibliography if one's aim is to produce an academic study.

Three areas of research into an old building might be its technical construction, its design and layout from the occupier's viewpoint, and the history of its ownership or tenancy. One could organise a bibliography of books, articles and manuscript sources under such headings as these. If research is wider than the investigation of a particular building – for instance a study of a building type or of the buildings of an industry, a locality or a class in society – other relevant headings will suggest themselves. Since architecture and building are incidental to most human concerns and to most historical writing, a bibliography may become weighed down with trifling references. Another danger is that references to the function served by a type of building may greatly outnumber references to the type of building itself, so that the tail wags the dog. A student of forge and foundry buildings would thus have to place some firm limit on his collection of references to metallurgy. Flexibility is called for in the organisation of a bibliography, so that the most important items can be kept in the forefront. A card-index or its computerised equivalent would seem to be the ideal form.

When it is necessary to clarify the correct bibliographical reference to an old or obscure work, there is no substitute for the *British Library General Catalogue of Printed Books*.

For recently published books, the *British National Bibliography* is important to anyone following a specialised line of inquiry. Its annual publication covers all books received by the statutary copyright libraries, and ephemeral lists appear at shorter intervals. Titles are in author sequence and there is a listing under the class numbers of the Dewey decimal classification system, which most libraries use. It may not be so helpful for a broad line of inquiry, because architecture may be split up between several places in the system. An investigator interested in rural cottage architecture might find relevant material in the vicinity of class 690 'building', 720 'architecture' or 333 'economics of land and housing' etc. Industrial archaeology is particularly troublesome to locate.

For periodicals, the equivalent comprehensive lead is the Library Association's annual *British Humanities Index*. Before 1962 the title of this was the *Subject Index to Periodicals*. The transactions of the various county archaeological societies are included in its scope, but by a strange omission not the periodicals *Vernacular Architecture* or *Post Medieval Archaeology*. From 1954 to 1966 the editors also produced *Regional Lists* on a county basis. These may enable a researcher to pinpoint local historical matter dispersed under many headings. They are typescript lists of abbreviated entries in alphabetical sequence, including ephemeral pamphlets. When the lists ceased publication, nothing seems to have taken their place; but some county archaeological societies' transactions and similar local history periodicals try to keep their readers abreast of local periodical literature.

Articles in over 400 specifically architectural periodicals can be traced through the *Avery Index to Architectural Periodicals* (2nd edn., 15 vols., Boston, Massachusetts, 1973, with subsequent supplements). The index is in alphabetical sequence under author and subject; the more frequently used subject headings constitute extensive bibliographies. In the words of the preface, 'architectural aspects of archaeology are included, as are those of the decorative arts and of interior design, and last, but definitely not least, the architectural aspects of city planning and housing'.

The Vernacular Architecture Group has performed a service in producing *A Bibliography on Vernacular Architecture* (David and Charles, 1972). This bibliography of books and articles covers the whole of the British Isles, both rural and urban buildings, construction, and the economic and social background. Its scope stops short at the Industrial Revolution, and there is a high concentration on farm and domestic buildings. It was published in response to the failure of more general bibliographies to deal coherently with vernacular buildings and their agrarian background.

The source and authority footnotes in works of research synthesis may be the starting point for the new researcher to discover primary sources. For medieval building and the evidence for construction and terminology the main authority is L. F. Salzman's *Building in England down to 1540* (reprinted with corrections 1967). M. W. Barley's *The English Farmhouse and Cottage* (1961) was the first work in which the potential of probate inventories was extensively exploited for purposes of domestic architectural history. Prof. Barley also contributed Chapter 10 to the *Agrarian History of England and Wales* vol. 4 (1967). In Chapter 11 of the same work, Peter Smith deals with Welsh rural domestic architecture. The work of the RCHM on domestic buildings other than the houses of the aristocracy is made more accessible in Eric Mercer's *English Vernacular Houses* (1975). For Wales, Peter Smith's *Houses of the Welsh Countryside* appeared in the same year. At a somewhat higher social level is Margaret Wood's *The English Medieval House* (1965; new edn., 1980), a work containing a very extensive bibliography and gazetteers of examples.

For classes of buildings regarded as industrial archaeology, useful gazetteers of examples and bibliographies of research are found in two series of volumes under the general title 'The Industrial Archaeology of the British Isles', one edited by Professor E. R. R Green and the other by Keith Faulkner. The latter makes particular use of the National Monuments Survey. Some publications in the sphere of urban or industrially sponsored housing tend to be descriptive without extensive analysis, or else economic history writing without detailed notice of design and construction. Impetus to research into working class housing came in 1971 with S. D. Chapman's (ed.) *The History of Working Class Housing*. This is proving a good field for academic research for those whose interests are not too narrowly architectural.

PRIMARY SOURCES

In each of the recent volumes of the Victoria County History the prefatory notes include lists of the relevant documents in the Public Record Office and in local archives, with their class numbers. Other frequently used sources are included in the note on abbreviations. The original editorial policy of the Victoria County History envisaged a splendidly comprehensive treatment of minor architecture, whether ecclesiastical, domestic or military.[47] Amongst the early volumes, however, only those for Surrey and Sussex show any serious attempt to follow it. None the less, as a lead to local history sources, particularly those in the Public Record Office, the V. C. H. is the very foundation of local history research. An editorial interest in architecture tends to be rediscovered in recent years. The post-war work of the V. C. H., with the advantage of far better organised local archives, has drawn away from the old concentration on the church and the manor.

Published guides dealing specifically with the classes of archives most likely to be helpful to the architectural historian are not numerous. In *Archives* vol. 2 (1953–6) is an article on 'Architectural Archives' by J. H. Harvey, and in the same volume 'Architectural History and its Records' by H. M. Colvin. The latter is republished as *A Guide to the Sources of English Architectural History* (Pinhorne's Handbooks no.1, 1967). It is arranged by class of building. Another guide is J. Harris's 'Sources for Architectural History in England' in the *Journal of the Society of Architectural Historians* vol. XXIV (1965). A bibliography of architectural conservation is John Harvey's 'Conservation of Old Buildings – a Select Bibliography' in *Transactions of the Ancient Monuments Society*, n. s. XVI (1969). A student's book is B. Alsopp's *The Study of Architectural History* (Studio Vista, 1970). The list of historical drawings and prints is M. W. Barley's *A Guide to British Topographical Collections* (C. B. A., 1974).

Since the war, the obscurely stored muniments of many local authorities have been organised and made accessible as a research facility to the public at large. In addition to the county record offices, diocesan record offices and the archive departments of many central governmental, religious, charitable and other bodies have adopted a similar openness. The guide to finding these collections is the latest edition of the Royal Commission on Historical Manuscripts' *Record Repositories in Great Britain* (HMSO). This booklet also gives leads to seeking out less accessible repositories.

The British National Archives

The British National Archives preserved in the Public Record Office are predominantly of interest to the medieval researcher, in contrast to the contents of local archives at county and diocesan level or below, which are mostly of post-medieval relevance. The British National Archives, extensively available in published form, must be considered before we can move on to consider local archives.

The index to the published British National Archives is the HMSO Sectional List no. 24, the latest edition of which should be obtained. This is amplified by the *Guide to the Contents of the Public Record Office*, especially vol. 1 (1963) which catalogues the originals and explains the significance of the various classes. The comprehensiveness of the Archives is due to the bureaucratic unity of the feudal system and the fortunate chance that the records of Chancery, with much that is relevant to the tenure of land and, by extension, of buildings, have survived well.

Under feudalism the only 'owner' of land was the Crown, and subjects held it in return for services. Landed property might be inherited under the feudal system, but if the heir was not of age to perform his military obligations to the Crown, the tenure would revert temporarily to the Crown in 'wardship'. Feudal tenure superficially resembles the modern idea of property, but at all times the Crown had a strong interest in keeping the fullest possible records of who held what, and what services, military or otherwise, were due in return.

Gradually, however, feudalism was overtaken by the strengthening of the rights of the subject. As services were commuted into money rents the basis was destroyed, and the last vestiges of feudalism were legally abolished in the time of Charles II. As the idea of absolute private property immune from royal interference was extended from the Tudor period onwards from the sphere of chattels to that of land and buildings, the new type of private owner started to create his own private records. So a dark age overcomes the records of property. Its feudal origins have had the most profound effect on the character of the English land law, and a modern guide to this very abstruse subject is A. W. Simpson's *An Introduction to the History of the Land Law* (1961).

Inquisitions

Escheats or inquisitions are a class of Chancery records. Inquisitions *post mortem* are records drawn up on the death of a feudal tenant in chief, their purpose being to inform the Court of Chancery of what precisely the late feudal tenant held. The juries compiling inquisitions *post mortem* usually identified parts of the holding by reference to the manorial tenants in actual occupation. They are available for the period from Henry III to Henry VII in calendar form, i.e. the parts of value to the historian are transcribed. For later inquisitions *post mortem* from the time of Henry VIII to the abolition of feudal tenures in 1660 only lists and indexes, i.e. alphabetical lists of references to persons, places and subjects, are available.

Inquisitions *post mortem* are not an original category of records, but a category devised by early keepers of the Public Records in an attempt to re-arrange them. The attempt also resulted in a class of inquisitions known as 'inquisitions miscellaneous', amongst which also are occasional detailed references to buildings. The following example is a splendid description of the buildings of a fourteenth-century manor:

> In the manor of Wylynton [Willington, Bedfordshire] the principal gate is completely ruined and carried away except the gate staples; the second gate is completely ruined; a third gate, with a watch tower to the entry to the mound and a drawbridge is much broken as regards timber, walls and roof. There is a hall of ancient fashion with a pantry and buttery and a passage and a kitchen annexed which used to be tiled but are now mostly unroofed, and the timber is old and in bad condition. There is a bakehouse of ancient fashion, old and in bad condition, mostly tiled and the rest unroofed. There is a chamber called knythystechambre of which the timber is doubtful; it is tiled but needs pointing. There is the foundation of another chamber newly laid, that is, resyns, bemes and stodes, annexed to the same chamber and no more. There is a chamber for the lord with a passage now ruined and nearly razed to the ground for want of both timber and roofing. There is another building called la Nuricerie, which is tiled but needs pointing, and the timber is in very bad condition and almost falling down. There is a building called la Chapelle entirely unroofed, but the timber can easily be mended. There is a building called la Garite which used to be a wardrobe for clothes, which is much ruined for want of both timber and roofing. There is a water mill of which the building is sufficient, but repairs are greatly needed to the wheel and the necessary parts working in the water, and to the defences against the water, namely the floodgates, the wier, and the foundations of the mill. There is another place a barn with a hewynhouse which is completely unroofed and the timber almost fallen to the ground. There is a dovecote kept in reasonable condition. The walls of the manor are of mud, and are altogether razed and destroyed. The whole could be repaired for £100 as the jurors believe.[48]

Enrolments

The Patent (i.e. open) Rolls extend from the time of King John to modern times. The published calendar extends from 1216 to 1575. There is a hiatus in the reign of Henry VIII. Many Licences to Crenellate are recorded.[49] The most interesting period is the succeeding reign of Edward VI, when the

Patent Rolls bear witness to the furiously active market in former Church property commenced in his father's reign. By Church property here is meant all manner of commercial and industrial premises. A typical item in 1548 records the grant of a messuage called the Plough, in Holborn, London, four boileries of salt water at Droitwich, Worcestershire; two cellars and a messuage called the Boars Head in Old Fish Street, London; a tavern called the Greyhound in St. Bride's; the Crown in the parish of St Botolph without Aldgate, etc., all being property confiscated from chantries.[50]

The Patent Rolls also preserve many town charters. The grant of the liberties of Reading given in the Patent Roll for 23 September 1560[51] records the exact boundaries of the town and gives much information about particular buildings and bridges. As the duty to repair the town's bridges had fallen to the Crown with the dissolution of the Abbey, the Mayor and Burgesses of Reading were granted permission to quarry the Abbey ruins for materials for this purpose.

The Close Rolls are a more numerous class of enrolments. A Statute of 1381[52] gave persons who had lost their deeds in the recent period of civil disturbance permission to bring other proof of title to the royal court and have it endorsed on the rolls. There was some attempt in later years to use the Close Rolls as a national register of all conveyances of freehold, but without success.

Liberate Rolls (the final 'e' is pronounced) consist of orders to the officers of the Exchequer to make payments. Those of the reign of Henry III have been calendared and are of importance for art and architecture.

A class of records only imperfectly covered in the British National Archives is the Common Pleas Fines. These records are not to be confused with the Fine Rolls of the Chancery. The Common Pleas Fines include an important type of document known as Feet of Fines (P.R.O. Class C.P. 25). The Common Pleas Fines run from the twelfth century to 1834. Almost from the start these Fines were used as a means for conveying what has now come to be called freehold property. An agreement or 'concord' between the two parties to the transaction was written three times on a single skin of parchment and the skin then cut into three. Each party was to have his own copy and the third part, the Foot of Fine, was retained as the Court's record. Only the very earliest Feet of Fines are published by the Record Commissioners.[53] Others are found amongst the publications of the Pipe Roll Society, and calendars and indexes may be sporadically available in local societies' collections and record offices.

Also not published are the Exchequer Rolls and the successive records of the Office of Works, though these are prime sources for the details of building terminology, costs, and methods. Two works using these records extensively are L. F. Salzman's *Building in England down to 1540* (reprinted 1967) and the series *The History of the King's Works* under the general editorship of H. M. Colvin.

Local records

At the heart of a county or other local record office collection are the records of the Quarter Sessions and of local government. Other statutory authorities' deposited records and the acquired papers of families, estates and businesses add to this and are likely to be of great value to the local researcher interested in buildings. Wills, probate records and the Bishop's transcripts of parish registers are similarly at the root of a diocesan record office collection. Either type of record office is likely to have an extensive collection of the invaluable Tithe Survey maps compiled around 1840.

In addition to such administrative, legal and property records, recent centuries have seen the creation of quantities of miscellaneous local history source material such as contemporary newspapers, trade directories, catalogues for the sale of estates and catalogues of commercial products. Such collections are likely to be well represented in reference library local history sections also. The Local Studies Collection of the Birmingham Reference Library exemplifies the variety of these miscellaneous records. The library has the status of a county record office for the West Midlands. Its miscellaneous collections cover Warwickshire, Worcestershire, Staffordshire, Herefordshire and Shropshire.

Local Acts of Parliament

From 1702 the collection has an almost complete set of local acts. Many refer to enclosures and other matters relevant to property development, as well as the usual coverage of plans legally required to be deposited by promoters of railways, canals etc.

Birmingham Corporation Records

The Corporation minutes from 1851 are held. The city was far from being the worst of nineteenth-century towns for slum conditions, but for what problem existed, and for the remedial measures taken – especially the development of Corporation Street as a slum clearance scheme – these records are central. At the turn of the century, furthermore, under the influence of Cadbury and Nettlefold, the city was well known for its advances in the new art of town planning.

Civic records

Records before incorporation start with the minutes of vestry meetings. These were first held at St Martin's in the Bull Ring and later they were held at the High Cross. The earliest Town Book to survive dates from 1723. From 1736 onwards there are Rate Books, an historically important register of property. There are electoral lists from the enfranchisement of the town in 1838, but these are difficult to use because the early ones list persons only by name and not by ward or address.

Other administrative archives are the constables' accounts from the eighteenth century to 1842 and the poor law records created by the overseers and guardians of the poor. The Workhouse records show the efforts of the guardians to obtain accurate information about the living and working conditions at mills to which they were in the custom of sending poor children as apprentices.

Directories

As a town heavily involved in small industry, Birmingham trade directories are of importance for industrial history and architecture. The earliest is of 1767, and many are well illustrated with views of buildings as well as products.

Trade catalogues

These are a source complementary to directories. Many eighteenth-century Birmingham manufacturers issued well-illustrated catalogues. Early trade cards are also often illustrated.

Newspapers

The local newspaper was *Aris's Birmingham Gazette*, started in 1741. Its early years were concerned mainly with national news, but from about 1860 it becomes an important source of local information. From the start, however, advertisements of houses and building plots for sale or lease are numerous. From a study of these advertisements, Chapman and Bartlett write:

> The only satisfactory way of tracing the evolution of working class housing in Birmingham is to study details of properties advertised for sale in *Aris's Birmingham Gazette* and other local newspapers for sample years over a period of a century or more from 1750. From this protracted exercise an unmistakable pattern of development emerges. It begins with the solid brick and slate merchant houses that were being built from the 1760s, when the geographical isolation that had limited Birmingham to a local market was broken by a series of canal links, which inaugurate the rapid commercial development of the town. The merchant houses were built on three or (occasionally) four storeys and were intended to accommodate a warehouse and counting house as well as domestic quarters for the family and its servants. In the 1760s newly built houses on this pattern mostly had gardens, or at any rate 'back land', sometimes with a convenient clay-pit. At the back of the house, often reached from the street by a gated arch, was also the stabling, pump, and, in course of time, workshop accommodation, known locally as 'shopping'. The back yard was frequently surrounded by a high brick wall (in the familiar manner of eighteenth century kitchen gardens), which was the obvious site for several workmen's cottages, built up to the wall 'blind-back' and sharing the communal pump and privies.[54]

Illustrations, maps and photographs

These are an extensive source. Early large-scale maps are reproduced in *Birmingham before 1800, Six Maps in the Local Studies Library* (Birmingham Reference Library, 1968). Estate maps and rentals for the leading landowners are numerous. There are many water-colours and engraved views of early Birmingham. The library houses the official photographic survey of Warwickshire commenced in the 1890s, with some coverage of Worcestershire and Staffordshire. Of the greatest importance, not only locally, is the collection of photographs started in 1860 by Sir Benjamin Stone, with its own catalogue. In addition to lantern slides, glass negatives, albums and scrapbooks, it comprises over 22,000 prints.

Manuscripts

This collection of about 100,000 items starts in the thirteenth century. This is a rich source for the more important local families, such as the Colmores. Some house contents inventories are very detailed, down to 'six small cakes, freshly baked . . .'. The parks of the important houses on the fringe of the growing town, particularly Aston Hall, are important in the process of releasing building land. The library is also the diocesan record office with the records of about 30 Birmingham churches. Local wills, first proved in the diocese in 1858, are held.

These miscellaneous records typify the classes of archival material to be found in library local studies collections, and probably also in record offices and museums. Any of this material can turn out to be invaluable to the local history and architectural researcher. More exceptional, in the Birmingham Local Studies Collection are the more than nationally important Boulton and Watt engineering archives, consisting of correspondence and about 36,000 working drawings. This firm was concerned, amongst many other things, with industrial power and lighting installations throughout the country and abroad during the Industrial Revolution, and the importance in architectural history of their drawings of mills and factories is brought out by the researches of Dr Jennifer Tann.[55]

There are very good guides to local history sources in general. D. Iredale's *Local History Research and Writing* (Enfield Press 1974 and Phillimore 1980) is a beginner's work; it discusses types of records, including those useful for industrial archaeology. Well-known guides are J. West's *Village Records* (1962), with examples; F. L. Emmison's *Archives and Local History* (1966); and W. E. Tate's *The Parish Chest* (3rd edn., 1969). W. B. Stephens' *Sources for English Local History* (1973) is arranged under subject divisions and includes examples of classes of record. The writings of Professor W. G. Hoskins include *Local History in England* (2nd edn. 1972), in which there are chapters on the topography of towns and on fieldwork in the study of buildings. The chapter on the 'Old Community' discusses many classes of possibly useful records. Recommended by Professor Hoskins is R. B. Pugh's *How to write a Parish History* (1954).

Most larger libraries and record offices display many works on local history, often shelved in a separate sequence. Together with books on the sentimental appreciation of villagery will be others ranging between topography, local agriculture, landed families and their seats, genealogy and heraldry and ramblers' tales. Old village and parish histories may be based on now-lost contact with nineteenth-century oral history, so that they themselves are now to be considered as primary source material.

Documentary evidence

From the viewpoint of the researcher interested in old buildings and turning to historical sources as a secondary line of inquiry, documentary evidence might help in several broad areas. It may concern buildings considered as construction, as manifestations of the requirements of their owners, and as identifiable property. These might be distinct aspects of a report on a building.

Construction
The useful paperwork of the building site is very likely to 'have perished. It is practically impossible to put up a building without drawings; but apart from those of an artistic nature, drawings are not apt to survive. Evidence

for the work of construction usually comes through records of payment. For buildings of a specialised nature, records range from the medieval Liberate Rolls recording expenditure on royal works, to the account books of companies and public undertakings in the modern era. The published National Archives are predominantly medieval; the surviving bulk of local and private records tends to belong to the last three centuries, with a dark age between.

Owners' copies of agreements with tradesmen occasionally survive. Plans defining the agreement or produced to aid the practical process of construction are rarer, except for work of high status: the utility of a document on the building site militates against its preservation. In any case, the bulk of material directly concerning site instructions to craftsmen, which the architectural historical researcher would most like to possess, was probably merely chalked on a wall or a floor and never committed to paper. Estate and business archives may be important to illustrate the owner's part in commissioning new building. They give a picture mainly of relations between socially and economically very unequal parties. The business papers of tradesmen rarely survive, and the business affairs of the lower ranks of society were seldom committed to writing at all. Records often refer to the cost of building operations or the cost of materials – often evidence in small detail. Particulars of the wages of craftsmen and labourers may be found in the evidence collected by contemporaries for the purposes of the Poor Law.

Use

A second possible area of documentary enlightenment deals with the layout of buildings and their adaptation to their owners' and occupiers' needs. This area of inquiry involves architectural illustration, whether produced for legal or artistic motives. Cartographical evidence is sparse before the nineteenth century, but very important where it can be found. Artistic illustrations of buildings in their settings, usually of a flattering type, are often found as embellishments in cartography and in commercial documents. Block plans sometimes accompany title deeds. Useful illustration may also occur in verbal form; for many (but not all) dioceses probate records are a valuable source of evidence for the names and furnishing of rooms in houses from the time of Elizabeth to the mid-eighteenth century, evidence from which architectural reconstruction is sometimes possible, and splendid evidence, furthermore, for the precise manner in which named types of room were used.

Property

A third great area is that of property, linking the ownership and occupation of buildings to actual families and individuals. The types of archival evidence here are very varied. Almost any source may identify people and where they lived. At the forefront of records of property are the owners' title deeds, though in counties where the modern process of registration of title has made headway there is an increased tendency to discard them. In present-day law it is not necessary in any case to trace title back more than 20 years, and many old title deeds have therefore been lost to the parchment requirements of the lampshade-making industry. Formerly, title depended crucially on the length of time it had been enjoyed (or so lawyers advised their clients) and the researcher sometimes, therefore, has the luck to find the history of the ownership of a building in which he is interested clarified for centuries back in one abstract of title, or one bundle of documents.

Related to title deeds are wills. The preservation of title deeds is somewhat random; the purchaser of property had more reason to retain them than the vendor, but no reason to deposit them in a public archive – sometimes a positive preference not to. The preservation of wills is better organised, having been a matter of ecclesiastical jurisdiction. Wills are an important part of diocesan archives. As the means of conveying property from person to person, title deeds and wills are legally precise.

For most purposes the complexities of a person's rights to property were reduced to a simple two-level scheme under various names: owner and occupier, otherwise freeholder and leaseholder, landlord and tenant. This is usually sufficient distinction for the historian. Generally a person possessing a 99 year lease or better interest was considered an owner, even though the term 'owner' is meaningless in the strict theory of English land law. An occupier not classed as an owner is usually a tenant under a lease for a shorter term than 99 years. Freehold and leasehold are the principal alternative names for the two levels of tenure; copyhold is a species of freehold of humble origin, usually confined to the ownership of cottages and smallholdings. Owner and occupier are the two categories of personal interest in property recognised in enclosure awards, in the late eighteenth-century land-tax records, and in the mid-nineteenth-century Tithe Survey. The same practical distinction is made in estate papers as 'landlord and tenant'. The expression 'in hand' is used to describe property owned and occupied by the same person.

Deeds

Deeds and related documents are central to the architectural researcher, and on occasions very good descriptions of groups of buildings may be found. There may be good evidence for the buildings of at least the upper levels of late medieval and later rural society. An instance is the arbitration in 1448 concerning a dower dispute over the use of Clay Hall at Tanworth in Arden, Warwickshire, between Maud, widow of John Fulwood, and her son Richard.[56] The arbitration grants Maud the rents of certain fields and

> The use of the room over the hall on the site of the manor of Fulwode until the said Richard has a chimney made below the hall, the said John Hubbard and Maud to give to the said Richard twenty shillings toward the cost of the chimney which is to be completed by the following Christmas, whereupon the said Maud is to occupy the room with the draught, and not the room over the hall, the said Maud to have reasonable use of the hall and to contribute a third of cost of repairs, and reasonable use of the parlour and chapel at convenient times, reasonable use of kitchen, bakehouse, brewhouse and malthouse to which she is to pay a third of the cost of reasonable repairs; also the elder barn, the nether orchard, the over shippon, the room above the garner and the third dove from every flight of the dovehouse, reasonable use of the out court for swine cattle and poultry, use of the garret over the gate to which she has to contribute a third of the cost of repairs and also a third part of the garden . . .

The two-courtyard arrangement of the buildings, probably with the barn between, fronted by the enlarged old manor house with its two main rooms heated and its unheated room below the hall stands out. Here is a detail of architectural improvement, the inserted chimney, traced to its immediate cause. And as Maud paid for a third of everything, its cost was evidently £3.

From this it will also be clear that not all documents in deed collections are straightforward conveyances of title.

Types of deed

For clarity the law has always used special names for the two principal parties to any transfer of property. The names indicate which is the active party making the deed and which the passive one gaining the property. The choice of terminology also indicates the nature of the transaction: if a recipient of property is called a *donee* one gathers that he is obliged in time to pass it on in accordance with a rule of inheritance by which he is bound. This is a useful legal shorthand.

For most transactions a pair of words are formed, one ending in '-or' (or '-er') signifying the active party, the other ending in '-ee' signifying the passive. Thus a *feoffment* is granted by a *feoffor* to a *feoffee*; a lease is granted by a lessor to a lessee and so forth.

Four primary types of deed are:

Type	Purpose	Names of parties	
		active	passive
Feoffment (Feoffamentum)	Conveys an estate in fee simple	Feoffor	Feoffee
Gift (Donatio)	Conveys an estate in limited fee, e.g. in fee tail	Donor	Donee
Grant (Concessio)	Conveys incorporeal hereditaments, e.g. an estate in reversion, rights of common, etc.	Grantor	Grantee
Lease	Conveys (out of a greater estate) an estate for life or lives, or a tenancy for years or at will	Lessor	Lessee

If the transaction is mutual between the two parties, the '-or' and '-ee' rule will not apply. There are two other types of primary deed frequently encountered, made between persons possessing equal estates (in the sense of both having fee simple, both a term of years, etc., though not necessarily property of the same value):

Type	Purpose	Names of parties
Exchange	Mutual exchange of equal estates	Exchangers
Partition	Mutual agreement to divide property held by the parties	Joint tenants, (Co)parceners (= female co-heirs), tenants in common

Another five types of deed are 'derivative', presupposing an earlier primary deed between the parties. The derivative deed then enlarges, confirms, alters, restores or transfers the interest or estate which was the subject of the primary deed:

Type	Purpose	Names of parties active	passive
Release or Quitclaim	1. To enlarge the relessee's inferior estate in possession 2. To renounce one's interest in jointly held property 3. To renounce in favour of a usurper 4. To renounce an expectation of reversion	Relessor	Relessee
Confirmation	To increase a tenant's estate or security of tenure	Confirmor	Confirmee
Surrender	To renounce a lease	Surrenderor	Surrenderee
Assignment	To convey an estate for life or for years	Assignor	Assignee
Defeasance	To defeat a primary deed (such as a mortgage)	(as in primary deed)	

The earlier deed may be recited in the initial section of the derivative one.

When a quitclaim renounces in favour of a usurper or squatter, the terms *disseisor* and *disseisee* may be used – but in this case the words refer to the previous usurpation, so that the disseisee releases to the disseisor, instead of the other way round.

The early law recognised *seisin* as the essence of title to property. Following the Statute of Uses (1536) a new type of deed came into existence to enable the parties to take advantage of the novel concept of 'use' in place of seisin. For a long time the law required the Statute to be cited in the preamble of a deed if this advantage were to be gained, where it is referred to as the 'Statute for Transferring Uses into Possession'. The true purchaser – *cestui que use*, in Law French – should be identified as the party 'to whose use' the apparent beneficiary or trustee receives the property. This is only the starting point of a mass of tortuously technical law, with springing and shifting uses, uses upon uses, and much else.

In property transactions the law has always favoured publicity and registration of title, whilst the parties have always favoured secrecy and evasion of registration. Seisin was subject to a public ceremony, but the conveying of use was private. The new law generated new types of deed:

Type	Purpose	Names of parties active	passive
Covenant to stand seised to uses	To convey an estate in possession to a kinsman	Covenantor	Covenantee

Type	Purpose	Name of parties active	passive
Bargin and Sale	To sell an estate in possession	Bargainor	Bargainee
Lease and Release (two deeds)	To sell a freehold	Lessor Relessor	Lessee Relessee
Revocation and new appointment	To declare who is to receive property under an earlier deed or will	Appointor	Appointee

Conveyance by Lease and Release became the classic post-medieval procedure. When it became clear under the Statute of Uses that seisin was no longer necessary for effective ownership, conveyance by Bargain and Sale was introduced for selling property to a non-relative. The same session of Parliament that passed the Statute in 1536 also enacted that no freehold would pass by Bargain and Sale unless registered in the Court within six months of the transaction. Lawyers needed to find a method of conveying secretly, and found the loophole that conveyances of estates less than freehold did not have to be registered: this gave rise to Lease and Release, first tested and validated by the Courts in 1621. The Lease is a Bargain and Sale for a year. This gave the lessee the use, and therefore by the Statute the 'possession'. In a deed dated the day following, the lessee then received a Release of the freehold and reversion: whereupon his estate was enlarged to fee simple.

The Conveyancing Act of 1841 made the initial lease unnecessary, so that Lease and Release was thereafter effected by a single deed. The method became extinct, however, under the Conveyancing Act of 1845.

Anatomy of a deed

As a precaution against fraudulent alteration, deeds are written without paragraph breaks or punctuation. None the less it is possible to break into the text at a number of significant points, as deeds follow standardised order and the sections have standard opening words written in enlarged lettering.

1 The Premises:

THIS INDENTURE... date and parties.

WHEREAS... The Recitals: previous deeds proving the vendor's title (which may be quoted at great length), agreements, mortgages, and any facts explaining the basis of the present deed.

NOW THIS INDENTURE WITNESSETH... The Testatum: the part containing the payment or rent etc. and the operative words which are the crux of the deed. The Testatum consists of three main parts: IN CONSIDERATION OF... the payment, rent, service etc.; HATH... e.g., bargained and sold ...; ALL... e.g. 'that capital messuage called Dale Hall ...'

2 The Habendum and Tenendum:

TO HAVE AND TO HOLD... Here is stated the extent of the title or interest conveyed.

3 The Stipulations:

RENDERING or YIELDING... The Reddendum: this stipulates what the grantor reserves to himself out of what is being granted, such as a rent to be paid.

TO THE INTENT THAT... If necessary the purpose of the deed is clarified.

PROVIDED... Here the deed seeks to anticipate an array of possible future outcomes and specifies how the effect of the deed is to be modified in each case. An intended marriage might not take place or might produce no heirs, a mortgage sum with interest might be paid, etc.

DOTH WARRANT... The warranty.

4 The Conclusion:

IN WITNESS... The names and seals of the parties and witnesses.

To go straight to the description of the property which is the subject of the deed one should look for the word ALL. Usually a description runs from a narrow and historically useful description:

> ... and also all that new erected Cotton Mill theretofore erected built upon the scite of an Old Corn Mill and some other buildings which were taken down and cleared away for that purpose therein mentioned to be situate and standing in or near Rocester aforesaid and to be then commonly called or known by the name of Rocester Mill and then or then late in the poss(essi)on of the said Richard Arkwright & Richard Bridden or one of them ...

to a comprehensive statement of the vendor's property intended to catch anything else which might have been forgotten, of almost no historical value at all:

> ... Together with all houses outhouses Edifices Buildings Mills Factories Barns Stables Cowhouses Yards Gardens Orchards Ways Wells Waters Watercourses Mill Dams Mill Fleams Wiers Goits Fisheries Trees Hedges ditches Gates Stiles Walls Fences Easements Profits Privileges Advantages rights members & Appurtenances whatsoever to the said messuage Cotton Mill Closes lands tithes heredit(ament)s & prem(ise)s thereby granted & released or expressed and intended so to be or any part or parts thereof belonging or in anywise appertaining ...

Fines and recoveries

Property might be conveyed by court judgement rather than by deed: the process involved a complex legal charade, a pretence of a dispute between the parties and a person known as the *common vouchee* who seems to be important but was probably merely the court crier. As this was not uncommon it is worth taking account of names given to the two parties.

The process started with the spurious issue of a writ of *praecipe* (demanding the return of the property in question). In the case of a *fine* the court action was commenced and then compromised; in the case of a *recovery* it was acted out to the full. Fines and recoveries are known in all periods down to their abolition in 1833. (They are known from the time of Henry II.) The main purpose of a fine was to enable a married woman to sell property in her own right, as the law did not permit her to convey property by deed during her husband's lifetime. The main purpose of a recovery was to enable the present owner of an entailed estate to free it of the rights of his heirs and anyone else possessing an interest.

In the first stage of a fine the vendor is called the *tenant, deforciant* or *defendant*; the purchaser is called the *complainant, demandant* or *plaintiff*. The purchaser requests permission to discontinue the action and a concord is drawn up; now the vendor is called the *cognisor* and the purchaser the *cognisee*. A note of the fine is enrolled in the records of the court, and a full record copied and delivered to each party. A fine is so called because it commences with the words 'This is the final agreement ... (haec est finalis concordia ...)'.

Fines were of four kinds, for details of which Blackstone should be consulted.[57]

Recoveries were invented by churchmen to evade the statutes of mortmain, and were used also by owners of entailed property to break the entail. They might be used to clear away old fetters before creating a new family settlement of property, as well as for outright sale. As in a fine, the purchaser pretended that he had formerly owned the property but been illegally ousted, and started his action. He is called the *demandant*. The other party, the vendor, is the *defendant*, otherwise the *deforciant* or the *tenant to the praecipe*.

In court the vendor called upon ('vouched') the *vouchee* to give a warranty for the vendor's title, the vouchee being the person whose reversionary interest in the property was, by prior agreement with him, to be extinguished. The vouchee then similarly called upon the *common vouchee*, the latter being a court servant not owning property. The latter duly failed to answer, so the court's judgement went in favour of the demandant. In the judgement the vendor is called the *recoveree*, the purchaser the *recoveror*. The purchaser received an absolute title registered in the court, all the old fetters of entail etc. being transferred to the fictitious compensatory property which would never be recovered from the common vouchee.

Probate records

Wills and inventories are of value for the study of property, and inventories have a special value for the study of domestic architecture. Wills may have the same importance as deeds; and inventories often name rooms and provide the means not only to reconstruct house-plans but to examine precisely how each room was occupied. When the deceased held leasehold property, leasehold being a chattel interest, it might be listed. The transcribing of probate inventories and their analysis is now a very flourishing local historical evening-class industry. Most inventories were deposited in diocesan record offices; the important ones proved in the archbishops' courts are at York at the Borthwick Institute (for York) or at the Public Record Office (for Canterbury). Probate became a civil matter in 1858.

Wills are very ancient. At first the proportion of his property which the testator might bequeath was limited, but gradually enlarged until the whole was included. In most of England this freedom was reached by the seventeenth century; it was extended to the province of York in 1692, to Wales in 1696, and to London in 1724.

The deceased's real property might be bequeathed in his will, but it might all be included without specific mention as 'residue' passing to his heir. Thus the will of Sir Richard Arkwright, which was proved at Canterbury on the 4th of September 1792, commences with seven cash legacies and then proceeds to give devise and bequeath to his heir, Richard Arkwright junior 'all my manors messuages lands and hereditaments as well freehold as customary or copyhold or leasehold with the rights members and appurtenances and also all the rest and residue of my personal estate of what nature or kind soever . . .'.

But the will, though typically unspecific about the extent of Sir Richard's considerable property, gives information about two buildings unfinished at the time it was written. Arkwright required

> . . . that my said son shall with all convenient speed complete in a proper manner the mansion house I have lately erected and also in a like and proper manner complete and finish the chapel I have lately built and that he shall by good and effectual conveyances endow or settle upon the minister or officiating clergyman of the said chapel for the time being the annual sum or payment of £50 . . .

The mansion was Willersley Castle, Matlock, commenced in 1782 but burned down before completion. Richard Arkwright junior completed it and also the chapel, consecrated in 1797, endowing a perpetual curacy in the gift of the family.[58]

An owner of property, contemplating death but reassuring everyone that his mind was yet sound, drew up his will in writing. Death supervened, and everyone whom it might concern searched for the latest-dated document they could find purporting to be the will. It was taken to the diocesan probate court (or the prerogative courts of the provinces of Canterbury or York, if the property was extensive enough for there to be chattels to the value of 100 shillings in two distinct dioceses). Here it was examined and 'proved', and an oath administered to the executor making him a temporary owner of the deceased's property entrusted with its disposal as willed.

For a period of about two centuries the manner in which the executor carried out this duty with regard to goods and chattels was closely supervised by the court. He was obliged, with the help of what expert local 'appraisors' he could find, to make out an inventory of all the deceased's goods and chattels with valuations. The purpose of the inventory was to verify the deceased's assets, that is goods and chattels with a value sufficient (assez) to discharge his debts. He then had to pay the debts in the order of priority prescribed by law, before paying legacies. Freehold ownership of buildings is outside the scope of inventories, as real property was not considered part of assets until 1830. The duties of the executor are clearly set out by Blackstone.[59]

Inventories are found among probate records from about 1650 to 1740. The chattels inventoried by executors and appraisors are usually what would be regarded as household goods and furniture – bedsteads, linen, pots and pans, the tools of the deceased's trade, and so forth. Often, as a matter of simple method, the contents are listed under room names, such as the 'upper parlour', the 'little red chamber', 'the cellar', and so on. There is evidence for the names, furnishing and uses of rooms, and, taken together, it may be possible to reconstruct the plan of the house if it conforms to an orthodox type. A few inventories concern a deceased who lived in part of a house or had goods in several houses, which is inconvenient for statistical analysis.

Probate inventories rarely deal with the chattels of the very poorest, but similar inventories were occasionally drawn up by Poor Law officers.

LITERATURE OF RECORDING

In 1756 Isaac Ware had concluded that evidence for the origins of architecture was lost, and that 'it is enough for us to acknowledge the defect of information, and while we trace the progress of the art . . . from reason, to say it is too old for history'.[60] Modern interest in the historical traditions of building starts with the realisation that systematic research in archives and careful recording of specimens offer the way to put developments into historical sequence. The rudimentary state of archaeological investigations at this time adds to the pessimism expressed by Ware; little was done apart from delving for sculptures and the uncovering of mosaic pavements or perhaps structures as unmistakable as a pillared hypocaust.[61]

The other main source of evidence, documentary research, had made no progress beyond the efforts of a few isolated pioneers such as Thomas Rymer to collect and publish even the most crucial ancient charters.

One of the influences on eighteenth-century ideas was the writing of the Roman architect Vitruvius, from the time of Augustus. Vitruvius had looked to the buildings of the barbarians of his time for the origins of architecture, and gives curious descriptions of them. For Vitruvius this had been a question of some importance, as he held that simple construction revealed the technical characteristics of materials, and that it was through the development of craftsmanship, coping with these materials, that the useful arts arose. Craftsmanship led a people from a state of barbarity and warfare to a peaceful civilisation.[62]

It was readily seen that the details of refined architectural ornament might be derived from practical features of construction in an earlier age; Sir William Chambers in 1759 produced a hypothetical design for a timber hut with exposed beam ends, supposed to be the origin of the details of the Doric order.[63] It was also a prevalent idea that the features of the Gothic style were derived from pagan sanctuaries in woodland groves, with the stems of tall trees giving rise to columns, and the branches arching together at the top giving rise to vault tracery. There was no clear idea of Gothic as a development from Romanesque. The 'wood and wicker' primeval Gothic was advocated by Sir James Hall as late as 1813.[64]

Architectural recording started with the attempts of antiquaries to recover better specimens of the classical orders and as a sideline to delving in the ruins of Italy for Roman and Greek sculptures, at a time when the aristocracy saw itself as heir to the manners of the Roman patrician class. Sir

William Chambers also made a resounding plea for the native Gothic architecture to be treated with as much interest:

> Would our dilettanti instead of importing the gleanings of Greece; or our antiquaries instead of publishing loose incoherent prints; encourage persons duly qualified, to undertake a correct elegant publication of our own cathedrals and other buildings called Gothic before they totally fall to ruin; it would be of real service to the arts of design; preserve the remembrance of an extraordinary stile of building now sinking fast into oblivion; and at the same time publish to the world the Riches of Britain, in the splendour of her ancient structures.[65]

There was quite remarkable progress in ideas during the period from the late eighteenth to the early nineteenth century, a period coinciding with the Industrial Revolution. There were many contributors to the 'debate' on the origins of the Gothic style of architecture in particular, a style thought of as being predominantly English. In *The Architectural Antiquities of Great Britain*[66] John Britton reviewed many of the prevalent theories and emphasised the development of Gothic architecture from Saxon and Norman origins and its later progress through phases largely anticipating those later to be defined by Rickman.

There was, in the same period, a new interest in the importance of documented research rather than merely conjectural theorising. With a new efficiency in government, a start was being made on making the national archives accessible for study. As early as 1764 commissioners were appointed to classify and calendar them. In 1800 the Royal Record Commission was set up.[67]

Popular demand for literature describing architectural antiquities was met by a quite new genre of writing – popular topography. John Britton produced, with E. W. Brayley, the first two volumes of *The Beauties of Wiltshire* in 1801. This was the first of nine works in the series 'The Beauties of England and Wales'. Britton was strongly in favour of preserving ancient monuments, and tried to found a society for the purpose. The new enthusiasm for places of interest other than the seats of the nobility was, however, strongly marked by Romanticism. There was a new appreciation of untamed landscape, and it might have been expected that this would encourage interest in geology and in simple buildings in local materials; but Romanticism was too sensational and superficial for this. 'The general intention of Picturesque travel', wrote Gilpin in 1794, 'is searching after effects'.[68] Tourists were keen to visit great mills and ironworks, and seek out 'gloom and terror as conducive to true emotions'.[69]

Another type of popular literature skirting an interest in the history of minor buildings is that of the *cottage orné* pattern books. This literature is so overlaid with aesthetic and moral ideas that it is of minimal extrinsic value. There is no interest in local materials as part of a local tradition, but every interest in the value of cottages as ornaments to a gentleman's property and in their character appropriate to the occupants. Thus Malton favoured the introduction of the classical pediment into cottage architecture, but considered that its effect would be suitably rustic and deferential if covered in thatch.[70] Choice of materials was essentially a moral one: 'The characteristic mark of a cottage is humility,' wrote Bartell in 1804, 'as if, conscious of its inferiority, it should appear to retire beneath the shelter of its friendly woods, which it would not do if it were fabricated of glaring colours and costly materials.'[71] It is quite unnecessary to suppose that the cottage orné fashion had anything remotely to do with what is now considered vernacular in architecture.

At a more academic level the study of architectural antiquities flourished in the literature on medieval ecclesiastical architecture, particularly the measuring and publication of drawings of Gothic buildings suitable for imitation in the religious revival of the early Victorian years. In 1835 Thomas Rickman published *An Attempt to discriminate the Styles of Architecture in England from the Conquest to the Reformation*, originating the terms 'Early English', 'Decorated' and 'Perpendicular' for the three salient phases of the Pointed or Gothic style, though the Ecclesiological Society preferred 'first, second and third pointed'. In 1849, admitting the arbitrariness of any classification of an evolving architecture, Edmund Sharpe proposed to change Rickman's Decorated and Perpendicular into 'Geometrical', 'Curvilinear' and 'Rectilinear'.[72]

Later authorities divided Gothic architecture on aesthetic grounds into Early and Late divisions, cutting across Rickman's Decorated Period. But all the later nineteenth-century writers acknowledge Rickman's contribution: he was 'the first to reduce chaos into order, and to show that the age of a building can be ascertained by the construction and the details, on the principle of comparisons with well known dated examples'.[73] Ecclesiastical architecture became a very widespread interest in the Victorian period. Leading societies were the Cambridge Camden Society, forming the nucleus of the London based Ecclesiological Society in 1846, and the Oxford Society for Promoting the Study of Gothic Architecture, which later changed its name to the Oxford Architectural and Historical Society. Both the Cambridge and Oxford societies were founded in 1839.

> However we may criticise the early church restorers, and with reason, and however hard we may find it to appreciate many of the new churches built at the time, we cannot escape from the recognition that it was the proselytising vigour of the Camdenians that brought an appreciation of ancient buildings – and by an easy extension, ancient monuments in general – into the lives of the English upper and middle classes in the 1840s as never before. For restorations or for new designs both societies built up archives of notes and drawings of medieval churches on as wide a front as possible. The Camdenians issued an elaborate questionnaire which was used by both societies, listing every possible feature of a church and its fittings in systematic order and under elaborate classified headings, the precursor of the record cards which were used by the staff of the English Ancient Monuments Commission.[74]

The new academic approach to architecture was widened to embrace domestic buildings with the publication of T. H. Turner's *Domestic Architecture*, continued after his death by J. H. Parker.[75] Much of the material for these volumes concerned houses of manorial or noble status, and a great deal of useful information on the way of life of people in these larger houses was collected. Illustration and information were not so readily found for the dwellings of the cottager, and an interest in the class of building which would now be more readily termed vernacular tends to appear later in the century when there were ideas of reviving traditional local architecture for a new vernacular style.

In 1889 Ralph Neville penetrated into this area with a study of cottage architecture in Surrey.[76] Neville was an architect, an assistant to Gilbert Scott, and seems to have had a particular interest in the training of pupils in Scott's office. He concentrated on examples of rural domestic architecture at an unpretentious level, 'omitting those of a more strictly architectural design and important nature'. He advocated the intensive study of the buildings of a district for purposes of professional education. Another work of local recording is the study of Snowdonia cottages by Hughes and North, who were also architects, in 1908.[77]

In 1916 C. F. Innocent produced *The Development of English Building Construction*.[78] Innocent acknowledged that old buildings might be studied for lessons in 'line, form and colour' but his main concern was to show their 'historic relationship to the building construction of the present time'.

A work of somewhat different character, full of novel ideas, is S. O. Addy's *The Evolution of the English House* (1898). Addy's work belongs to a central European tradition of scholarship, intensely interested in primitive origins.[79] Addy drew heavily on German writings on farmhouse types. He shows great interest in the etymology of building terms wherever it might assist understanding. His book went out of print after the Great War, but a second edition was brought out by Summerson in 1933 using notes compiled by Addy.

Much was published in illustration of local domestic architecture in the early years of the present century, including E. Guy Dawber's *Old Cottages and Farmhouses in Kent and Sussex* (1900), *Old Cottages in the Cotswold District* (1904); W. Curtis Green's *Old Cottages and Farmhouses in Surrey* (1908) commencing Batsford's Old Cottage series; Stuart Dick's *The Cottage Homes of England*, illustrated by Helen Allingham; Sydney R. Jones' *The Village Homes of England* (1912) and *English Village Homes and Country Buildings* (1936); and H. Batsford and C. Fry's *The English Cottage* (1938).

M. W. Barley's *The English Farmhouse and Cottage* (1961) uses the intensive work that has been done, particularly since the war, on the analysis of probate inventories and other important sources of extra information on domestic life and architecture.

The great development of the present century has been the establishment of Royal Commissions for Historical Monuments in England, Scotland and Wales, and the recording work which they have initiated. The destruction of architecture in the south east during the war led to the setting up also of the National Buildings Record, now renamed the National Monuments Record and merged with the English R.C.H.M. More recently, at a local level there has been the establishment of numerous County Sites and Monuments Record Departments. The discovery has also been made since the war that industrial buildings and the domestic buildings of the Industrial Revolution cry out for the attention of the historian and the architectural recorder.

Archaeological and historical societies and Adult Education classes are avenues for amateur interest. Amateur interest compensates to some extent for the loss of professional interest in historical study amongst architects. Recording is no longer dominated by architects researching for correct details for their buildings in historical style (at least, one hopes that era is past, although the professional demoralisation of the '70s has taken its toll, and in the early '80s there have been some sad recrudescences of Palladianism and similar nonsense, even commissioned by universities). Architectural history should settle into being a disinterested academic study, pursued by laymen in architecture as much as by architects. No architect can be said to take an intelligent interest in his professional work unless he is aware of its history, but historical research should be a tool of the trade only of the professional conservationist who needs to be able to carry out repairs correctly.

Amateur recording groups have distinguished themselves in the annual BBC 'Chronicle' competitions. It is largely up to amateur enthusiasts to fill the gap left by the waning of professional interest amongst architects in the history of building and buildings. Local recording groups are important, and the best, like the Ludlow group, publish prolifically. Most historic towns wait for similar scrutiny. The field is open for the amateur who sees architecture in its place in social, technical and economic history.

Glossary

Abacus A slab forming the topmost member of a column capital

Aggregate Material providing bulk in a mortar, plaster or concrete; usually sand and (in concrete) gravel

Aisle The lateral part of a building between a longitudinal arcade and an outside wall

Aisled hall A hall divided into a central nave and two lateral aisles by means of longitudinal arcades or rows of columns, with a single roof overall

Aisle plate The wall-plate on an aisle wall

Aisle tie A tie-beam from arcade post to outside wall

Angle bead A three-quarters-round timber bead fixed to a salient angle of a wall, serving as a screed for plastering and as a means to resist damage at the corner; also called Staff bead

Apse (1) Originally a half-domed semicircular recess inside a building; (2) a polygonal or round-ended termination of a church sanctuary

Arcade (1) A line of regularly spaced columns or piers with arches connecting them one to another; (2) also loosely used for a line of posts and bracing in a framed aisled building

Arcade plate A longitudinal beam carried on arcade posts, serving as a support to rafters

Arcade post One of several posts standing in a line, similar to the columns of an arcade, in an aisled building

Arch (1) A structure within a wall consisting of a series of wedge-shaped blocks spanning in a curve from abutment to abutment, each block caused by gravity to press against its neighbours (c.f. **Dome** and **Vault**); (2) any head of an opening in curved form, even if only superficially resembling an arch in the first sense

Arch brace A curved diagonal member in the top corner of a timber frame; one of a pair of curved timbers rising from a principal to a tie-beam or a collar

Architrave (1) Originally, a beam spanning from column to column; hence (2) the lowest division of an entablature; and (3) a decorative moulding covering the joint between a door or window frame and the surrounding wall, the traditional architectural form from which derives the second sense

Archivolt (1) Properly the intrados (soffit or reveal) face of an arch; (2) sometimes used for the moulded decoration following the curve of an arch on the wall face (the word in this sense perhaps considered similar to 'architrave')

Arris The sharp edge where two surfaces meet in a salient angle

Ashlar (1) Carefully squared masonry constructed in regular courses with aligned perpend joints (c.f. **Rubble**); (2) one of a set of short vertical timbers in the plane of the inside face of a flat-topped wall, rising from the inner end of a sole piece to the underside of a common rafter

Attic (1) Originally the top part of a classical façade, decorated with the Attic order; (2) a storey wholly or partly within a roof

Axial (or central) chimney A chimney at the centre of a cross wall between cells (the defining feature of a class of house plans)

Baffle entry An entrance to a house facing the side wall of a chimney stack (the defining feature of a class of house plans)

Baluster A supporting post under a handrail

Balustrade A handrail and balusters

Banker mark The signature mark on a stone made by a banker mason

Barge-board A fascia, often decorative, fixed to the verge of a roof to conceal the roof carpentry and the top edge of the wall

Barrel roof A roof with a ceiling of barrel vault shape

Barrel vault A semi-cylindrical vault

Base cruck A cruck (where an arcade post might have been used) rising to an arcade plate

Bay A unit of a repetitious structure in the longitudinal direction, extending between a consecutive pair of cross frames or trusses

Bay line The meeting line of two bays

Bay window A projecting window at ground level (c.f. **Oriel**)

Bead A small round moulding

Bed The plane of stratification of sedimentary rock; a horizontal joint in masonry

Blade A cruck

Blind arcade A series of arches, often standing on pilasters, as a projecting decoration on the face of a wall

Bond Systematic principle in laying bricks to achieve interlocking

Boss A large stone at the crossing point of ribs in masonry vaulting, usually treated as a decorative feature

Box frame System of framing on which roof trusses are carried on the tops of wall frames (contrast cruck framing); alternatively called 'Post and Truss'

Brace A diagonal member stiffening a frame

Bressummer (1) A sill beam to an upper storey wall frame; (2) a large beam such as that carrying masonry over a shop-front or large fireplace

Broach A half-pyramid shape used to achieve a transition between an arris and a chamfer

Butt purlin A side purlin extending only from bay line to bay line, jointed to the sides of principal rafters (c.f. **Through purlin**)

Buttery A service room for the storage of drink, below the cross passage of a hall house

Camber A slight upward curve in a beam

Came In window glazing, a lead bar grooved on either side

Cantilever The end of a beam projecting beyond its support

Cap The ornamental top of a column or post

Carpenter's mark A numeral carved on timber during trial assembly to identify which members belong together at joints

Casement A window opening on hinges (c.f. **Sash**)

Catslide A roof extended to cover a lean-to part in one slope

Cell A unit of domestic accommodation, either an apartment for an individual or a space for a distinct function (c.f. **Bay**, which refers to the structural unit)

Cellar (1) Originally, a store house or store room; (2) a room or rooms wholly or partially below ground

Cement A calcined composition of lime and clay with special setting and hardening properties, including Roman cement (patented 1796) and Portland cement (patented 1824)

Centre A temporary support while laying voussoirs

Chamber (1) An upstairs room (c.f. **Loft**); (2) A private room

Chamfer (1) An arris cut back ('bevelled') to present a plane surface at 135° to each face; (2) a moulding in a similar position

Chevron (1) Originally, a rafter; hence, an inverted V shape; (2) a zigzag ornament

Clapboard (1) Originally, an oak board to be shaped into a barrel stave; (2) a tongue-and-grooved board in external wall cladding (the American use of this word is different)

Clay lump Lumps of clay like large but unfired bricks used for walling

Cleat In framing, a block fixed to the side of one member to support another

Close studding Walling with timber posts set at a distance apart not much greater than their own width

Clunch A soft limestone from the lower beds of the chalk, used for carving or for inferior walling

Cob A mix of clay (marl or chalk) with gravel, dung and straw, used for walling. (c.f. **Clay lump**)

Coin See **Quoin**

Collar (beam) A horizontal member in a truss tying a pair of principals or rafters together at mid-height

Collar purlin A longitudinal member in roof framing upon which collars rest at their mid points

Column A thin vertical structural support in stone or in a material architecturally imitating stone, consisting of base, shaft and capital

Common (adj.) One of a regularly spaced set (of rafters, joists etc.) acting in unison

Coping The top course of a wall, exposed to the weather

Corbel A stone etc. projecting from a wall to carry the end of a rib or beam or other source of concentrated load.

Core (1) The interior of a wall; (2) an imperfectly burned lump of limestone, incapable of slaking properly

Cornice (1) The topmost element of a Classical entablature; (2) a projecting course at or near the top of a wall

Cottage (1) Originally, the dwelling of a member of the cottar class in feudal society; (2) later, the small dwelling of a member of the labouring class, loosely contrasting with 'house'; (3) in modern times, also a small dwelling suited to retirement or retreat, irrespective of class

Couple A pair of rafters or principals

Course A layer of stones or bricks

Crown glass Glass made in disc form (c.f.**Muff glass**)

Cross frame A frame on a bay line. (c.f. **Wall frame**)

Cross wall A wall at right angles to the ridge line

Crown post An upright member in roof construction which stands on the mid-point of a tie-beam and supports a collar purlin, and usually is braced to each

Crow steps Steps ornamenting a gable parapet

Cruck One of a pair of inclined, and usually curving, timbers rising from near or at ground level, the lower part carrying wall framing (if present) and the upper part serving as a roof principal. Some crucks consist of two timbers jointed together. **Full cruck** from at or near ground level to apex; **base cruck** from at or near ground level to underside of arcade plate; **raised cruck** from just below wall-plate to apex; **middle cruck** from just below wall-plate to underside of collar beam; **upper cruck** from top of tie-beam to apex

Cruck spur A short horizontal timber from the back of a cruck to a wall-plate

Curvilinear style In English Gothic architecture, the later subdivision of the Decorated style

Cusp A projection remaining between two hollows (foils) on the edge of a window opening

Dado Wall panelling carried up to waist height only

Dais A raised platform at the superior end of a hall

Daub Dense clay mixed with chaff used to plaster over wattle or similar panels

Decorated style In English Gothic architecture, the highly ornamented second phase from the late thirteenth to the mid-fourteenth century, defined with special reference to stone window tracery (subdivided into the Geometric and Curvilinear styles)

Dentil One of a row of small projecting blocks in a cornice (originally a feature of the Ionic order)

Diaper A pattern of evenly spaced diagonal lines crossing each other

Dome A vault over a circular space, usually with voussoir courses circular in plan

Dormer window A window standing up above the plane of a roof

Double pile plan A plan two cells deep

Dragon A beam in floor construction running diagonally to a corner, supporting the inner ends of trimmed floor joists on either side; the use of a dragon beam enabled two adjacent faces to be jettied

Drawbar A stout bar used to hold a door shut, otherwise sliding back into a hole in the wall

Dressings Stronger or decoratively 'dressed' masonry used at corners, around openings, in strings and cornices, etc.

Droved (adj.) Dressed with a broad chisel (masonry)

Dutch gable A gable with a parapet ending in ornamental curves

Eared architrave An architrave moulding stepped as if to outline an extended lintel at the head of the opening

Early English style In English Gothic architecture, the first phase from the late twelfth to the late thirteenth century, defined with special reference to stone window design and characterised by the absence of tracery other than plate tracery

Eaves A roof overhang; the bottom edge of a roof slope (c.f. **Verge**).

Entablature The horizontal part, usually carried on columns or pilasters, at the top of a Classical façade, consisting of architrave, frieze and cornice

Entasis The slight swelling in the shaft of a classical column

Extrados The outer curved face, not normally visible, of an arch or vault

Fair tooled (adj.) dressed in regular manner with a point (masonry)

Fascia (1) Originally, a band in clothing; (2) one of the bands into which the architrave of an entablature may be divided; (3) a facing to a floor-edge in a stair-well; (4) any elongated panel such as the name board above a shop-front

Fastening An additional part inserted into a joint to tighten it and to prevent the members from coming apart

Finial The ornament at the tip of a pinnacle or a ridge

Firehood A large smokehood

Fire window A small window lighting the space beneath a firehood

Floating coat In plastering, the second coat, consisting of fine stuff and a little hair

Flushwork A wall facing of knapped flints

Foil (1) Originally, a leaf; (2) a small arc between the cusps of a window, small symmetrical windows being termed 'trefoil', 'quatrefoil', etc., according to the number of foils

Framed construction Construction consisting of rod-like members jointed to one another at their ends

Frieze (1) The middle element of a Classical entablature, usually ornamented; (2) a decorated or sculptural band

Furrowed (adj.) Dressed in regularly spaced parallel grooves with a point (masonry)

Gable The triangular part of a wall between the verges of a roof

Geometric style In English Gothic architecture, the earlier subdivision of the Decorated style

Groin The arris formed by two vaults meeting at or near right angles

Gypsum A white mineral, calcium sulphate combined with 21 per cent of water. It is heated to drive off most of the water and ground to produce plaster of Paris for plastering and for alabaster

Half timber (1) Originally, signified those buildings in which the ground storey was of brick or stone and the parts above timber-framed; (2) later used indiscriminately for any visibly timber-framed construction

Hall (1) The principal room of a medieval house, usually distinguished from private apartments at the superior or 'upper' end and from service rooms beyond an entrance cross passage at the 'lower' end; (2) in later times the lobby or room first entered in a house, if serving no other purpose

Halling Wall tapestry in wealthier Tudor houses

Hammer beam A short horizontal timber at the base of a roof truss, projecting into the interior of the building, its projecting end supported on a substantial strut or bracket and carrying much of the roof load (a large and important roof may contain two or three tiers of hammer beams)

Hammer post The post standing on a hammer beam

Header A brick seen end-on in a wall; a bond stone penetrating two thirds through the thickness of a wall

Hip An external corner formed in a roof slope (c.p. **Valley**)

Hipped roof A roof in which there are slopes towards the end walls as well as to the sides

Hood A smoke canopy over a fireplace

Hydraulic (adj.), referring to mortar: capable of setting chemically in the absence of air, especially under water

Impost The surface which bears the thrust of an arch or vault

Intrados The inner curved face of an arch or vault

Jack roof A large raised part along the apex of a(n industrial) roof, to let smoke and heat out

Jamb (1) Originally, a leg; (2) the upright post of a frame in an opening

Jetty The overhang where a floor projects over the face of the wall beneath, giving increased area to the upper storey

Joist A common floor or ceiling beam

Jowl The enlargement at the top (or occasionally at the bottom) of a post to provide sufficient bulk where a complex carpentry joint is needed

King post An upright post from tie-beam to ridge

Label mould A projecting dripstone over a window, stepped down at either side of the window opening

Lancet A narrow Gothic window without tracery

Lap joint A joint in which a recess is cut in the face of the main member to receive the shaped end of the secondary member.

Lime mortar Mortar, the setting constituent of which is lime (rather than cement)

Lime plaster Plaster, the setting constituent of which is lime (rather than cement)

Lime putty Fat lime slaked, ground and matured for several months, used as a constituent of finishing plaster or in fine joints in brickwork

Lintel An unframed beam at the top of an opening

Loft A floored space entirely within a roof

Louvre A small raised part at the apex of a (domestic) roof, around the edge of which smoke or heat may escape; c.f. **Jack roof**

Mason's mark *see* **Banker mark**

Mortar The bedding material between stones or bricks

Mortise A socket cut in the side or end of one member to form a joint with the tenon cut at the end of another member

Moulding A continuous linear profile applied or carved at the junction line of two plain surfaces or at an edge to achieve a visually satisfactory transition

Muff glass Glass made in cylinder form then cut and opened flat (c.f. **Crown glass**)

Mullion An upright member in window tracery

Niche A cavity in a wall to recieve a statue or an ornament

Ogee The geometrical form where two opposed quarter circle curves are placed end to end: also called a *cyma*. Where the curves run from horizontal through vertical to horizontal (e.g. in Classical cornice mouldings) it is a *cyma recta*; where from vertical through horizontal to vertical (e.g. in some Gothic window tracery) it is a *cyma reversa*. Properly an ogee is a cyma reversa, and the cyma recta should be termed a *back ogee*, but the word ogee is used indiscriminately.

Ogive (1) Properly, the groin or groin rib of a vault; (2) this word often used wrongly for an ogee curve

Open hall A hall with no ceiling to conceal the roof timbering

Oriel A bay window to an upper floor not carried down to ground level

Outshot An additional small room under a lean-to roof

Panel A solid filling in a frame

Pantry A room for food storage

Parget Originally, plastering (especially with relief ornament); more recently, the lining of flues with plaster and cow dung

Parpend A stone appearing on both faces of a wall

Passing brace A very long brace in a truss, passing across several other members

Pediment The triangular extension of an entablature to form a gable; the same feature in miniature used to ornament the head of a door or window

Perpend An upright joint between bricks or stones

Perpendicular style In English Gothic architecture, the third phase characterised by an emphasis on vertical ornament, defined with special reference to stone window tracery, prevailing from the second half of the fourteenth century until superseded by Renaissance styles

Pier Several meanings, including (1) a part of a masonry wall viewed end-on; (2) a pilaster; (3) the solid part between openings in a wall; (4) a supporting pillar for a bridge or an arch; (5) an ironwork or similar structure supporting a large instrument

Pitch The angle of slope of a roof, measured from the horizontal

Plaster of Paris Dried and ground gypsum, a paste made from which dries and sets rapidly with slight expansion; in plastering, a constituent of the stuff used for finishing and moulding

Platband (1) The projection between two flutes of a column; (2) a horizontal moulding, the height of which much exceeds its projection; an especially common detail in brickwork, where three courses at an upper floor level project slightly to shed rain from a vulnerable part of the wall

Plate A fully supported horizontal timber

Plate tracery Tracery appearing to be formed by piercing a flat surface with a group of apertures

Plinth The bottom part of a wall or column-base, beneath any ornament; a thickened part of a wall at ground level

Point A small mason's chisel

Pozzolana Crushed volcanic ash (from Pozzuoli near Naples) used as a natural cement

Pricking up coat The render coat in plastering, scored to create a key for the next coat

Principal post A post where a wall frame and a cross frame meet, to which part of the roof load is brought

Principal rafter A rafter at a bay line carrying one or more purlins upon which common rafters rest

Purlin A longitudinal member in roof construction at or near mid-height receiving the load of common rafters and transmitting it to the cross frames or walls; purlins may be 'side purlins' or 'crown purlins'

Queen post An upright member in a truss not on the centreline

Quicklime Calcium oxide, produced by calcination of limestone or chalk, used as the basis for most mortar and plaster

Quirk A recess at the side of a moulding

Quoin (1) A salient corner of a wall; (2) a better stone selected for this position

Rafter A roof beam running from ridge to eaves

Rebate A rectangular recess in the edge of a member, especially the hollow in a doorframe

Render The first coat of plaster, consisting of coarse stuff

Respond A pilaster supporting an arch spanning out from the wall

Ridge piece (ridge purlin) The member in roof carpentry into or on which the heads of common rafters are fixed

Roofer A stone used in the manner of a roofing tile. Synonyms 'tilestone' or, less satisfactorily, 'stone tile'

Rubble Walling stones dressed with the hammer or axe, or roughly chiselled (c.f. **Ashlar**)

Run (vb.) To sieve (plaster or lime putty)

Rustication Rough finish and exaggerated joints given to masonry to give the appearance of strength

Sash A window which opens by sliding (c.f. **Casement**)

Scantling A structural timber sawn on all four faces; its dimensions

Scappled (adj.): dressed with the pick-end of the mason's hammer

Scarf A joint connecting two members end to end in line

Scissor brace A brace rising from a wall-plate to the mid-height of an opposite rafter, forming a scissors-like cross with its pair

Screens passage A cross passage behind the screen of a hall, separated from it by a spere

Setting coat In plastering, the final coat

Side purlin A purlin directly supporting common rafters; side purlins may be classified into 'butt purlins' and 'through purlins'

Slake (vb.) To add water to quicklime in order to convert it to hydrate of lime for bricklaying or plastering

Smoke bay A bay in a building without upper floor or ceiling by which smoke can reach a louvre in the roof

Smokehood A canopy over a hearth

Solar An upper private room in a hall

Sole piece A short horizontal timber across the head of a wall, forming the base of a triangle between rafter and ashlar

Soffit The lower face of a member or structure, especially of a beam, arch or ceiling

Spandrel One of the two roughly triangular spaces outside the curve of an arch

Spere (1) Originally a movable screen in a hall protecting the occupants from view and from draught when an outer door was opened: (2) a cross frame including two aisle posts between which the movable screen might be placed

Springing The point or line from which the soffit of an arch or vault rises

Sprocket A short timber added to the foot of a rafter to create an extended eaves at shallower pitch

Squinch An arch or corbelling diagonally across the corner of a room

Stancheon An upright structural member in wrought metal, e.g. rolled steel

Stop The decorative termination of a chamfer

Stretcher An oblong brick or stone seen side-on in a wall

String course A projecting horizontal course in a wall

Strut A short structural member resisting compression along its length

Stucco Originally, plastering; more recently, external plastering brought to a smooth surface

Stud A minor upright member in framed wall carpentry

Stuff Plasterer's material, which may be coarse, fine or gauged: coarse stuff is slaked lime, sand and hair; fine stuff is lime putty, sand and a little hair; gauged stuff is lime putty and gypsum

Tenon A projection of reduced cross-section formed in or near the end of a member and designed to form a joint when pushed into a mortise in another member

Tension brace (a possibly inappropriate term for) A diagonal member in the bottom corner of a timber framed wall, jointed at its foot to a sill or beam and at its head to a post, and serving to resist distortion in the plane of the frame

Thorough band A bond stone through the thickness of a wall

Through purlin A purlin running from end to end of a roof over the backs of rafters (c.f. **Butt purlin**)

Tie-beam A beam serving to maintain the distance apart of two wall frames, especially the beam into which the feet of a pair of principal rafters are fixed

Toft A house site or a back yard; 'Toft and Croft' is house site and paddock

Tracery Thin stone members subdividing a window, especially in Gothic architecture; extended in the late Gothic period to the decorative treatment of walls and vaults

Transom A horizontal member in window tracery

Trass Crushed volcanic ash, used as a natural cement

Truss A triangulated frame spanning a void

Trussed rafter A common rafter braced to its pair; a 'trussed rafter roof' is a continuous rather than a bay structure, the rafters transmitting their load directly to the walls without the intermediary of purlins

Tudor arch A depressed, four-centred Gothic arch

Tumbling Inclined brickwork courses at the verge of a gable, meeting it at right angles; the tumbled brickwork is usually set out in a series of triangles toothed into the ordinary courses

Tunnel vault A barrel vault

Vault An arch elongated in the direction of its axis, with voussoirs laid in bonded courses, and covering an area

Verge The sloping edge of a pitched roof

Vernacular (adj.) (1) Originally, using popular language rather than Latin or Law French; (2) (in architecture) characteristic of local tradition. 'Vernacular architecture' seems at first to have meant (sensibly) modern building in an indigenous traditional style; but this is now called 'neo-vernacular' and the simple adjective is applied to the old architecture under study.

Voussoir A (usually wedge-shaped) stone used in

the construction of an arch or vault

Waggon vault A barrel vault

Wall frame A frame parallel to the roof ridge line

Wall-plate A longitudinal timber at the top of a wall upon which the feet of the common rafters rest; where the walls are timber-framed, the top member, called the 'top plates' serves also as the wall-plate

Wealden house A house with a hall between two jettied wings and a continuous eaves

Wind brace A timber bracing a purlin to a principal rafter

References

1 A. H. Pitt-Rivers, *King John's House, Tollard Royal, Wiltshire*, 1890 (Privately printed)

2 W. Stubbs, 'On the present state and prospects of historical study' (lecture delivered May 17, 1876) in *Lectures on Medieval and Modern History*, ii, 1876, p. 41 (Clarendon Press)

3 M. Beresford and J. G. Hurst, *Deserted Medieval Villages*, 1971 (Lutterworth Press, London)

4 C. F. Fox, *The Personality of Britain*, National Museum of Wales, 1932 (Cardiff)

5 M. W. Barley, *The English Farmhouse and Cottage*, 1961, p. 4 (Routledge & Kegan Paul)

6 E. Mercer, *English Vernacular Houses*, 1975, p. 1 (R.C.H.M.)

7 R. A. Cordingley, 'British Historical Roof-Types and their Members: a Classification' in *Trans. Ancient Monuments Soc.*, 1961

8 Sir Cyril Fox and Lord Raglan, *Monmouthshire Houses*, vol. I, p. 39 (Welsh Folk Museum, St Fagans)

9 J. T. Smith, 'Timber Framed Building in England', *Archaeol. Journal*, 1965

10 M. Wood, *The English Medieval House*, 1965 (J. M. Dent)

11 W. G. Hoskins, 'The Rebuilding of Rural England 1570-1640' in *Past and Present*, Vol. IV, 1953, p. 44ff, reprinted in *Provincial England*, 1963, p. 131ff (Macmillan & Co.)

12 See H. Hobhouse, *Thomas Cubitt, Master Builder*, 1971 for a study of the early origins of contracting in gross (Macmillan & Co.)

13 E.g. at Fazeley: see J. Tann and L. D. W. Smith, 'Early fireproof housing in a Staffordshire factory village' in *Post Medieval Archaeology*, Vol. VI, pp. 191-7

14 Sanitary Inquiry, House of Lords Sessions Papers, 1842, XXVII

15 Local Reports of the General Board of Health: see *B.C.L.* [*British Library General Catalogue of Printed Books*] to 1975 (1981), Vol. 98, pp. 1519-1573

16 Sanitary Inquiry, op. cit., England, Report no. 12, pp. 192ff

17 H. Adams, *Joints in Woodwork: a paper read before the Civil and Mechanical Engineers' Society on 1 March 1877*, 1894, p.8

18 George Sturt, *The Wheelwright's Shop*, 1934; chap. VII 'The Sawyers' describes itinerant sawyers at work in the early years of this century (Cambridge University Press)

19 L. F. Salzman, *Building in England down to 1540*, 1967, p. 343; J. Moxon, *Mechanic Exercises*, nos. IV and VI (1678) also illustrate this type of saw and give a detailed description of the art of using it

20 Rees's *Cyclopaedia*, 'Sawing'

21 Salzman, op. cit., p. 202

22 Especially C. A. Hewett, *The Development of Carpentry 1200-1700, an Essex Study*, 1969, (David & Charles) and *English Historic Carpentry*, 1980, (Phillimore)

23 R. Neve, *The City and Country Purchaser and Builder's Dictionary*, 2nd edn., 1726 (republished by David and Charles, 1969); R. Harris, *Discovering Timber-Framed Buildings*, 1978 (Shire Publications)

24 *cogging, cocking* or *caulking* is now differently

understood as 'when a cog or solid projecting portion is left in the lower piece at the middle of the joint', Adams, op. cit., p. 21

25 T. Tredgold, *Elementary Principles of Carpentry*, 1820 (London)

26 Salzman, op. cit., p. 317

27 C. Tomlinson, ed., *Cyclopaedia of Useful Arts and Manufactures*, 1854, 'Nails' (London)

28 'Fore locke bolts hath an eye at the end, wherein a forelock of iron is driven to keep it from starting backe' J. Smith, *Seaman's Grammar*, 1627 (London)

29 *English Gilds*, E.E.T.S. No. 40, p. 367 (Early English Text Soc., London)

30 Wm. Harrison, *Description of England*, 1577

31 Statute 17 Edw IV c. 4

32 F. N. Knoop and G. P. Jones, *The Medieval Mason*, 1933, pp. 47, 192; L. F. Salzman, op. cit., p. 121n, p. 126

33 See especially R. Lister, *Decorative Wrought Ironwork in Great Britain*, 1957, and *Decorative Cast Ironwork in Great Britain*, 1960 (G. Bell & Sons, London)

35 R. and J. A. Brandon, *Analysis of Gothic Architecture*, 1847, vol. 1 (Rimell & Son, London)

35 T. Bannister, 'The First Iron Framed Buildings' in *Architectural Review*, 107, April 1950

36 Bannister, op. cit., p. 236

37 H. R. Johnson and A. W. Skempton, 'William Strutt's Cotton Mills, 1793–1812' in *Trans. Newcomen Soc.*, 30, 1956

38 J. Smeaton, *A Narrative of the building of the Eddystone Lighthouse*, 1791, Vol. III, ch. iv

39 L. J. Vicat, *Recherches expérimentales sur les chaux de construction, les bétons et les mortiers ordinaires*, Paris, 1818 (Trans. Capt. J. T. Smith, London, 1837)

40 For the art of using a camera effectively see Terry Buchanan, *Photographing Historic Buildings*, R.C.H.M., 1983

41 In 1948 Professor R. A. Cordingley introduced the system in a paper read before the British Association for the Advancement of Science, describing the programme of research into rural houses and cottages begun under his leadership five years earlier. See 'A Scheme for the investigation of English Rural Dwelling Types' in *The Advancement of Science*, VI, April 1949, pp. 123–4

42 An offprint of this publication with slightly abridged introduction was published in 1976, and may be purchased from the Ancient Monuments Society, St Andrew by the Wardrobe, Queen Victoria Street, London EC4V 5DE

43 H. R. Johnson and A. W. Skempton, op. cit.; T. Bannister, 'The First Iron Framed Buildings' in *Architectural Review*, 107, April 1950, pp. 231–46

44 F. W. B. Charles, 'The Timber-framed Buildings of Coventry', *Trans. Birm. and Warwickshire Arch. Soc.*, Vol. LXXXVI, 1974, p. 115n

45 E. Wiliam, 'A Cruck Barn at Hendre Wen, Llanrwst, Denbighshire' in *Trans. Anc. Mon. Soc.*, new series, Vol. XXI, 1976

46 Choisy uses these projections to good effect in *L'art de bâtir chez les Romains*, 1873, to illustrate vault construction.

47 H. A. Doubleday and W. Page, *A Guide to the Victoria County History of the Counties of England*, 1903 (Constable)

48 'An inquiry into several manors in Bedfordshire and Buckinghamshire, in the King's hand by the death of Elizabeth, late wife of John Mowbray of Axholme, during the minority of the heir, 10 May 50 Edw III (i.e. 1376)' in P.R.O. *Calendar of Inquisitions Miscellaneous*, vol. 3, no. 1013. Reproduced by permission of the Controller of Her Majesty's Stationery Office.

49 Listed in Turner and Parker, *Some Account of Domestic Architecture in England*, Vol. III, pt. 2, 1859, p. 401ff

50 *Calendar of Patent Rolls 1547–8*, p. 352

51 *Calendar of Patent Rolls 1558–60*, p. 283ff

52 5 Ric II Statute 1 c. 8, 'Remedy for lost Deeds'

53 Record Commissioners' Publications no. 21

54 Chapman and Bartlett, 'The Contribution of Building Clubs and Freehold Land Society to Working-class Housing in Birmingham' in S. D. Chapman, ed., *The History of Working Class Housing*, 1971 (David & Charles)

55 Esp. J. Tann, *The Development of the Factory*, 1970 (Cornmarket Press, London)

56 Archer Deeds, Shakespeare Mem. Lib., Stratford, transcribed by Mrs Mollie Varley

57 Blackstone's *Commentaries*, Book 2, chap. 21, 'Of alienation by Matter of Record'

58 Pigot, *Directory of Derbyshire*, 1828

59 Blackstone's *Commentaries*, Book 2, chap. 32, 'Of title by Will and Administration'

60 Isaac Ware, *A Complete Body of Architecture*, 1756, Book III (Osborne & Shipton, London)

61 Thomas Telford's excavation at Wroxeter in Shropshire in 1788 to rescue evidence for a large Roman bath house, for example, described in his *Autobiography* and the accompanying *Atlas*, 1838 (London)

62 Vitruvius, *De Architectura*, Book II, chap. i

63 Sir W. Chambers, *Treatise on the Decorative Part of Civil Architecture*, ed. J. Gwilt, 1825, plate 1 facing p. 106 (Priestley & Weale, London)

64 Sir James Hall, *Essay on the Origins, History and Principles of Gothic Architecture*, 1813 (London)

65 Chambers, ed. Gwilt, op. cit., p. 129

66 J. Britton, *The Architectural Antiquities of Great Britain*, 1807–35. In the essay on Malmesbury Abbey Church (in vol. 1) Britton lists the styles as Anglo-Saxon (597–1066), Anglo-Norman (1066–1189), English (1189–1272), Decorated English (1272–1461) and Highly Decorated or Florid English (1461–1509).

67 See *Guide to the Contents of the Public Record Office*, Vol. II, p. 2 (H.M.S.O.)

68 Rev. W. Gilpin, *Three Essays on Picturesque Beauty*, 1794, p. 41 (Blamire, London)

69 E. A. L. Moir, *The Discovery of Britain: the English Tourists 1540–1840*, 1964 (Routledge & Kegan Paul)

70 J. Malton, *Essay on British Cottage Architecture*, 1798 (London)

71 E. Bartell, *Hints for Picturesque Improvements*, 1804, p. 11 (J. Taylor, London)

72 E. Sharpe, *A Treatise on the Rise and Progress of Decorated Window Tracery in England*, 1849 (London)

73 C. H. Parker, *ABC of Gothic Architecture*, 1888, p. 4 (J. H. & J. Parker, Oxford)

74 S. Piggott, 'The Origin of the English County Archaeological Societies' in *Trans. Birmingham and Warwickshire Archaeol. Soc.* for 1974, LXXXVI

75 T. H. Turner, *Some Account of Domestic Architecture in England*, vol. 1, 'from the Conquest to the end of the thirteenth Century', 1851; J. H. Parker, ibid. vol. II, 'from Edward I to Richard II' 1853; ibid. vol. III, parts 1 and 2, 'from Richard II to Henry VIII', 1859 (J. H. & J. Parker, Oxford)

76 R. Neville, *Old Cottages and Domestic Architecture in South-West Surrey*, 1889 (Billing & Sons, Guildford)

77 H. Hughes and H. L. North, *The Old Cottages of Snowdonia*, 1908 (Jarvis & Foster, Bangor); reprinted by the Snowdonia National Park Society, 1979

78 Reprinted by David & Charles, 1971

79 The same tradition underlies the founding of a number of Scandinavian open air museums, starting with Skansen in Stockholm in 1873

Index